Moving Image and Sound Collections for Archivists

Moving Image and Sound Collections for Archivists

ANTHONY COCCIOLO

ALA Editions

CHICAGO 2018

Society of American Archivists
www.archivists.org

This edition published by ALA Editions, an imprint of the American Library Association, 2018.

Printed in the USA by Lightning Source.
POD-1

ISBN: 978-0-8389-1740-4

Graphic design by Sweeney Design, kasween@sbcglobal.net.

Note: All figures and photographs were created by Anthony Cocciolo unless otherwise stated.

To Steven

Table of Contents

Introduction

This book has been written for every archivist (or archivist in training) who has opened a box or file cabinet or otherwise unearthed some carrier of moving image and sound and has wondered what to do. You may have not recognized the format, you may have not known if it held video or audio, and you may have not known how to describe the item. It is even possible that you did not recognize it as a carrier of moving image and sound. I can already see our great-grandchildren using CDs as coasters! For every archivist who has struggled with moving image and sound records—maybe even pretending that tape or disc was not so different from a file folder and would fit nicely in an acid-free box nestled among paper records—this book is for you.

My primary job is teaching aspiring archivists and other information professionals at Pratt Institute's School of Information in New York City. I often find that students have familiarity with some moving image formats, such as VHS tapes and DVDs, but often have little exposure to other formats. I check their knowledge during the first week of the class Projects in Moving Image and Sound Archives, when I present students with a box full of moving image and sound media and ask them to sort the media into three types: carrier of moving image and sound, carrier of sound only, and none of the above. A three-minute countdown adds to the pressure. I witness the students get flustered as they attempt to distinguish between some things that look nothing alike and others that are very similar. Try telling the difference between a MiniDV tape, a DAT tape, and a microcassette in a rush! Often, the students encounter formats that they have no personal experience with, and as a result, they make some classification mistakes.

Professional archivists who work primarily with paper records often encounter media that they are not familiar with. One archivist interviewed for this book noted that she emailed photos of unfamiliar media to an audiovisual digitization firm to get more information. Another archivist hired a consulting company with expertise in audiovisual media to survey and help identify media in the collections. Although both are great strategies, they highlight a common theme: professional archivists are often not trained to work with audiovisual materials. This is not surprising, as management of moving image and sound archives has not been a significant component of graduate archival education programs.[1] However, is this really a problem? Can't archivists simply rely on outside expertise to address this lack of know-how? The answer is, inevitably: it depends. But while it may be helpful to rely on outside experts, all archivists should possess some familiarity with audiovisual formats and know when to ask for help with more complex issues. Large archival institutions, such as large university or government archives, will in many cases be able to hire specialists to address their audiovisual collections. Also, larger institutions often have more robust fund-raising infrastructures, which open up funding opportunities from federal, state, local, and private sources that can support audiovisual projects. For smaller archives, including archives run by lone arrangers, obtaining outside expertise may be more of a challenge—hence the reason for this book. The goal of this book is to provide guidance on managing archival moving image and sound collections, especially for those archivists who may need to develop their own expertise or who interact with experts in their own institution or among external partners. The information in this book is based on published sources; information delivered by professionals at conferences; personal experience in research, teaching, and consulting in the area of moving image and sound records; and examples from archival practice based on interviews with archivists engaged in audiovisual projects. Interviews were conducted with archivists over the telephone and discussed issues such as types of materials stewarded, digital preservation reformatting, interacting with vendors, user access and legal issues, and fundraising for audiovisual projects, among other relevant issues.

The intended audience for this book is primarily the general archivist who may deal primarily in non–moving image and sound materials, such as paper records, and not the moving image archivist. For this reason, the book emphasizes formats that are likely to appear in a nonspecialized archive among other types of records. For example, the general archivist is likely to find many VHS tapes and (hopefully) no nitrate film prints. Since not everything can be included in a single book, and my experiences are more in general than in specialized archives, the focus here will be on the needs of the general archivist.

This book can certainly be of interest to other professionals who handle moving image and sound records, such as media asset managers, metadata specialists in television and film, independent filmmakers, and documentary filmmakers. The book may also be of interest to personal digital archivists, who may be interested in preserving family or community memories. Knowing that such individuals may happen to pick this book up for assistance with their moving image and sound assets, I have attempted to clearly define the meaning of any archivist-specific language, and I have included a glossary.

A further goal of this book is to speak directly to the realities of today's archival environments by first acknowledging the intense resource constraints that many repositories face. This book looks for applicability not only to large, well-endowed university or government archives, but also to community archives, historical societies, and lone arrangers, who have increasing needs and flat or declining resources. For this reason, the book attempts to help the archivist make sensible choices with the limited resources on hand, such as choices related to collection reformatting or setting up digital preservation infrastructure. In sum, the book assumes that work related to moving image and sound collections needs to be balanced among many competing resource-intensive demands.

It should also be noted that this book is targeted specifically at archivists and not necessarily at multimedia librarians. Library multimedia departments often circulate films on DVD, Blu-ray, or other formats with the goal of making this content available for academic, scholarly, and other uses. This content can range from obscure independent films to Hollywood blockbusters. While the archivist, like the librarian, may need to concern himself with providing access to moving image and sound content, the archivist has an underlying responsibility to balance preservation with access. Archives preserve unique or rare content, such as oral history projects, and thus need to take into account preservation needs as well as access needs. The multimedia librarian can always order another copy of a blockbuster film on Blu-ray if the copy on hand gets damaged or lost, but mishandling the master copies of archival moving image and sound content may result in the complete disappearance of this content. Thus, while the multimedia librarian and the archivist may share some common objectives, such as helping users access moving image and sound materials, the role of preservation significantly distinguishes their roles.

With some noted exceptions, this book takes the position that preservation of and access to moving image and sound records is best advanced by reformatting them to digital formats (if they are not already digital) and engaging in digital preservation of those assets. The literature on moving image and sound preservation and access has long emphasized reformatting of materials. For example, Jerry McWilliams wrote in his book *The Preservation and Restoration of Sound Recordings* (1979) that once a vinyl disc "has been played about ten times, it is a good idea to tape it and play the tape from that point on" because "some deterioration of sound quality will occur under the best playback conditions."[2] Recommendations to reformat continued into the 1990s from archivists such as Christopher Ann Patton, who promoted the position that "a copy will have to be made for research use so that the original recording is not damaged or worn out."[3] Today, the consensus is that preservation of and access to moving image and sound recordings is best advanced through reformatting to digital formats, with the exception of film, which is discussed in more depth in chapter 8, "Film Collections." For example, William Chase, in the *ARSC Guide to Audio Preservation*, writes that "carrier deterioration and technical obsolescence make reformatting to digital files the only way to ensure future access to legacy format sound recordings."[4] Video expert George Blood notes that "all historic video formats must be migrated into file-based digital format."[5] Audiovisual archivist Joshua Ranger—in a blog post titled "For God's Sake, Stop Digitizing Paper"—argues that "for almost all formats in almost all cases, reformatting is required to preserve the signal or image, and in a growing number of cases it is absolutely required to provide any degree of access beyond looking at the physical object."[6] Anyone who has ever had a researcher return a VHS tape that has been "eaten" by a VCR or tried to find a working U-matic tape player on eBay should be able to sympathize with this logic.

Despite calls from audiovisual archivists for preservation reformatting, archivists often provide visitors with the "archival" or "master" media item, be it a VHS tape, audiocassette tape, or some other item. Archival educator and researcher Karen F. Gracy provides some reasons this practice continues. She conducted a short survey of sixteen archivists responsible for digitization and distribution of moving images and found that "resources, technological expertise, and copyright" were the major impediments to digitization.[7] Although these are admittedly serious obstacles, this book aims to help the archivist begin to overcome them, while acknowledging that there will continue to be times when providing the master media item to the researcher may be the only feasible option. But if we are to be serious about preservation and access, then digital reformatting is a practice worth striving for, even in resource-constrained environments. I am optimistic that archivists can make some headway in this area. For the last several years, I have had my students engage in digital reformatting of audio and video recordings in collaboration with the Lesbian Herstory Archives, creating today what is one of the largest digitized audiovisual lesbian, gay, bisexual, and transgender (LGBT) archives available online, including thousands of hours of interviews, oral histories, and events, among other types of recordings.[8] If this can be achieved with no paid staff and no outsourced conversion, there are likely a number of similar arrangements that can be devised through the use of volunteers as well as through collaborations with local educational institutions. Solutions that address reformatting, including through DIY (do-it-yourself) reformatting, vendor-supported reformatting, and other options, are explored in this book.

One challenge is that the literature on reformatting of moving image and sound records is rather sparse, especially compared to resources on reformatting still images. For example, there is no video equivalent for Cornell University Library's excellent *Moving Theory into Practice: Digital Imaging Tutorial*, which provides guidance on reformatting still images.[9] This book aims to fill in some of these gaps, while also recognizing that technology changes quickly, so it is important not to be too specific about what hardware and software to use. For example, Cornell's tutorial warns those digitizing to use CRT (cathode-ray tube) computer monitors for verifying digitized works. This was sound advice in 2003 but is simply anachronistic today as progressive-scan displays, such as LED and LCD, have improved dramatically. Therefore, more basic principles will be emphasized, rather than what button to push when or what conversion device to buy now.

The eleven chapters of this book are intended to provide solid grounding for general archivists to manage their moving image and sound collections. The first part provides more general practices that can be used regardless of media types, while the second part provides guidance for specific media formats.

The first chapter looks at the topic of appraisal of moving image and sound records, which is the process of determining what records have permanent value and should be maintained by an archives. Chapter 2 addresses the topic of accessioning, arrangement, and description, which includes steps for taking custody of records, physically arranging them, and creating metadata records for them using various methods. Chapter 3 addresses legal and ethical issues, such as donor issues, copyright, and fair use, among other topics, which are essential for making moving image and sound collections available. Chapter 4 explores the topic of digital preservation, which is essential to the preservation of moving image and sound works, as nearly all new records are created through digital technology. Chapter 5 explores options for providing access to collections, looking at ways to do it yourself over the web and other options for making moving image and sound collections meaningful to users. Chapter 6 explores issues in interacting with moving image and sound producers, such as oral history makers and documentary filmmakers, with the goal of ensuring the long-term persistence of their work and possible transfer of such works to an archives.

The second part of the book provides guidance specific to media types. Chapter 7 explores the topic of managing audio collections, including formats, housing, storage, and digital conversion procedures. Chapters 8, 9, and 10 follow a similar pattern, exploring film collections, analog video collections, and digital video collections, respectively. Chapter 11 explores issues in archiving complex media, an umbrella term that captures a wide variety of media that do not easily fit into the category of "digital video," such as records embedded in software such as educational CD-ROMs. An epilogue explores some future considerations for moving image and sound archiving.

This book would not be possible without the help of many people. I would like to thank my colleagues on the SAA Publications Board for their useful feedback on drafts of this book, specifically Chair Christopher J. Prom and Nicole Milano—the book's shepherd—as well as the reviewers of the manuscript, who provided essential feedback. Further, I would like to thank the several dozen individuals who are referenced throughout this work and whose advice, research, and experience are essential components of this book. In particular, I would like to thank the archivists who agreed to be interviewed for this book, including Elizabeth Charlton, Sarah Gesell, Rachel Grove, Lisa Lobdell, and Christina Zamon. I would also like to thank my colleagues at Pratt Institute, including the faculty, administration, and students, for their encouragement and for providing an environment in which this book could be written. I would specifically like to thank my graduate assistant for the spring 2016 term, Allison Chomet, for her assistance on the manuscript. Further, I am thankful for the use of libraries and the services of librarians, including Pratt Institute Libraries, New York University Libraries, Columbia University Libraries, and the New York Public Library.

I hope this book offers useful advice and intriguing ideas on managing moving image and sound collections to the seasoned archivist, aspiring archivist, or anyone interested in the topic. I welcome your feedback and comments for future revisions of this book. You can reach me at acocciol@pratt.edu, on Twitter at @acocciolo, and through my website, www.thinkingprojects.org.

Anthony Cocciolo
New York, 2017

NOTES

[1] Further, audiovisual records are not specifically mentioned in the curriculum section of SAA's *Guidelines for a Graduate Program in Archival Studies* (2016), http://www2.archivists.org/prof-education/graduate/gpas/curriculum, permalinked on December 8, 2016, at https://perma.cc/NCE2-F5L6.

[2] Jerry McWilliams, *The Preservation and Restoration of Sound Recordings* (Nashville, TN: American Association for State and Local History, 1979), 57.

[3] Christopher Ann Patton, "Whispers in the Stacks: The Problem of Sound Recordings in Archives," *American Archivist* 52, no. 2 (1990): 274–80. Also see Christopher Ann Patton, "Preservation Re-Recording of Audio Recordings in Archives: Problems, Priorities, Technologies, and Recommendations," *American Archivist* 61, no. 1 (1998): 212.

[4] William Chase, "Preservation Reformatting," in *ARSC Guide to Audio Preservation,* ed. Sam Brylawski, Maya Lerman, Robin Pike, and Kathlin Smith (Washington, DC, and Eugene, OR: ARSC, CLIR, and Library of Congress, 2015), 110.

[5] George Blood, *Refining Conversion Contract Specifications: Determining Suitable Digital Video Formats for Medium-term Storage* (Washington, DC: Library of Congress, 2011), http://www.digitizationguidelines.gov/audio-visual/documents /IntrmMastVidFormatRecs_20111001.pdf, permalinked on April 5, 2016, at https://perma.cc/L58A-38NV.

[6] Joshua Ranger, "For God's Sake, Stop Digitizing Paper," *AVPreserve Blog,* August 25, 2014, https://www.avpreserve.com /blog/for-gods-sake-stop-digitizing-paper-2/, permalinked on September 14, 2016, at https://perma.cc/6DRP-44H6.

[7] Karen F. Gracy, "Distribution and Consumption Patterns of Archival Moving Images in Online Environments," *American Archivist* 75, no. 2 (2012): 446.

[8] Herstories: Audio/Visual Collections, http://herstories.prattsils.org, permalinked on August 30, 2016, at https://perma.cc /NET4-Q83W.

[9] Cornell University Library Research Department, *Moving Theory into Practice: Digital Imaging Tutorial* (2003), http://library .cornell.edu/preservation/tutorial/contents.html, permalinked on April 21, 2016, at https://perma.cc/7SST-6TD2.

PART I

ARCHIVAL PRACTICES FOR MOVING IMAGE AND SOUND COLLECTIONS

CHAPTER 1

Appraisal and Reappraisal

OVERVIEW

In archives, appraisal is the process by which records are determined to have archival or permanent value.[1] It is important to note that appraisal does not refer to monetary value or assigning the market value for a work, but rather to the designation of a record as having continuing value.[2]

Reappraisal is the process by which the value of items originally deemed to have archival or permanent value is second-guessed, and the preservation-worthiness of the records is reevaluated.[3] Records that no longer have permanent value can be deaccessioned, which means they can be offered to another institution, returned to the donor, or destroyed.[4]

Appraisal is often thought to be the most significant activity in which archivists engage. F. Gerald Ham, former president of the Society of American Archivists, described it as "our most important and intellectually demanding tasks as archivists."[5] This view is clearly understandable, given that appraisal decides what will become part of the historical record. Because of this monumental responsibility, the literature on archives appraisal has been extensive and vigorous, especially during the last two decades. At my own institution, a semester-long course is taught on archives appraisal alone, with much of the time devoted to engaging with this extensive literature. Although a thorough investigation of the literature on this topic is beyond the scope of this book, I discuss some relevant appraisal concepts with pertinence to moving image and sound collections, as well as some new ideas on appraisal.

BRIEF HISTORY OF ARCHIVES APPRAISAL

It is nearly impossible to discuss archives appraisal without beginning with Sir Hilary Jenkinson, an influential British archivist and the author of *A Manual of Archive Administration* (1922).[6] Jenkinson is particularly notable in that he believed that archivists should not engage in appraisal but rather should preserve all records transferred to their custody.[7] If selection was to take place, the creators and not the archivist should do it. The vast growth of modern bureaucracies after World War II and the subsequent deluge of information made appraisal necessary and Jenkinson's view untenable. In the United States, T. R. Schellenberg provided the framework that addressed this deluge and made appraisal a central part of archivists' work.[8] As articulated in his 1956 book *Modern Archives: Principles and Techniques*, records with permanent value had evidential value, informational value, or both. Records of evidential value were those that provided information about the organization and function of the creating organization. Records of informational value were those that informed about people, places, conditions, and events in the society in which the organization functioned.[9] In Schellenberg's view, "archivists should be empowered to review all records that government agencies propose to destroy," and they "should make judgments on the value of records in terms of their ultimate usefulness to the people and the government, using whatever professional assistance they can obtain either from public officials or from scholars."[10] Thus, records could be retained for reasons beyond the consideration of their original creators, including societal implications and other historic value.

Schellenberg's granting of permission to professional archivists to make judgments about what had permanent value was not to everyone's liking. For example, in 1995 David Bearman noted that "all selection and appraisal based on trying to create a representative record will fail simply because it is being carried out by people living in the present."[11] To make archives appraisal more systematic, Helen Samuels borrowed some thinking from the social sciences and led the development of functional analysis, in which records are retained in consideration of the major social functions of the institution that created them. For example, Samuels recommends that records in higher education be retained in the context of seven major functions: 1) confer credentials, 2) convey knowledge, 3) foster socialization, 4) conduct research, 5) sustain the institution, 6) provide public service, and 7) promote culture.[12] Functional analysis continues to be developed, specifically by better attuning it to resource-constrained contexts.[13]

A criticism often applied to formal appraisal processes is that they prioritize the records of senior officials or society's elites and do not capture the fullness and diversity of communities. As my French teacher in high school, Mrs. Karlsson, would have described it, archives often collect the works of the "crème de la crème" of society. In writing about moving image archives, Sam Kula notes that moving image archivists "can just as easily distort the record with poor choices as do their colleagues working with the written record," rendering a record that only reflects a "preponderance of 'official' images from big government and big business" and leaving out "moving images at the margins of society and outside the industrial/capitalist mainstream."[14] Because of this possibility, he argues that moving image archivists "need to move outside the boundaries of the moving image industries to reach out to amateur and independent image-makers, all types of artists working in film and video, and image-making on the margins of society, to ensure that their collections are truly reflective of the entire society."[15]

An example of an appraisal approach that prioritizes high-level leaders—as opposed to an approach that seeks records from a diversity of persons—is the capstone approach adopted by the US government for managing email records. Under this approach, email records are permanently retained at the level of the user account only for "high level policy/decision makers" and their immediate staffs, and other email accounts are discarded after a set period of time.[16] Because of the massive quantity of email records produced by the federal government and the cost of maintaining them, some selection is indeed necessary. However, some critics could point to this as further proof that archives only reflect the records of elites.

APPRAISAL OF MOVING IMAGE AND SOUND RECORDS IN THE LITERATURE

A notable issue with appraisal, as it is discussed in the archives literature, is that most of it does not apply particularly well to moving image and sound records. Archival educator Karen F. Gracy writes, "I would argue caution in the wholesale application of appraisal theory to moving images, as most appraisal models were not designed with moving images in mind."[17] Kula agrees, writing, "Whatever the approach to appraisal, archival literature offers little in the way of concrete and practical guidance."[18] A major reason Kula notes this might be the case is that while most archivists appraise records at varying groupings (e.g., record series such as "correspondence" or "meeting minutes," folder level, etc.), moving image records are usually considered at the item level. One factor is the cost of preserving a moving image record, which is considerably higher than the cost to preserve a box of paper records. Another factor is often the lack of inherent relationships between a moving image record and other moving image records—relationships that often exist with paper records. This of course is not always the case. For example, oral history projects are often created by a single source around some larger theme, and the records can be logically grouped together by this shared origin. Similarly, moving image records such as television programs can often be grouped into seasons and series. A related issue that Kula notes is that many moving image and sound records often do not have much evidential value because they do not reveal how their production company or administrative entity functioned. This is especially true of fictional works, which may have enormous informational value (e.g., revealing the values of the society that produced the work) but little if any evidential value. This would not hold true for items like recordings of meetings or events of an organization, which would clearly have evidential value.

Despite the gaps in the appraisal literature in addressing the needs of moving image collections, Kula finds that there are some appraisal ideas that are useful for selecting moving image records. The first is the idea that old age should be respected, which he notes was espoused in 1901 by H. O. Meissner, head of the Prussian Privy State Archives. Kula finds that "moving images have suffered so extensively from benign neglect by archivists and curators that all moving images produced before 1930 can be regarded as incunabula," or the earliest traces of the form and hence most valuable.[19] Further, "all broadcast television before 1970 should be acquired, as so much of what was broadcast live before 1960 has been lost, and so much of what was recorded on videotape in the sixties has been wiped."[20] He notes that other factors to evaluate in selecting moving image and sound works include the "complex question of aesthetics"—as difficult and subjective as this can be.[21] Other selection criteria are firsts and milestones, such as the first sound film. The last selection criteria include universal retention, such as retaining all the works of a specific producer or director. It should be noted that Kula's views on moving image appraisal are clearly influenced by his work at the film, sound, and television section of the National

Archives of Canada, and thus some of these points may only make sense when viewed in terms of a national collecting scope.

Although Kula does not explicitly state these criteria—perhaps because they are too obvious—an additional factor in moving image appraisal is the extent to which the record is unique or rare. For example, a recent Hollywood movie on Blu-ray would not be a rare or unique item. In this case, the Blu-ray format is a highly compressed version of the original format, which would likely be in digital cinema or 35 mm film format. Lastly, an additional aspect to consider is if the item held is the highest fidelity version. For example, VHS, DVD, and Blu-ray have tended to be consumer-oriented formats that eliminate some visual information for the sake of convenience and cost. For professionally produced works, there are typically higher fidelity versions, such as film, high-resolution computer files, or professional videotape formats. However, many community archiving projects, such as oral history projects, are likely to use consumer formats such as VHS. Thus, ensuring that you are archiving an item that is rare or unique and that the version you have is the highest fidelity version are important—if somewhat obvious—considerations.

ISSUES IN AUDIOVISUAL APPRAISAL

Methods for conducting archives appraisal—or even engaging in appraisal—are debated. For example, archival researcher and educator Anne Gilliland suggests that appraisal of digital records may no longer be feasible and that archivists should consider embracing records in their totality.[22] She notes: "More consequential to ponder and debate at this moment is the very real possibility of the death of appraisal with regard to born-digital records. Appraisal was an idea of its time. It is not an idea of this time."[23] The reason Gilliland believes that appraisal may not be possible is the "volume of digital documentation being created today and the profoundly networked nature of organizational and personal activities in the digital realm that makes it difficult to identify points of decision making or to establish institutional boundaries around records."[24] However, archivists such as Geof Huth disagree. Huth writes that the Jenkinsonian notion that archivists shouldn't appraise is "a bit batty," arguing that "appraisal, in the end, determines everything about archives" and is needed with digital records "to contain the flow."[25]

The appraisal of born-digital records is deeply needed, and with an urgency not found in paper records. The reasons are twofold. The first reason is characteristic of any born-digital record, whether it is a moving image or not, and that has to do with the cost of digital preservation. It can be very expensive. Although I explore some ways to keep the cost down in chapter 4, especially for low-resourced institutions, there is still a significant cost. Equally important are the indirect costs of digital preservation, which include the environmental impact of powering data centers as well as the waste produced in both making the computer hardware and disposing of it at the end of its life cycle. Paper is famous for being able to endure "benign neglect," often still communicating information after being stored in the worst of conditions. Digital information does not endure benign neglect nearly as well as paper, and although digital preservation has a chance of being very good at preserving records, the cost requires archivists to be somewhat choosy about what we preserve digitally.

The second reason that appraisal is needed for born-digital records is specific to moving image content. Appraisal is needed for digital moving image records because the files are unusually large, especially when compared to other types of records, and they can easily overwhelm a digital repository's capacities if their inclusion is not very judicious. Consider the following example from my experience working as an electronic records consultant for a grant project at an art museum in the United States. During that time, the museum's theater department transferred to the archives eight 6-terabyte (TB) RAID—redundant array of independent disks—devices, which included high-definition video recordings of many of the theater's events from the last several years. (See figure 1-1.) This would not have been problematic if we had unlimited space; however, our repository for all archival assets was initially set at 10 TB. Although the repository could grow to a certain extent, should all 48 TB be permanently retained? This was not the only occasion that moving image records presented such a problem at the museum. Analysis of network storage for files that could be removed from active network storage to archival storage showed that one hundred of the largest files were videos with file extensions such as .MP4, .MOV, .AVI, .FP7 (Final Cut Pro 7), .DV, and .MTS (high-definition video format).[26] For example, one awards event contained 75 gigabytes (GB) of video spread across seven files that fully captured the event. These examples illustrate the need for not only appraisal but also an expanded conceptualization of appraisal to accommodate the unusual demands that moving image records present.

Figure 1-1. One of eight 6 TB disk arrays transferred to an art museum archives in 2014.

Back to Gilliland's earlier assertion: has it become significantly more difficult to distinguish a record from a nonrecord? I would argue that it has not. However, what has changed are the tools necessary for procuring documentation from the digital realm. In some cases, it may be necessary to pull down records from the web by using web archiving or other bulk extraction tools, including extracting information from cloud-based social media services such as Facebook, Instagram, and YouTube. Pulling information from the web can get quite technical and might require the use of APIs (application programming interfaces) and the creation of scripts to download records to an institutional archive.[27] Although additional tools are needed for gathering such documentation, what is a record of personal or institutional activity continues to be fairly clear.

NEW APPROACHES TO APPRAISAL OF MOVING IMAGE RECORDS

Appraisal is significantly limited by the concept that it is ultimately about whether to keep or not to keep. However, in the world of born-digital records and digitized records, it is necessary to modify our notion of appraisal to include a third element: *to keep in what form.* Before I explain this notion further, I will offer some background on digital archiving.

First, it is important to distinguish digitized records from born-digital records. "Born-digital" refers to records that originate on computers, for which there may (or may not) be an analog equivalent, such as a printout. Born-digital records are different from collections created through digitization, which creates digital versions or surrogates of materials that originated on paper, film, or another analog medium. In the library, archives, and museum community, when digitizing an item—say a photograph or a video—it is common to produce a master copy that adheres to some defined standard and is as faithful to the original as possible. The rationale for creating a master is that it can be the definitive source for a number of derivatives (e.g., copies for the web or DVDs). Since it is as faithful to the original as possible, the original will not need to be digitized again. This also has the advantage of keeping the master from being exposed to harm through the digitization process. For example, in the case of a photograph, the extensive light produced by a scanner could slowly fade the color of the photograph. In the case of video, it eliminates the risk that the original video will get jammed in the player and damage the tape itself.

Another benefit of maintaining the highest fidelity masters relates to display technology. Display technology continually advances, as seen in the recent shift toward ultra high-definition television from high-definition and standard-definition television. Since each iteration of display technology has a higher resolution, being able to make use of the best quality copy of moving image records will help ensure that those images look as good as possible. The final advantage is that the digitized master may become the true master, displacing the original if that original media becomes unplayable from obsolescence or physical deterioration.

Despite the benefits of keeping a digital master, there are some drawbacks. The first is that the files are often much larger than their lower fidelity (or lower resolution) equivalents, making them more difficult to move and share. The second drawback is that the master files have to be managed, which takes time and resources and could be burdensome if the files are not accessed often (or ever), as may be the case when lower resolution copies satisfy researcher demand.

With digital archiving, the concept of archiving the original or highest resolution copy of an object as the master is common practice. Lower resolution copies, or copies that may make use of lossy compression (compression that discards information that the algorithm developer thinks the viewer will not notice), are generally thought to be acceptable for researcher access but should not be considered archival masters. With digital still images, the practice of creating a digital master as well as an access copy is considered best practice. For example, many libraries, archives, and museums create uncompressed TIFs as their master files and use JPGs for access.[28]

The question becomes at what point an archivist should consider not only whether to keep or not to keep but also a third option: to consider the form in which an item is kept. In the digital library and archive literature, *uncompressed* has become synonymous with *archival* or *master*, and *compression* with *access*.[29] However, at what point does the reality of digital preservation cost induce archivists to consider retaining lossy, compressed moving image records? How much savings can compression offer? And what records should be compressed? These issues will be explored in the following example.

During the art museum electronic records project mentioned earlier, I surveyed a number of large born-digital video collections. For example, one collection included six .MOV files totaling 165 GB that recorded a two-day meeting for a new initiative by the education department. During this meeting, a camera was set on a tripod, offering a wide view of the conference table. The purpose of the meeting was to plan a new educational initiative, and so the recording clearly had permanent value. However, was it necessary to preserve the high-definition footage in the format that came off the camera? Compression could reduce the size of the collection by 72 percent with no readily discernible visual or auditory differences. The only real downside of the compression process is that it would take approximately 45 minutes to compress one large video file while running on the background of a modern laptop. Is this a sensible course of action?

I would argue that in this case it is essential to consider the mission and collecting scope of your archives. At an art museum, it is clear that any recordings that have any potential to be exhibited, whether on film or television or in a gallery, should not be subjected to lossy compression, and the highest fidelity copy should be retained. Further, anything that could be classified as an artwork, such as performance art, or that includes artists speaking about their work or process should not be lossy compressed. However, for records like routine staff meetings, where the information is essential but retaining the highest fidelity copy is too costly, lossy compressed versions are satisfactory for meeting future researcher demand.

Ultimately, the argument for keeping the highest fidelity copy comes down to the importance of the visual information conveyed in the image and its relevance to the mission of the archives and the parent institution. In the case of the art museum, moving image records with evidential value—such as ones that demonstrate the functioning of the organization—are often better candidates for lossy compression than other records. For recordings of meetings, spoken language is the primary carrier of information, and the value of the visual information is to augment the information contained in the spoken language (e.g., facial expressions, gestures, responses by listeners, clarifying the identity of the speaker, etc.). To help decide in what form a moving image record should be kept, figure 1-2 identifies some considerations and examples from an art museum context.

	Accession, highest fidelity form	Accession, reduced fidelity	Deaccession
Evidential value	Illustrate significant organizational activity relevant to the collecting scope.	Illustrate significant organizational activity relevant to the collecting scope.	Illustrate routine administrative activity with limited or no relevance to the collecting scope.
Informational value	Illustrate the people, places, conditions, and events relevant to the collecting scope.	Illustrate the people, places, conditions, and events relevant to the collecting scope.	Illustrate people, places, conditions, and events that are largely irrelevant to the collecting scope.
Visual information	Visual information is important to the overall record and may exhibit some historic or artistic value, especially with respect to demonstrated evidential and/or informational values.	Visual information offers limited information and no historic or artistic value, especially with respect to evidential and/or informational values, and can be poorly composed.	Visual information offers limited information and no historic or artistic value, especially with respect to evidential and/or informational values, and can be poorly composed.
Examples from an art museum context	*Evidential:* A noted architect takes the viewer on a tour of a new museum building she designed. *Informational:* A performance artist enacts her latest work.	*Evidential:* A daylong staff meeting to discuss a new educational initiative, with camera recording unattended on a tripod. *Informational:* Video interviews with anonymous museum visitors for an internal study on their response to an exhibition.	*Evidential:* A staff training on how staff can use their health savings accounts. *Informational:* A DVD of a Hollywood film that was found among a departed staff member's belongings.

Figure 1-2. Appraisal decision matrix that takes into account the form in which a record will be kept.

It should also be noted that the use of lossy compression for select records makes the most sense in moving image records, such as video, and not sound records. The reason for this is that sound records, even the most high-fidelity recordings, are not that large, especially compared to video. For example, a very high-fidelity digitization of an hour of analog audio can result in a file about 1 GB in size.[30] However, one hour of digitized standard-definition video can result in file sizes of 100 GB or more.[31]

An upside to this approach is that it takes into account the value of the moving image records with respect to all other digital records contained within a repository. For example, is it sensible that a single video should occupy more resources (e.g., disk space) than the textual records of an entire archives? Does a single video warrant the same disk space requirements as tens of thousands of textual documents? For some moving image records, especially those that have significant value, this can be a fair trade-off. However, other moving image records should be considered in light of the overall resources they will require over time and the impact they have on the overall archiving enterprise.

Since the cost of producing digital video is much lower than film and even lower than analog video (e.g., there is no need to buy videotapes), digital video is being produced at a remarkable rate. For this reason, videographers sometimes leave cameras rolling and produce more raw footage than needed. Thus, while the highest fidelity version of a completed video project could be retained, video elements not used in a completed video may be good candidates for lossy compression (or even deaccessioning). However, this is of course dependent on the content itself, the subjects included, and the persons implicated, as well as the mission of the archives and the parent institution. What is important is that the archivist consider the "keeping in what form" issue in his mind, because the file size demands presented by raw footage or cameras kept recording all day are likely to overwhelm most if not all digital repositories.

It is worth noting that the "keeping in what form" issue is not that unusual when considered in relation to developments in digital preservation. For example, an accepted practice in digital preservation is to convert records from formats for which it is difficult to ensure persistence (e.g., proprietary file formats that are no longer vendor supported) to formats better suited for long-term preservation (e.g., openly documented, text-based formats).[32] Even with paper-based records, there is some past precedent for considering the "keeping in what form" issue. For example, some archives photocopy highly acidic materials like newspaper clippings onto acid-free paper and dispose of the original clippings.[33] Acts like this are about preserving the information and not harming the other nearby records with excessive acid. What is notable about this practice is that it requires the transformation of the original format to a new format, thus requiring the archivist to consider the "keeping in what form" issue and the best ways to ensure the persistence of information.

Taking into account the "keeping in what form" issue allows for archives to have more flexibility in collecting moving image materials. More and more, archivists are being presented with terabytes of high-fidelity video footage and are turning them away because they feel their only responsible option is to keep the highest fidelity master versions, and they do not have the resources (e.g., disk space) for keeping such material. Because moving image materials are so large, and they are in a sense in competition with other records for valuable repository resources such as available disk space, there is a danger that archivists will not collect these materials because they fear they will consume all available resources.

A further issue is that keeping slightly less high-fidelity versions of moving image material has not been proven to fail to meet user needs. Gracy notes that the expectations of image quality by users have not been explored and that there may be a "gap between moving image archivists' conceptions of image quality and perceived image quality of digital surrogates by users of those materials."[34] She suggests that varying user communities, such as psychologists, visual anthropologists, historians, and media studies scholars, may have different expectations of image quality. In this case, it may be sensible to forgo a binary approach and select image quality dimensions that are appropriate to the user community, in addition to other factors aforementioned.

TECHNICAL APPRAISAL

Because of the variety of formats in which audiovisual material may occur, including on digital and analog carriers, some level of technical appraisal is necessary. Huth, in writing about appraising digital records, distinguishes appraisal from technical appraisal, which involves assessing the technical characteristics of records for their ability to be prepared for permanent retention. Findings from technical appraisal can influence overall appraisal decisions.[35] The notion of technical appraisal is useful for moving image and sound records, which often require some level of technical appraisal of considerations including specialized equipment needed to play back the media, file formats of digital records, the possibilities for reformatting or migrating for preservation and access, and the digital preservation infrastructures available for storing such files.

REAPPRAISAL

Archivists may well encounter media in their processed collections, leading them to consider reappraisal, or the need to reevaluate past appraisal decisions to assess the preservation-worthiness of records. For example, an archivist may come across media that is inadequately described and wonder what is on the recording—and is it worth keeping? For media that are inadequately described or labeled, there is no other way to engage in reappraisal than to watch or listen to the media item. Christopher Ann Patton notes that this may well frustrate the archivist more versed in paper records because the media "cannot be 'scanned' or skimmed quickly by sight alone" and that "'speed reading' is generally not an option."[36] However, this can also be what is fun about appraising audiovisual records: a limited set of uniform media types yielding unexpected and infinite possibilities upon playback.

However, what are archivists to do if they do not have the playback equipment? There are a number of options for gaining intellectual access. If you have a large quantity of media in this format, it may make the most sense to purchase a player. (See the appropriate chapters in this book for information about playback of specific media types.) As mentioned in these chapters, *never insert or load an archival media item in a player that you are not familiar with*. Rather, buy a "test" tape or other media item on a site such as eBay, and ensure that the playback works correctly and does not damage the media before inserting your archival item into the player. This is also a good idea for players that have not been used in a while. For example, the test tape I use with U-matic VTRs, containing a music video, was purchased on eBay. (See figure 1-3.)

Figure 1-3. U-matic test tape and U-matic VTR.

If you have a small quantity of the media type and do not expect to receive many more items in this format, another option is to outsource the digitization to gain access to the content. Upon receiving the digitized contents back, you may realize that the content does not have permanent value, and thus the digitized files and original media can be deaccessioned. This option can appear a bit wasteful but can be an effective and efficient solution for repositories that have some funds to spare.

A third option is the collectivist strategy, in which archivists share their resources through informal and formal means so that other archivists and collections can benefit. This can be somewhat challenging for large institutions that may have policies stating for whom and for what reason institutional equipment can be used. However, if these barriers can be overcome, this solution holds a great deal of promise.

There are a number of initiatives underway that look to pool resources for common benefit. For example, the XFR Collective, which grew out of the New Museum's *XFR STN* exhibition of 2013, has helped artists and others transfer videotapes to digital formats via their equipment and share it through the Internet Archive.[37] With regard to obsolete born-digital formats, Ricky Erway of OCLC has argued for the creation of SWATs (software and workstations for antiquated technology), which are "organizations or institutions that are willing to put their expertise to use for the benefit of the broader community by providing specialized services to institutions with limited resources."[38] Further, some libraries have begun lending audiovisual equipment, and this is a great way to gain intellectual access to media. For example, the library at my home institution—Pratt Institute—began circulating 16 mm film projectors to students, faculty, and staff.[39] These projectors have piqued the interest of archival students and faculty, who were interested in them as a way to gain access to the contents of films that were stewarded in their collections.

Federal funders such as the National Endowment for the Humanities (NEH) have begun offering grants that allow libraries, archives, and museums to act as pools of resources and expertise to facilitate community digitization. For example, NEH's Common Heritage grant program looks to fund digitization events, where community members can bring in items such as audiovisual recordings for digitization.[40] These grants require that public programming is also an integral part of the event. Grants such as these offer great opportunities to interact with the community and also provide means to purchase playback equipment.

Other collectivist strategies have been envisioned. In a somewhat fanciful idea, Emily Gore of the Digital Public Library of America has argued for the creation of "Scannebagos," Winnebagos outfitted with "mobile scan centers that would enable the digitization of collections from small, local cultural heritage institutions that may not otherwise have access to these services."[41] Although not a reality yet, ideas such as Scannebagos and SWATs, among others, indicate a growing interest in collectivist strategies for digitization.

Beyond such initiatives, one of the most promising solutions for gaining access to the intellectual content of media is through leveraging the network of archivists within your local community. You never know if you don't ask: "I have six U-matic tapes in my collection. Can I come by and watch them on your player?" This may be a challenge for rural archivists, who—unlike archivists in cities—may not have nearby colleagues to depend on. In cases such as these, it may be necessary to develop more diffuse networks and share resources through snail mail, similar to interlibrary loan.

Part of a reappraisal process could also include a preservation assessment. For example, a preservation assessment could identify records that are problematic because they contain mold. However, a reappraisal process could identify those same records as no longer having permanent value, and thus the preservation actions needed to deal with the mold could be avoided by deaccessioning the material.

Thus, reappraisal and preservation assessment are intimately connected. Although beyond the scope of this book, recommended resources for proceeding with reappraisal and preservation assessment include *Guidelines for Reappraisal and Deaccessioning* from the Society of American Archivists and the University of Illinois at Urbana-Champaign's "Preservation Self-Assessment Program."[42]

EXAMPLE FROM ARCHIVAL PRACTICE
Archives of Emerson College
Boston, Massachusetts

Throughout this book, examples from published sources, interviews, and personal experience will help situate moving image and sound archives in practical archival contexts. To that end, the first example is based on an interview with Christina Zamon, formerly head of archives and special collections at Emerson College in Boston, MA (2007–16), and since 2016 head of special collections and archives at George State University.[43] The focus of my questions was on her work at Emerson, a private college specializing in communication and the arts. The example highlights strategies she used in selecting media for digitization that aimed to promote both preservation and access.

Zamon began at Emerson as a lone arranger and used her experience to write the book *The Lone Arranger: Succeeding in a Small Repository* (2012). By the time she left Emerson, two additional archivists had been added to the staff. When she began work at Emerson, Zamon noted there were large quantities of audiovisual items. There was not playback equipment for all media types, and she did not necessarily want to play back some of the older media, recognizing that effort was better spent in reformatting them to digital formats for preservation and access. Thus, a system was developed of digitizing or migrating media on demand by hand-delivering it to a local digitization vendor; the returned digitized files would be stored on an Emerson IT server. Patrons would access the digitized files however they needed them, such as through the web, USB flash drive, or optical disc.

Experiences with digitization on demand led Zamon to look more closely at her audiovisual collections. This led her to hire an intern to do an initial assessment of what audiovisual items were present and where they were stored. This assessment was used to inform the development of a Preservation Assistance Grant for Smaller Institutions from the National Endowment for the Arts that would permit the archives to hire AVPreserve—a consulting company with expertise with audiovisual materials based in Brooklyn, NY—to perform a full assessment. The grant application was successful, and AVPreserve was hired. Zamon expected AVPreserve to find about 5,000 to 5,500 audiovisual items; however, the tally was closer to 10,000 items in nearly all possible media formats, including U-matic, VHS, open-reel audio and video, 16 mm and 35 mm film, Blu-ray, DAT, Betacam, Betamax, and Digibeta, among other formats. She notes that "any format from the last fifty years we had at least one instance of. We did not know that we had such variety. We had a lot more of it than we thought we did."

As the archives continued to acquire more and more audiovisual materials, Zamon recognized that it needed a more proactive digitization approach than digitization on demand permitted. She decided to reallocate funds from an unused budget line to reformat media each year. She also used unspent funds left in the department's budget at the end of the fiscal year to reformat media. When moving from digitization on demand alone to proactive digitization, the archives needed to make its own selection decisions. Criteria were developed that prioritized items that had both high research value and rare formats over items that had low research value and were in fairly common formats. For example, some open-reel video as well as some DAT tapes were identified as having high research value and were recognized as endangered formats and thus were sent off for digitization. Media on VHS, which was fairly inexpensive and easy to digitize, was generally deprioritized unless it was of high research value. Any commercial works under copyright, such as those that could still be purchased, were deprioritized as well.

As part of its final report, AVPreserve provided digitization pricing information and a vendor list, including George Blood LP in Philadelphia and MediaPreserve in the greater Pittsburgh area. These vendors were especially useful for digitizing more obscure formats. For formats that were relatively easy and inexpensive to digitize, such as VHS or U-matic tapes, Zamon could also use Mass Productions in the Boston area.

Once digitized masters were created, they were stored on a hosted digital preservation platform called Preservica.[44] Via Preservica, the plan is to store preservation master files in Amazon's Glacier service, which is effectively "dark storage" where files cannot be quickly pulled up, and to store access files in Amazon's S3 service, where files can be quickly pulled up over the web.[45] By the time Zamon left Emerson, the plan was to store approximately 25–30 TB of preservation masters in Amazon's Glacier and 2 TB of access copies on S3 via Preservica.

CONCLUSION

Appraisal determines what gets incorporated into archival holdings and included in the historic record and has tended to result in one of two actions: to keep or not to keep. However, I have advocated for expanding the notion of appraisal to include a third dimension: keeping in what form. This dimension recognizes that moving image records present unique challenges because of their large file sizes and that it does not behoove archivists to use a binary approach. Rather, the form a record is stored in should be determined with respect to the mission and collecting scope of the archives and the evidential and informational values inherent in the record. This approach allows for the incorporation of born-digital and digitized moving image content into archives while taking into account their value and preservation demands in relationship to all digital records being stewarded. The chapter concludes with an example from archival practice, where a lone arranger makes audiovisual media available to researchers through a digitization-on-demand process, which paves the way for a proactive reformatting program guided by selection criteria.

NOTES

1. Richard Pearce-Moses, "Appraisal," in *A Glossary of Archival and Records Terminology* (Chicago: Society of American Archivists, 2005), http://www2.archivists.org/glossary/terms/a/appraisal, permalinked on March 31, 2016, at https://perma .cc/H9EK-69QZ.

2. Ibid., "Monetary appraisal," http://www2.archivists.org/glossary/terms/m/monetary-appraisal, permalinked on March 31, 2016, at https://perma.cc/N6J2-EBLC.

3. Ibid., "Reappraisal," http://www2.archivists.org/glossary/terms/r/reappraisal, permalinked on March 31, 2016, at https:// perma.cc/W5E8-CLWD.

4. Ibid., "Deaccessioning," http://www2.archivists.org/glossary/terms/d/deaccessioning, permalinked on March 31, 2016, at https://perma.cc/DV2H-7HAJ.

5. F. Gerald Ham, "The Archival Edge," in *A Modern Archives Reader*, ed. Maygene F. Daniels and Timothy Walch (Washington, DC: National Archives and Records Administration, 1984), 326.

6. Sir Hilary Jenkinson, *A Manual of Archive Administration* (Oxford: Clarendon Press, 1922).

7. Terry Eastwood, "Towards a Social Theory of Appraisal," *The Archival Imagination: Essays in Honour of Hugh A. Taylor*, ed. Barbara Craig (Ottawa: Association of Canadian Archivists, 1992).

8. Frank Boles, *Selecting and Appraising Archives and Manuscripts* (Chicago: Society of American Archivists, 2005).

9. T. R. Schellenberg, *Modern Archives: Principles and Techniques* (Chicago: Society of American Archivists, 1956), http://www .archivists.org/publications/epubs/ModernArchives-Schellenberg.pdf, permalinked on March 31, 2016, at https://perma.cc /F5TC-A7R2.

10. Ibid., 32.

11. David Bearman, "Archival Strategies," *American Archivist* 58, no. 4 (1995): 383.

12. Helen Willa Samuels, *Varsity Letters: Documenting Modern Colleges and Universities* (Chicago: Society of American Archivists, 1992).

13. Marcus C. Robyns, *Using Functional Analysis in Archival Appraisal: A Practical and Effective Alternative to Traditional Appraisal Methodologies* (Lanham, MD: Rowman & Littlefield, 2014).

14. Sam Kula, *Appraising Moving Images: Assessing the Archival and Monetary Value of Film and Video Records* (Lanham, MD: Scarecrow Press, 2003), 128.

15. Ibid., 33–34.

16. "NARA Bulletin 2013-02," National Archives and Records Administration, http://www.archives.gov/records-mgmt/bulletins /2013/2013-02.html, permalinked on March 31, 2016, at https://perma.cc/8T97-B5FE.

17. Karen F. Gracy, *Film Preservation: Competing Definitions of Value, Use, and Practice* (Chicago: Society of American Archivists, 2007), 80.

18. Kula, *Appraising Moving Images,* 24.

19. Ibid.

20. Ibid., 41.

21. Ibid., 43.

22. Anne J. Gilliland, "Archival Appraisal: Practising on Shifting Sands," in *Archives and Recordkeeping: Theory into Practice*, ed. Caroline Brown (London: Facet, 2014), 31–61.

23. Ibid., 54.

24. Ibid., 49.

25. Geof Huth, "Module 14: Appraising Digital Records," in *Appraisal and Acquisition Strategies,* ed. Michael Shallcross and Christopher J. Prom (Chicago: Society of American Archivists, 2016), 14, 26.

26. Anthony Cocciolo, "Challenges to Born-Digital Institutional Archiving: The Case of a New York Art Museum," *Records Management Journal* 24, no. 3 (2014): 238–50.

27. Several examples of bulk extraction tools are included in this project: Anthony Cocciolo, "Community Archives in the Digital Era: A Case from the LGBT Community," *Preservation, Digital Technology & Culture* 45, no. 4 (February 2017): 157–165, https://doi.org/10.1515/pdtc-2016-0018, permalinked on August 31, 2016, at https://perma.cc/B9AD-2M7H.

28. An example of digitization standards resulting in master and access images is the Federal Agencies Digitization Initiative (FADGI) Still Image Working Group's *Technical Guidelines for Digitizing Cultural Heritage Materials: Creation of Raster Image Master Files*, 2009, http://www.digitizationguidelines.gov/guidelines/FADGI_Still_Image-Tech_Guidelines_2010-08-24.pdf, permalinked on March 31, 2016, at https://perma.cc/8G5L-5LVP.

29. Ian Bogus et al., *Minimum Digitization Capture Recommendations* (Chicago: Association for Library Collections and Technical Services Preservation and Reformatting Section, 2013), http://www.ala.org/alcts/resources/preserv/minimum -digitization-capture-recommendations#video, permalinked on March 31, 2016, at https://perma.cc/HKM4-UUEX.

30. Assumes that audio is digitized at 24-bit/96 kHz (or 24 bits are sampled 96,000 times per second).

[31] Assumes that standard definition video is digitized using 10-bit uncompressed YUV.

[32] Digital preservation standards that require format migration include OAIS. For more information, see Brian Lavoie, *The Open Archival Information System (OAIS) Reference Model: Introductory Guide,* 2nd ed. (York, UK: Digital Preservation Coalition, 2014).

[33] Goodluck Israel Ifijeh, "Newspaper Preservation in Developing Countries: Issues and Strategies for Intervention," in *Preserving Local Writers, Genealogy, Photographs, Newspapers, and Related Materials,* ed. Carol Smallwood and Elaine Williams (London: Scarecrow Press, 2012).

[34] Karen Gracy, "Perceptions of Image Quality in Digital Moving Image Surrogates" (poster presented at the Society of American Archivists Annual Meeting Research Forum, Cleveland, OH, August 18, 2015).

[35] Huth, *Appraising Digital Records.*

[36] Christopher Ann Patton, "Whispers in the Stacks: The Problem of Sound Recordings in Archives," *American Archivist* 53, no. 2 (1990): 276.

[37] XFR Collective, "Our History," https://xfrcollective.wordpress.com/about/our_history/, permalinked on August 31, 2016, at https://perma.cc/4KAF-XYZR.

[38] Ricky Erway, *Swatting the Long Tail of Digital Media: A Call for Collaboration* (Dublin, OH: OCLC Research, 2013), 3, http://www.oclc.org/content/dam/research/publications/library/2012/2012-08.pdf, permalinked on August 31, 2016, at https://perma.cc/ZN88-VMDA.

[39] Pratt Institute Libraries, "Visual and Multimedia Resources," https://library.pratt.edu/services/visual_multimedia_resources/, permalinked on January 27, 2017, at https://perma.cc/P4P6-BLME.

[40] National Endowment for the Humanities, "Common Heritage," http://www.neh.gov/grants/preservation/common-heritage, permalinked on August 31, 2016, at https://perma.cc/5PLM-7AMJ.

[41] "Scannebago," *Wikipedia,* https://en.wikipedia.org/wiki/Scannebago, permalinked on December 6, 2016, at https://perma.cc/LB66-XDNF.

[42] Peter Blodgett et al., *Guidelines for Reappraisal and Deaccessioning* (Chicago: Society of American Archivists, 2012), http://www2.archivists.org/sites/all/files/GuidelinesForReappraisalAndDeaccessioning-May2012.pdf, permalinked on March 31, 2016, at https://perma.cc/P3MB-CNQ5; Preservation Self-Assessment Program (Urbana-Champaign: University of Illinois, 2015), https://psap.library.illinois.edu/, permalinked on March 31, 2016, at https://perma.cc/T94B-KZCB; Jennifer Hain Teper, "The Preservation Self-Assessment Program: A Tool to Aid in Preservation and Conservation Prioritization," *The Book and Paper Group Annual* 34 (2015): 159–63.

[43] Christina Zamon, telephone interview by the author, December 2, 2016.

[44] Preservica, http://preservica.com/, permalinked on April 21, 2016, at https://perma.cc/Q2VQ-T7GU.

[45] Amazon Glacier, https://aws.amazon.com/glacier/, permalinked on December 6, 2016, at https://perma.cc/4WXZ-WLQS; Amazon S3, https://aws.amazon.com/s3/, permalinked on December 6, 2016, at https://perma.cc/X6RN-AGVP.

CHAPTER 2

Accessioning, Arrangement, and Description

This chapter discusses the topic of accessioning, arrangement, and description of collections with moving image and sound materials, including steps for taking custody of records, physically arranging them, and creating metadata records for them using various methods. However, before we delve into this topic, some brief background is necessary.

ACCESSIONING

Archives should have a well-articulated procedure for accessioning materials into their holdings. Typically, archives assign an acquired collection an accession number and provide a basic inventory of the contents of the collection. In creating an accession record, it is useful to note the presence of audiovisual material or digital media (which can also contain audiovisual information), the quantity of these items, specific format, and any physically obvious condition issues. (Please consult the relevant chapters in this book for determining the format and adding condition notes related to media.) Chapter 6, "Interactions with Moving Image and Sound Producers," offers advice on working with creators during donation. If this information is recorded well and the collection stays in the backlog for an extended duration, the relevant boxes can be quickly identified if resources become available for conducting format migration. See the sample accession record in figure 2-1, modified from Kathleen D. Roe's seminal book *Arranging and Describing Archives and Manuscripts*:[1]

Date rec'd 12/12/2004	Accession no. 13464-2004	Location West Alcove, Range 1 Shelf 2–3
Creating individual/organization Katherine Valdez		
Title Synchronized swimming collection		
Quantity 17 cubic feet		
Approximate Dates: 1930–1990		
General contents: Video tapes, photographs, autographs, letters, scrapbooks, various written materials		
Donor/transferring agency: Professor Katherine Valdez		
Accessioned by: Kayla Johnson	**Date:** February 21, 2003	

Box list: Katherine Valdez Synchronized Swimming Collection			
Contents	**Box number**	**Location**	**Notes**
Videotapes	1–3	Range 1, Shelf 2	20 VHS tapes, 7 MiniDV tapes, 1 U-matic SP tape
Photographs	4–7	Range 1, Shelf 2	
Audiotapes	8–9	Range 1, Shelf 2	28 compact audiocassettes
Scrapbooks	10–14	Range 1, Shelf 3	
Topical files	15–16	Range 1, Shelf 3	
Electronic files	17	Range 1, Shelf 3	12 3.5-inch floppy disks, 2 5.25-inch disks, 5 250 MB Zip disks, 2 USB hard disks (500 GB)

Figure 2-1. Sample accession form.

The accession form need not be a paper form. Archivists can use archival management systems such as Archivists Toolkit or ArchivesSpace to record and manage incoming accessions.[2] Non-archives-specific tools such as Microsoft Access or Filemaker Pro can also be used to document accessions.

Current best practice is to image digital media that contain electronic files on accession.[3] Imaging creates a bit-for-bit copy of the media; this disk image should be retained, as it is an exact replica that can replace the original media if the original fails while in storage. The images can then be stored in trustworthy digital repositories, and when the time comes to process the collection, the disk images can be used rather than the original digital media. If resource constraints prevent imaging of media on accession, then at a minimum the media information (media type and quantity) should be maintained in the accession record. Chapter 11, "Complex Media," discusses disk imaging in more depth.

At the time of accessioning, archivists should have donors sign a donor agreement. The donor agreement will be discussed at length in chapter 3, "Legal and Ethical Issues."

PHYSICAL STORAGE

Recommended practice for archivists is to store paper records in acid-free boxes and acid-free folders.[4] The reason is that "acid can migrate from . . . poor quality enclosures to the records within," and "corrugated cardboard boxes emit substantial quantities of peroxides and acid by-products, which are especially harmful to records in closed containers."[5] The damage caused by acidic boxes and folders may not initially be evident from a few years of exposure, but "the damage caused to records by acid—whatever its source—is conclusive."[6] Further, the acid in boxes acts to erode the structure of the box over time, making it brittle and more likely to break down. To determine if a folder or a box has acid in it, pH pens are available that measure the acidity of the paper. Many options exist, such as pens with digital readouts and pens that leave ink that changes color if there is acid in the paper.[7]

Should archivists place moving image and sound media into acid-free boxes? Further, should they arrange paper records with moving image media together in the same box? Guidance from the International Association of Sound and Audiovisual Archives (IASA) indicate that there is no reason not to place media into acid-free boxes.[8] Storage of archival audiovisual media should strive to eliminate exposure to dusts and other pollutants, and acid-free boxes have the advantage of adding an extra layer of protection than that provided by shelves alone. Since some media, such as large film reels, will not fit into a typical banker's box (10" x 12" x 15"), large media are better suited for storage directly on shelves. This includes all grooved discs, such as vinyl discs, which are best kept upright on shelves in sleeves designed for discs, as pressure from other nearby objects can deform a disc and the grooves that contain the sound.[9] Also, the IASA standard recommends that all audio and video "carriers, discs, tapes and any cassettes should be stored upright."[10] Films, however, should be stored flat or horizontally in rigid containers that protect the reels from dust or physical damage.[11] Lastly, media should not be tightly packed so as not to damage each other and to prevent the weight of the box from becoming untenable or threatening the integrity of the box.

While arranging media with paper records is an option, one aspect to consider is the humidity and temperature of the storage environment. Chapters 7 through 11 will discuss the recommended best practice in storage of each type of media; however, the storage temperatures and relative humidity for some media are typically colder and dryer than most paper collections require. For example, for paper records, the Northeast Document Conservation Center recommends a maximum temperature of 70°F with 30–50 percent relative humidity; for tape collections, IASA and the Association of Recorded Sound Collections (ARSC) recommend a temperature of 46–54°F with 25–35 percent relative humidity.[12] Thus, best practices in a storage environment may induce archivists to store their paper and media in separate rooms. However, many small archives may only have a single room or facility and will need to adopt a temperature and humidity range that works well for more than one kind of material. Further, some archives may have a single room and little or no control of temperature or humidity, in which case the separation of media from paper material makes little sense.

DESCRIBING MOVING IMAGE COLLECTIONS USING ARCHIVAL METHODS

As mentioned in the previous chapter, moving image and sound collections are often considered on the item level rather than as a grouping of records, as is typical of paper records. With paper records, group-ings can include the collection level (e.g., "Herman Baca Papers") and record group (e.g., "Committee on Chicano Rights"), followed by series-level grouping (e.g., "Correspondence," "Newsletters," etc.).[13] This is unlike most moving image materials available for checkout from library multimedia departments that have interrelationships imposed by librarians to help promote access through subject headings (e.g., "Feminists—United States—Biography") and genres (e.g., "documentary films").

Like library multimedia departments, many moving image archives create primarily item-level metadata. For example, the Association of Moving Image Archivists (AMIA) *Compendium of Moving Image Cataloging Practice* (2001) surveys moving image archivists on their cataloging practice and notes that only one out of twenty-seven archives create group-level metadata records for all moving image collections.[14] It is not surprising that the one group to consistently create group-level metadata records is an oral history–centered archive—the Fortunoff Video Archive for Holocaust Testimonies, now at Yale University. Oral history projects often originate from a common source or provenance, which is as important to document as the content of the oral history itself. Information about the origination of the oral history project, including information about the project team, is valuable information that points to the context in which the oral histories were created, which can have eventual bearing on the content itself. For example, choosing to ask an interviewee certain questions and not others is not only context but also acts to constitute the record. Documenting context is the cornerstone of archival practice and is one of the aspects that distinguishes archival practice from other metadata-creation practices like library cataloging.[15] Oral history projects also often include textual documentation, such as transcripts and rights release forms, which benefit from being intellectually arranged (if not physically arranged) with the recording media.

As of the 2001 survey, many of the moving image archives studied created MARC (Machine Readable Cataloging) records, which are well suited for retaining information like title, description, cre-ator, and technical information (e.g., carrier), but may not be well suited for describing the provenance or origination of a collection. MARC is the standard data structure for storing most library catalog records. An excerpted sample of a MARC record for a circulating film on DVD from the Pratt Libraries is illustrated in figure 2-2.

Existing standards for moving image cataloging, like the Library of Congress's Archival Moving Image Materials (AMIM2), stress creating item-level MARC records. Because item-level records describe an item (e.g., a film reel or several film reels), being able to intellectually arrange moving image records with their respective paper records is not typically possible with MARC records. Examples in AMIM2 suggest that paper records and recorded media get grouped together only through notes fields such as the following:

> (MARC field 544) The papers of Edward W. Brooke are serviced in the Manuscript Reading Room of the Library of Congress (see LC bibliographic record mm81058347) and the audio materials in this collection are serviced in the Recorded Sound Reference Center of the Motion Picture, Broadcasting, and Recorded Sound Division.[16]

245 00 United in anger : l ba history of ACT UP / l cJim
Hubbard and Sarah Schulman present a film by Jim
Hubbard; directed by Jim Hubbard; produced by
Sarah Schulman, Jim Hubbard.

264 1 [United States] : l bUnited in Anger, Inc., l c[2014]

264 4 l c©2014

300 1 videodisc (93 min.) : l bsound, color; l c4 3/4 in.

336 two-dimensional moving image l btdi l 2rdacontent

337 video l bv l 2rdamedia

338 videodisc l bvd l 2rdacarrier

344 digital l boptical l gstereo l 2rda

346 l bNTSC l 2rda

347 video file l bDVD video l eregion 1 l 2rda

380 Documentary film.

610 20 ACT UP (Organization) l xHistory.

610 20 ACT UP New York (Organization) l xHistory.

650 0 AIDS (Disease) l xPolitical aspects.

650 0 AIDS activists l zUnited States.

Figure 2-2. Excerpted sample MARC record for a circulating
film on DVD.

Julia Child Papers, 1920–1993

I.   Biographical
II. Correspondence
     a.   Personal
     b.   Cookery
     c.   Fans
     d.   Publishers
     e.   Lawyers
     f.   TV Companies
III. Teaching
     a.   Cooking classes
     b.   TV programs
     c.   Cooking demonstrations
IV. Writings
V.   Publicity
VI. Audiovisual
     a.   Photographs
     b.   Audiotapes
     c.   Videotapes

Figure 2-3. Sample archival arrangement
from Roe.

Despite the tendency of moving image archives to not always create group-level records, that does not mean that it has not been done and that such collections would not benefit from such description. Further, sources on archival arrangement and description indicate that creating group-level records first can help expedite making collections available to researchers, especially when there are not sufficient resources to create item-level records. Pam Hackbart-Dean and Elizabeth Slomba, in *How to Manage Processing in Archives and Special Collections*, note that "although item-level description is often a great way to access difficult-to-describe materials, this level of description is labor-intensive," and archivists should "consider processing audiovisual collections at the series and collection level, which will emphasize the overall content of series and collection."[17] Daniel Santamaria, in his book on extensible processing for archives, further supports this view, noting that media of the same format can be grouped together and basic information such as quantity and condition notes can be maintained.[18] He notes that some of this information can be recorded during the initial accession process, when the records are initially transferred into the archives, and then reused in finding aids. Further, several examples from Roe's *Arranging and Describing Archives and Manuscripts* indicate that group-level description of audiovisual material is an option. She provides an example of an arrangement in figure 2-3; note the grouping of audiovisual material at the end.[19]

In figure 2-4, an excerpted finding aid as an access point to an audiovisual collection, specifically an oral history project, is provided. (For the sake of brevity, some reformatting has taken place, such as removing the following elements: Arrangement, ID, Acquisition Method, Appraisal Information, Preferred Citation, Processing Information, Alternate Extent Statement, and all Series 2 information, including subseries. The full finding aid is available online.[20]) Noteworthy aspects of the finding aid, such as the work of putting the media items into a larger context, are noted in the right column.

Figure 2-4. Excerpted finding aid providing access to oral history collection. Reproduced with permission, Archives of the American Field Service and AFS Intercultural Programs.

Oral History Collection, ca. 1985–2012 **By Nicole Milano** **Collection Overview** **Predominant Dates:** 1999–2007 **Creator:** AFS Intercultural Programs **Extent:** 6.0 Cubic Feet (5 boxes) **Languages:** English, Spanish, Castilian, French **Abstract** The Archives of the American Field Service and AFS Intercultural Programs (AFS Archives) and AFS Intercultural Programs, Inc. staff have launched several initiatives to document the rich history of AFS through audio and visual oral history interviews. The Oral History Collection contains select transcripts, photographs, written histories, preparatory questionnaires, and more than 150 hours of audio and visual interviews with World War I and II ambulance drivers, present and former AFS Intercultural Programs staff, and prominent student exchange program Returnees over a period of nearly two decades. **Scope and Contents of the Materials** The AFS Oral History Collection contains more than 150 hours of audio and visual interviews with World War I and II ambulance drivers, present and former AFS Intercultural Programs staff, and prominent student exchange program Returnees over a period of nearly two decades. The collection also includes select transcripts, photographs donated by ambulance drivers or taken during their interviews, written histories, and preparatory questionnaires and instructions for the interviews. The interviews give insight into various aspects of AFS history, including life as an ambulance driver in World Wars I and II, working with Stephen Galatti for the early student exchange programs, and the development and expansion of AFS Intercultural Programs, Inc. For more information on the oral history initiatives, see the individual series and subseries descriptions.	*The collection overview provides a broad sense of what is in the collection and the overall size of the collection, in terms of physical dimensions and also intellectual content (e.g., total listening hours).*
Acquisition Method: The World War II Oral History Project (which became known as the AFS Legacy Project) consisted of audio interviews completed by the American Field Service (AFS) ambulance drivers and sent to the AFS Archives at various dates, beginning in 1999. The World War I interviews were conducted or coordinated by William Foley, an AFS collector and AFS Archives volunteer. All other interviews were conducted through AFS Intercultural Programs, Inc. and the Archives of the American Field Service and AFS Intercultural Programs (AFS Archives), and all audio and visual material was transferred to the AFS Archives at various dates.	*Provides background on how the collection came to exist, thus putting the "stuff" into context.*

(continued)

(Figure 2-4 continued)

Box and Folder Listing

Series 1: Pre-Legacy Interviews, ca. 1985–1995
This series includes interviews, the bulk of which are audio, conducted by AFS Intercultural Programs staff and volunteers prior to the AFS Legacy Project oral history initiative, which began in 1999.

For more information on the oral history initiatives, see the individual subseries descriptions.

> **Subseries 1A:** World War I Driver Interviews, ca. 1985–1987— Box 1
> This subseries includes cassette tapes of interviews conducted with World War I ambulance and camion drivers (including Edward S. Ingham and Edward A. Weeks, Jr.) by AFS collector and AFS Archives volunteer William Foley between 1985 and 1987.

> **Subseries 1B:** Staff Interviews, ca. 1985–1987—Box 1
> This subseries includes cassette tapes and transcripts (drafts) of undated staff interviews conducted with early and longtime staff members of AFS, including Robert M. Applewhite, Dorothy "Dot" Field, and Stephen H. Rhinesmith. These interviews were used in preparation for Orrick's 1991 publication about the AFS student exchange programs entitled *The First Thirty Years: 1947–1976.*

> **Subseries 1C:** World War II 50th Reunion Interviews, 1995—Box 1
> This subseries includes cassette tapes of interviews conducted with World War II ambulance drivers and former staff (including Henry M. "Bud" Wagner and Mr. and Mrs. John C. Cobb II) at the 50th anniversary reunion for the World War II ambulance drivers held in Williamsburg, Virginia, in 1995.

> **Subseries 1D:** World War II Interviews, 1988
> This subseries includes one audio interview on a cassette tape conducted with World War II ambulance driver James A. Doughty, which was not part of a particular project or reunion. The interview was conducted by former AFS Archivist L. D. Geller in St. Augustine, Florida, on April 6, 1988. There is also a list of questions available for this interview.

Series and subseries group together related materials and provide additional detail beyond what is provided in the Collection Overview. Note how the individual who initiated the project is noted, which is an important aspect of the series' provenance and further reason for grouping together those materials.

Subseries 1D may be small in size (it contains only a single cassette) but is its own subseries because of its distinct provenance.

A feature of this online finding aid is that it not only documents the whole collection in terms of both its physical and intellectual dimensions, it also allows access to select digitized items, allowing users to listen to or watch oral histories. Additionally, the user can readily see how an individual item is grouped with other items. The following example illustrates an item-level record of a digitized oral history from the same collection. Note how users are able to see how an item is part of a larger subseries, series, and collection, and how they can zoom out to view these larger sets of groupings.

In figure 2-5, the item-level record and excerpted finding aid were created by archivist Nicole Milano in Archon, an archival management system that makes use of archival standards, specifically *Describing Archives: A Content Standard* (DACS) and Encoded Archival Description (EAD).[21] Archival management systems, unlike general content management systems, specifically allow for the organization of information into hierarchies (collection, series, subseries) and actively make use of such archival standards. Other archival management systems include Archivists Toolkit, ArchivesSpace, and Access to Memory (AtoM).[22] Since these systems all make use of EAD, finding aids encoded as EAD can be transferred from one archival management system to another.[23] Content management systems, such as Omeka, Drupal, Joomla, WordPress, and others, do not by default support archival descriptive standards

Legacy Project: Arthur Howe, Jr. | Archives of the American Field Service and AFS Intercultural Programs

Available: http://brandcenter.afs.org/CMS/sharedbin/afs-history-and-archives/oral-history-platform /4_002_2B_Howe.mp4

Title: Legacy Project: Arthur Howe, Jr.

Date: 2002 September 21

Description:

Interviewee: Arthur Howe, Jr.

Interviewee AFS Affiliation: World War II Driver (Major—ME 2), Staff, Life Trustee

Interviewer: Douglas Manger

Length: 52 minutes 40 seconds

Location: Baltimore, MD

Phys. Desc: Also available as an audiocassette, 2 MiniDVs, 4 VHS tapes, and WAVE file created at 44.1kHz/16-bit.

ID: 4_002_2B_Howe

Repository: Archives of the American Field Service and AFS Intercultural Programs

Found in: Oral History Collection, ca. 1985–2012 -> Series 2: Legacy Project, 1999–2012 -> Subseries 2B: Legacy Project, 2002–2012

Creators: Howe, Arthur, Jr. (1921–)

AFS Intercultural Programs

Subjects [abbreviated]:

Allied Forces. Mediterranean Theater

Ambulance drivers

World War, 1939–1945—Campaigns—Africa

World War, 1939–1945—Campaigns—France

World War, 1939–1945—Campaigns—Germany

World War, 1939–1945—Campaigns—Italy

Yale University. Class of 1943

Publisher: Digitized by the Pratt Institute's School of Information and Library Science in 2012.

Rights: All rights reserved by AFS Intercultural Programs. Permission to reproduce or use this oral history must be submitted in writing to the Archives of the American Field Service and AFS Intercultural Programs.

Languages: English

Figure 2-5. Item-level record for oral history. Reproduced with permission, Archives of American Field Service and AFS Intercultural Programs.

such as DACS and EAD; however, archivists may use them in other ways. For example, archivists may use Omeka to catalog and present individual items to users, and they may use Wordpress to present finding aids to users.

Although a thorough discussion of DACS and EAD are beyond the scope of this book, a brief discussion of these standards is warranted.[24] DACS specifies a set of rules for writing content that goes into an EAD-encoded finding aid. For example, DACS specifies how an archivist should format a date (e.g., 2018 June 12), name a person (e.g., use the familiar name like Jimmy Carter, not James Earl Carter), and which pieces of information are required in a finding aid and which ones are optional. EAD is the machine-readable version of the finding aid, rendered as XML (Extensible Markup Language). Thus, one finding aid is equivalent to one EAD record, which may represent hundreds of boxes and thousands of items. For example, the scope and content note of the AFS finding aid may be represented with EAD in the following way:

```
<ead>
<eadheader>[Basic information about the finding aid, such as the title]</eadheader>
<frontmatter>[More basic information about the finding aid, like the publisher]</frontmatter>
<archdesc>
<scopecontent>The AFS Oral History Collection contains more than 150 hours of audio and visual inter-
views . . . </scopecontent>
</archdesc>
</ead>
```

Figure 2-6. Excerpted sample finding aid represented as EAD.

Using tools like XML editors (e.g., Oxygen XML editor[25]), users can verify that their EAD complies with the EAD standard. Fortunately, the archival management systems mentioned earlier create EAD files for you, so you do not necessarily need to hand-code EAD. However, many archivists find it useful to know how to do this.

DACS-compliant finding aids can also be used to support providing access to media that are not available online. The "Conditions Governing Access" field of a finding aid—required of all finding aids that are DACS compliant—can highlight any physical access and technical access limitations related to the media. Possible examples, pulled from the DACS standard, include:

> "The audiocassettes are located in cold vault storage and must be acclimated before delivery
> to the research room."[26]

> "Parade recorded on Super 8 film."[27]

For media that cannot be played because the institution does not have playback equipment nor will it be able to digitize the media on demand, it would be appropriate to make this clear to the user in the conditions governing access. This can be as simple as:

> "U-matic videos cannot be viewed because a player is not currently available."

> "Eight mm films cannot be viewed because a projector is not currently available."

ITEM-LEVEL DESCRIPTIVE PRACTICES

Describing archival materials by creating finding aids that use the DACS and EAD standards is an option that may make a lot of sense in cases where all other collections are described this way, in cases where the groupings are significant, or in cases where an archivist wants to link individual items back to their parent groupings (e.g., be able to see how an item is part of a larger collection and be able to get some background on the collection as a whole). Thus, finding aids and EAD are particularly valuable where the hierarchical structure and interrelationships are important to understanding the overall record. Using a finding aid approach also makes sense for collections that are predominantly paper based, with audiovisual material only a part of this larger whole. Also, as mentioned earlier, creating group-level records can make collections known to researchers with less labor than creating item-level records. However, there are alternatives, most of which emphasize creating item-level records.

Creating item-level records is becoming increasingly important for preservation, both in terms of knowing what you have and planning for reformatting. Further, providing access to audiovisual recordings almost always requires item-level records, as illustrated in figure 2-5. Joshua Ranger, an audiovisual archivist, argues that "unlike an MPLP-like approach that can successfully limit description to the collection or series level, the ability to plan budgets, timelines, equipment needs, and other preservation plans that unequivocally impact access is directly tied to the documentation of some degree of item-level knowledge about one's collection."[28] MPLP ("more product, less process") is an archival processing strategy developed by Mark Greene and Dennis Meissner that aims to reduce processing backlogs by dedicating less effort to certain labor-intensive steps, like physical arrangement and item-level description.[29]

Item-level standards include the AMIM2 standard, which is an older standard that has been put in place by the Library of Congress and is used by several moving image archives.[30] AMIM2 records are output as MARC records. Other groups, such as library multimedia departments, may describe moving image collections using AACR2 (Anglo-American Cataloguing Rules) with MARC record output. This standard has been replaced by the RDA (Resource Description and Access) standard, which also outputs MARC records.[31] Despite this, AACR2 records will continue to be around for a long time, as some catalogers continue to use this format.[32] Although creating MARC records that adhere to the AMIM2, RDA, or AACR2 standards will not be further discussed in this book, interested readers can find useful guidance for implementing these standards in the notes for this chapter.

There are alternative descriptive standards that do not rely on creating MARC records, which can be complicated to create and difficult for novices to understand. One way to describe moving image and sound records is to use the Dublin Core standard, which can be supplemented with the PBCore standard. The Dublin Core standard was designed to describe web resources using fifteen simple and flexible fields that can be repeated, such as title, description, and creator.[33] The PBCore standard (short for Public Broadcasting Metadata Dictionary Project) was created to supplement the Dublin Core standard by providing technical metadata and other information that is relevant for maintaining moving image collections.[34] For example, PBCore provides fields to specify the physical media (if it exists), the digital media (if it exists), and information on the encoding (e.g., "WAV" or "H.264/MPEG-4"). Having technical metadata on the media and digital files can help promote preservation. For example, being able to easily locate all the Betamax tapes in your archives for digitization or knowing that you have digital videos in a proprietary format or encoding that are no longer supported by a vendor can help expedite identification of media for migration to more sustainable formats.

Some content management systems (CMSs), digital asset management systems (DAMs), and media asset management systems (MAMs) have begun to support PBCore. One of the simplest and easiest CMSs that has some limited support for PBCore is Omeka, a free, open-source software that works well for providing access to audiovisual media.[35] For the last several years, my students at Pratt Institute have been using it to make oral histories and other audiovisual media available from local archives, such as the Lesbian Herstory Archives and Archives of the Center for Puerto Rican Studies, among others.[36]

An advantage of Omeka is that it also allows the creation of hierarchical collections of items, thus simulating some of the functionality of a finding aid.[37] However, it should be noted that although this may simulate a finding aid, these metadata records are not exportable to DACS/EAD finding aids, thus inhibiting some potential interoperability benefits (e.g., being able to transfer entire finding aids from one archival management system to another).

To start using Dublin Core and PBCore standards to describe moving image and sound collections, first identify the fields you would like to use. You can browse the available fields on the DC and PBCore websites.[38] Since PBCore includes dozens of fields, it is likely that you will not use them all. Also, simple CMSs such as Omeka do not implement all the features and fields available in these standards. Information that you would want to retain includes descriptive, administrative, and technical metadata. Descriptive metadata lets you and your users search for content and understand what is contained in the record. Administrative metadata, such as knowing the physical location, helps the archives manage the asset. Technical metadata, which can be considered a type of administrative metadata, communicates technical aspects that are relevant to preserving and rendering the record (e.g., communicating the relationship between the digitized content and its original media). The example in figure 2-7 illustrates a Dublin Core/PBCore record from the Herstories Audiovisual Archive created by students at Pratt Institute's School of Information on behalf of the Lesbian Herstory Archives:[39]

In this example, a single VHS tape has been digitized to create a master copy and an access copy. Using the PBCore specification, the differences between the master and access copies could be articulated through creating two instances. However, as mentioned earlier, Omeka does not implement all features of PBCore such as the ability to create instances, so in this example this functionality is handled by repeating fields and adding the "[master]" and "[access]" labels. This example provides some of the most relevant descriptive and technical metadata and is by no means a comprehensive list. Each repository needs to decide which descriptive and technical metadata it wants to create and maintain. Opening files and viewing their technical properties can retrieve much of the technical metadata. For example, in VLC Player, you can hit CTRL (Windows) or Command (Macintosh) and the "i" key to pull up technical properties of a video.[40] There are also some automated methods for retrieving technical metadata.[41] In this example, the technical metadata points to aspects like video encoding, which is useful to know if a particular encoding method is no longer being supported and the content needs to be migrated to another format. Other information, such as file size, aspect ratio, and image dimensions, helps to confirm for users (and the repository) that what they are looking at is indeed what has been accessioned and described by the archives.

For audio collections, the descriptive metadata are similar to the metadata retained for video collections. One important distinction is that many audio formats have two sides (e.g., side A or 1 and side B or 2), and it is important to decide up front if separate metadata records will be created for each side or if one metadata record will represent the entire recording. For simplicity's sake, a single metadata record for a single audio carrier is recommended; however, the details of the sides should be provided. An example is provided in figure 2-8.

Schema	Field	Example
Descriptive Metadata		
DC	Title	Lesbian Herstory Archives Daughters of Bilitis Video Project: Linda Lopez, Tape 1 of 2, 1988 October 22
DC	Subject	Lesbian—United States—History Lesbian and Gay Experience Lesbians—United States—Identity
DC	Description	Linda Lopez is interviewed in 1988. She talks about growing up in the South and how she fared as a lesbian living in a conservative community . . .
DC	Creator	Linda Lopez [interviewee]
DC	Creator	Manuela Soares [interviewer]
DC	Date	1988 October 22 [date created]
DC	Rights	Copyright the Lesbian Herstory Archives . . .
DC	Language	en-US
DC	Format	Video recording
DC	Identifier	Special Collection 202, tape MV42
DC	Coverage	San Francisco, CA
Technical Metadata		
PBCore	formatPhysical	VHS NTSC SP
PBCore	formatEncoding	DV Video [master]
PBCore	formatEncoding	MPEG4/H264 [access]
PBCore	formatDuration	02:03:25
PBCore	formatFileSize	28 GB [master]
PBCore	formatFileSize	525 MB [access]
PBCore	formatFrameSize	720X480 [master]
PBCore	formatFrameSize	320X240 [access]
PBCore	formatAspectRatio	4:3
PBCore	formatIdentifier	linda_lopez_tape1of2_1988oct22.avi [master]
PBCore	formatIdentifier	linda_lopez_tape1of2_1988oct22.mp4 [access]
Administrative Metadata		
Other	physicalLocation	Box 2

Figure 2-7. Example of Dublin Core augmented with PBCore metadata record for a video recording.

Schema	Field	Example
Descriptive Metadata		
DC	Title	Audre Lorde, Reading from 13th Moon Series 1982 (Tape 1)
DC	Subject	Lesbians Feminists African American feminists African American women—Poetry
DC	Description	[Side A] A poetry reading from Audre Lorde . . .
DC	Description	[Side B] Lorde discusses her next poem . . .
DC	Creator	Audre Lorde
DC	Publisher	WBAI Radio Station
DC	Date	1982 [date created]
DC	Rights	Reproduced with permission by the Lesbian Herstory Archives . . .
DC	Language	en-US
DC	Format	Audio recording
DC	Identifier	SPW1169
Technical Metadata		
PBCore	formatPhysical	Compact Cassette
PBCore	formatEncoding	WAV [master]
PBCore	formatEncoding	MP3 [access]
PBCore	formatDuration	00:31:42 [Side A]
PBCore	formatDuration	00:29:23 [Side B]
PBCore	formatFileSize	548 MB [master, Side A]
PBCore	formatFileSize	29 MB [access, Side A]
PBCore	formatFileSize	508 MB [master, Side B]
PBCore	formatFileSize	28 MB [access, Side B]
PBCore	essenceTrackSamplingRate	96 kHz [master]
PBCore	essenceTrackBitDepth	24 [master]
PBCore	essenceTrackDataRate	128 kbps [access]
PBCore	formatIdentifier	spw1169_A.wav [master]
PBCore	formatIdentifier	spw1169_A.mp3 [access]
PBCore	formatIdentifier	spw1169_B.wav [master]
PBCore	formatIdentifier	spw1169_B.mp3 [access]
Administrative Metadata		
Other	physicalLocation	Basement, Audio shelf #2

Figure 2-8. Example of Dublin Core augmented with PBCore metadata record for an audio-only oral history.

EXAMPLE FROM ARCHIVAL PRACTICE
Archives of the Kinkaid School
Houston, Texas

Although creating item-level metadata or aggregated finding aids may be noteworthy long-term goals, some archives find that they need more basic information about their audiovisual collections before they can engage in more extensive descriptive or reformatting work. To provide an example of this type of activity, an example is provided based on an interview with Sarah Gesell, archivist for the Kinkaid School in Houston, TX.[42] Her interview illustrates a lone arranger's initial work on her moving image and sound records.

The Kinkaid School—a prekindergarten through high school college preparatory school—was founded in 1906, and an archives was founded in the 2000s to document the rich history of the school. Gesell is the third archivist to hold the position. Recognizing that audiovisual collections were inadequately arranged and described, she began an audiovisual project with the first phase dedicated to creating an inventory of media in the archives.

To begin this process, Gesell created a FileMaker Pro database—intending it to only be temporary—with the following information fields: title, date, year, type of content, creating department, description, media format, housing type, digitized (Y/N), digital format, location, and accession number. She also noted preservation issues such as mold, mildew, or an active state of decay such as vinegar syndrome. (See chapter 8, "Film Collections," for more information.) During this inventory, she found that there were at least four hundred unique items and sets of duplicate items, including reel-to-reel audio, 8 mm film, Super 8 film, compact audiocassette, VHS, CD, DVD, Hi8 video, and DAT audiocassette. During the inventory process, she was able to weed nonarchival teaching materials, such as Hollywood or educational films. Sets of materials spread across multiple containers have been intellectually reunited and will be physically reunited during the next phase of the project. Media with mold were quarantined in oversized Ziploc bags. Depending on their historical value for documenting the school, some moldy media will be cleaned and digitized, while others (including mystery items) will be considered for deaccessioning. Plans are being developed for reformatting, which will most likely take place off-site, with specific procedures and formats to be included in the plan.

When files come back from vendors, Gesell plans to store the files on network storage provided by the school's IT department, knowing that digital storage and preservation planning will be required. In terms of storing the original carriers, she found that relocating all media onto one set of shelves, while maintaining the intellectual linkages, has been helpful in getting a handle on audiovisual materials.

CONCLUSION

What is the best methodology for describing collections with moving image and sound records: creating group-level records or item-level records? The answer is inevitably both. Group-level records allow for the audiovisual materials to be quickly discoverable, and they illustrate the relationships between moving image materials and other parts of a collection. However, item-level records are very useful in planning a digitization initiative, doing an assessment of the preservation needs of a collection, and making digitized content available. Thus, the group level is a great place to start, but eventually building out item-level records is a worthy goal. I am particularly compelled by approaches that integrate group-level records, such as DACS finding aids, with item-level records, including their digitized or born-digital contents. For example, AtoM, a Canadian archival description and access software, helps facilitate this by making available DACS finding aids with their group-level descriptions and providing an interface for linking in digitized items—with item-level metadata like Dublin Core—into their respective series or folder.

Fairly new access initiatives give additional reason to create item-level records. For example, the Digital Public Library of America (DPLA), "a national digital library that aggregates digital collections metadata from around the United States," requires that digitized content be made available through item-level records and has not, at the time of writing, accepted digitized content that is linked in through a finding aid.[43] Hence, being able to participate in such initiatives, in collaboration with libraries, museums, and other cultural institutions, inevitably requires the creation of item-level records.

This chapter concluded with an example from archival practice where an archivist undertook an audiovisual inventory project across all collections, recording information about the media as well as preservation issues. This inventory can then be used not only for finding media but also for prioritizing reformatting.

NOTES

1. Kathleen D. Roe, *Arranging and Describing Archives and Manuscripts* (Chicago: Society of American Archivists, 2005).

2. Archivists Toolkit, http://www.archiviststoolkit.org/, permalinked on March 30, 2016, at https://perma.cc/FZ8A-PL25; ArchivesSpace, http://www.archivesspace.org/, permalinked on March 30, 2016, at https://perma.cc/QA9K-EK35.

3. AIMS Work Group, *AIMS Born-Digital Collections: An Inter-Institutional Model for Stewardship* (2012), http://dcs.library .virginia.edu/files/2013/02/AIMS_final.pdf, permalinked on March 30, 2016, at https://perma.cc/3V9R-XR7E.

4. Mary Lynn Ritzenthaler, *Preserving Archives and Manuscripts*, 2nd ed. (Chicago: Society of American Archivists, 2010).

5. Ibid., 86.

6. Ibid., 186

7. Retailers in North America of acid-free boxes, folders, and pH pens include Gaylord (http://www.gaylord.com/, permalinked on March 30, 2016, at https://perma.cc/2YNY-8G4X), Hollinger Metal Edge (http://www.hollingermetaledge.com/, perma-linked on March 30, 2016, at https://perma.cc/SJ7B-7CNS), Talas (http://www.talasonline.com/, permalinked on March 30, 2016, at https://perma.cc/873B-L5J4), University Products (http://www.universityproducts.com/, permalinked on March 30, 2016, at https://perma.cc/L64X-2HSU), and Demco (http://www.demco.com/, permalinked on April 24, 2016, at https://perma.cc/5NWV-VXU3), among others.

8. Dietrich Schüller and Albrecht Häfner, eds., *Handling and Storage of Audio and Video Carriers*, IASA-TC05 (London: International Association of Sound and Audiovisual Archives, 2014).

9. Jerry McWilliams, *The Preservation and Restoration of Sound Recordings* (Nashville, TN: American Association for State and Local History, 1979).

10. Ibid., 50.

11. National Film Preservation Foundation, *The Film Preservation Guide: The Basics for Archives, Libraries, and Museums* (San Francisco: National Film Preservation Foundation, 2004), http://www.filmpreservation.org/preservation-basics/the -film-preservation-guide-download, permalinked on March 30, 2016, at https://perma.cc/9WHU-P8F5.

12. Sherelyn Ogden, *Temperature, Relative Humidity, Light, and Air Quality: Basic Guidelines for Preservation* (Andover, MA: Northeast Document Conservation Center), https://www.nedcc.org/free-resources/preservation-leaflets/2.-the -environment/2.1-temperature,-relative-humidity,-light,-and-air-quality-basic-guidelines-for-preservation, permalinked on March 30, 2016, at https://perma.cc/L3RT-CSML; Schüller and Häfner, *Handling and Storage of Audio and Video Carriers*; Carla Arton, "Care and Maintenance," in *ARSC Guide to Audio Preservation*, ed. Sam Brylawski, Maya Lerman, Robin Pike, and Kathlin Smith (Washington, DC, and Eugene, OR: ARSC, CLIR, and Library of Congress), 52–76.

13. Example of finding aid from Herman Baca Papers, MSS 0649, Special Collections and Archives, University of California, San Diego, http://www.oac.cdlib.org/findaid/ark:/13030/kt867nd0km/, permalinked on September 2, 2016, at https:// perma.cc/5BYF-P4H4.

14. Abigail Leab Martin, *AMIA Compendium of Moving Image Cataloging Practice* (Beverly Hills, CA: Association of Moving Image Archivists, 2001).

15. Kathleen D. Roe, *Arranging and Describing Archives and Manuscripts*.

16. AMIM Revision Committee, *Archival Moving Image Materials: A Cataloging Manual*, 2nd ed. (Washington, DC: Library of Congress Cataloging Distribution Service, 2000, Appendix C, 10.

17. Pam Hackbart-Dean and Elizabeth Slomba, *How to Manage Processing in Archives and Special Collections* (Chicago: Society of American Archivists, 2013), 48.

18. Daniel A. Santamaria, *Extensible Processing for Archives and Special Collections: Reducing Processing Backlogs* (Chicago: Neal-Schuman, 2015).

19. Kathleen D. Roe, *Arranging and Describing Archives and Manuscripts*.

20. Finding aid for Oral History Collection, ca. 1985–2012, Archives of the American Field Service and AFS Intercultural Programs, http://www.afs.org/archon/index.php?p=collections/controlcard&id=5, permalinked on September 2, 2016, at https://perma.cc/5V8J-MCGC.

21. Archon website, http://www.archon.org/, permalinked on March 30, 2016, at https://perma.cc/57BD-URSS; Society of American Archivists, *Describing Archives: A Content Standard*, 2nd ed. (Chicago: Society of American Archivists, 2013), http://files.archivists.org/pubs/DACS2E-2013_v0315.pdf,, permalinked on April 24, 2016, at https://perma.cc/UT92 -YVE2; Daniel Pitti, "Encoded Archival Description (EAD)," in *Understanding Information Retrieval Systems: Management, Types, and Standards*, ed. Marcia Bates (Boca Raton, FL: Taylor & Francis, 2012), 685–97.

22. Access to Memory (AtoM), https://www.accesstomemory.org/en/, permalinked on March 30, 2016, at https://perma.cc /ZM6D-K985; Archivists Toolkit, http://www.archiviststoolkit.org/, permalinked on March 30, 2016, at https://perma .cc/K7X6-BDK9; and ArchivesSpace, http://www.archivesspace.org/, permalinked on March 30, 2016, at https://perma .cc/829M-H8UQ.

23. Although EAD records can be transferred from one archival management system to another, sometimes minor edits are required to get the record to import correctly.

24 More information on DACS and EAD can be found in Sibyl Schafer and Janet M. Bunde, "Standards for Archival Description," in *Archival Arrangement and Description*, ed. Christopher J. Prom and Thomas J. Frusciano (Chicago: Society of American Archivists).

25 Oxygen, http://www.oxygenxml.com/, permalinked on March 30, 2016, at https://perma.cc/FN8M-TN8N.

26 Society of American Archivists, "Physical Access," in *Describing Archives: A Content Standard*.

27 Society of American Archivists, "Technical Access", in *Describing Archives: A Content Standard*, http://www2.archivists.org/standards/DACS/part_I/chapter_4/3_technical_access, permalinked on December 6, 2016, at https://perma.cc/YB9Y-EY8F.

28 Joshua Ranger, *What's Your Product? Assessing the Suitability of a More Product, Less Process Methodology for Processing Audiovisual Collections* (New York: AVPreserve, 2012), http://www.avpreserve.com/wp-content/uploads/2012/08/WhatsYourProduct.pdf, permalinked on March 30, 2016, at https://perma.cc/GQ9Y-YGKG.

29 Mark A. Greene and Dennis Meissner, "More Product, Less Process: Revamping Traditional Archival Processing," *American Archivist* 68, no. 2, (2005): 208–63.

30 AMIM Revision Committee, *Archival Moving Image Materials*.

31 Colin Higgins, *Cataloging and Managing Film and Video Collections: A Guide to Using RDA and MARC 21* (Chicago: ALA Editions, 2015).

32 Yuji Tosaka and Jung-ran Park, "RDA: Resource Description and Access—A Survey of the Current State of the Art," *Journal of the Association of Information Science and Technology* 64, no. 4 (2013): 651–62.

33 Dublin Core website, http://dublincore.org/, permalinked on March 30, 2016, at https://perma.cc/R8E4-TPTN.

34 Nan Rubin, "The PBCore Metadata Standard: A Decade of Evolution," *Journal of Digital Media Management* 1, no. 1 (2012): 55–68.

35 Omeka website, http://www.omeka.org, permalinked on March 30, 2016, at https://perma.cc/U8BS-PJHM.

36 Herstories: Audio/Visual Collections, http://herstories.prattinfoschool.nyc/omeka/, permalinked on August 30, 2016, at https://perma.cc/NET4-Q83W; Voces Digital Audio Archive, http://voces.prattsi.org/, permalinked on September 2, 2016, at https://perma.cc/LT3K-SNGG.

37 Requires the installation of the CollectionTree plugin, http://omeka.org/add-ons/plugins/collection-tree/, permalinked on March 30, 2016, at https://perma.cc/8JFX-ZZBL.

38 PBCore, http://pbcore.org/, permalinked on March 30, 2016, at https://perma.cc/LLQ6-XJQB; and Dublin Core, http://dublincore.org/, permalinked on March 30, 2016, at https://perma.cc/R8E4-TPTN.

39 The record presented here has undergone some revisions from the version available online.

40 VLC Player, http://www.videolan.org/vlc/, permalinked on March 30, 2016, at https://perma.cc/54SN-DSGW.

41 Dave Rice, "Automating PBCore Technical Metadata," AVPreserve, https://www.avpreserve.com/pbcore-instantiationizer/pbcore-instantiationizing/, permalinked on March 30, 2016, at https://perma.cc/JH9T-GTH7.

42 Sarah Gesell, telephone interview by the author, December 2, 2016.

43 Lisa Gregory and Stephanie Williams, "On Being a Hub: Some Details Behind Providing Metadata for the Digital Public Library of America," *D-Lib Magazine* 20, no. 7/8 (2014), http://www.dlib.org/dlib/july14/gregory/07gregory.html, permalinked on March 30, 2016, at https://perma.cc/TE97-QNTF. Some recent developments indicate that DPLA may be moving to include EAD records in their collections.

CHAPTER 3

Legal and Ethical Issues

Legal and ethical issues arise at every stage in the work of the archivist: before and after accessioning a collection, during arrangement and description, and as researchers access the collection, whether it is through a web browser or a library's video terminal. This chapter will not attempt to impart all legal and ethical considerations an archivist must make. Other resources, such as Menzi Behrnd-Klodt and Christopher J. Prom's edited volume, *Rights in the Digital Era*, provide a thorough overview of the topic.[1] However, this chapter will offer some important legal and ethical considerations, especially as they relate to moving image and sound collections.

COPYRIGHT BASICS

When it comes to audiovisual recordings like interviews created after February 14, 1972, copyright law dictates that work is copyright protected for the life of the creator plus 70 years.[2] When a work is copyrighted, it gives the copyright holder certain rights. This includes the right to make copies of the work and the right to perform the work publicly, among other rights. As soon as an interviewer hits the stop button on a tape or digital recorder, anyone who has contributed original creative work to that recording has copyright protection. Although the underlying facts of a recording like an oral history may not be copyrightable, the particular expression of the oral history—such as the creative arrangement of words, sentences, and paragraphs—is copyrightable. The same applies to musical works, interviews, and other creative works. If a corporate body or organization creates the work, the duration of the copyright is 95 years from its first publication or 120 years from date of creation, whichever comes first.[3]

Unfortunately for sound recordings, things are not so straightforward for recordings before February 14, 1972, which are not covered by federal copyright law but are often covered by state statutory and common law.[4] Heather Briston notes that "when managing collections with sound recordings, it is easiest to assume that they remain under copyright."[5] However, Columbia Law School professor June Besek writes that "creating digital copies [of pre-1972 unpublished recordings] solely for preservation purposes is extremely unlikely to be actionable under state law, civil or criminal."[6] In her report, Besek analyzes the state laws in California, Illinois, Michigan, New York, and Virginia and highlights differences in the law that impact pre-1972 sound recordings; she also uses legal cases to explore their implications for a number of different types of recordings, such as radio interviews, oral histories, and interviews by journalists. This resource should be consulted when attempting to make pre-1972 sound recordings available digitally.

After the copyright ends, the work enters the public domain, where the exclusive rights of the copyright owner end. Typically, works created before 1923 are in the public domain.[7] At this point, anyone is able to copy the work for whatever use they deem fit. Crediting the author is an ethical but not necessarily legal obligation of the user.

COPYRIGHT AND DONOR AGREEMENTS

Because of the extensive amount of time a work remains in copyright—a work made by a young person can easily be under copyright for 135 years—it is important for archives to get not only physical ownership of moving image and sound records but also copyright. Getting copyright of the work allows for digital reformatting of the work and greater ease in making the work available online. A simple donor form is included in figure 3-1 that transfers both physical ownership and copyright.

Many artists, including photographers and filmmakers, among others, are hesitant to give over their copyright. One method to work around this is to seek a bequest, which includes the donation of copyright through a will. For a discussion of this issue and ways to talk about it with prospective donors, see chapter 6, "Interactions with Moving Image and Sound Producers."

For past donations, if copyright was not transferred via a donor agreement, or if no formal donor agreement was signed, it is possible to go back to donors and get them to sign a new agreement that also transfers copyright. For deceased copyright owners, the copyright is managed by the estate for the length of the copyright (typically seventy years after death). The "estate" often refers to the deceased donor's spouse or children. A will can also designate copyright control for the donor's work. When an estate or creator cannot be located or contacted, a work then becomes an orphan work. The Society of American Archivists provides a useful workflow for determining if a work should indeed be considered an orphan work.[8]

Front Runners New York
PO Box 230087
Ansonia Station
New York, NY 10023

Donor Agreement

I hereby donate the collection described below to Archives of Front Runners New York (FRNY), as an unrestricted gift, and transfer to Archives of FRNY **legal title** and **copyright** to the contents in as far as I hold them, except for any limiting conditions specifically stated below.

I agree that any materials in the collection which are not to be retained by Archives of FRNY shall be disposed of by Archives of FRNY as it sees fit or shall be returned to me or my designee if so stated below.

Collection description:

_____

_____

_____

_____

Limiting conditions or restrictions:

_____

_____

_____

Donor name, mailing address, and email address:

_____

_____

_____

Signed by:

_____   _____
Donor signature   Date

Accepted by FRNY History and Archives committee representative:

_____   _____   _____
Print name   Signature   Date

Figure 3-1. A simple donor form that transfers physical ownership and copyright.

COPYING COLLECTIONS WHEN COPYRIGHT IS NOT TRANSFERRED

In some cases, copyright cannot be secured because the donor or estate is unknown or cannot be reached. In this case, there are options for doing digital reformatting and some very limited online access.

Section 108: Library and Archives Exemption

Under Section 108 of the Copyright Act of 1976, up to three copies of a work can be made if there are significant preservation concerns.[9] This would be in cases where a replacement copy cannot be obtained through the market, and the ability to preserve the work is inhibited by deteriorating or obsolete media. Much of twentieth-century audio and video media are on deteriorating carriers, so reformatting for preservation's sake is not such a legally risky endeavor for a nonprofit archives with a public service component.[10] When a work is reformatted to a digital format for preservation reasons, it does not necessarily mean that it can then be put online and thus published globally. Rather, the digitally preserved copy can be accessed in much the same way as the deteriorating copy—on-site at an archives facility.[11]

Section 107: Fair Use

Despite the limitations of section 108 of the Copyright Act, section 107—or the fair use section—offers some limited options for making copies of copyrighted work. Fair use allows for copying small amounts of copyrighted work and making it available to researchers if four criteria are met:

- Purpose: educational and scholarly use, criticism and commentary, news reporting, transformative use, parody
- Nature: published work, factual or nonfiction based, important to educational objectives
- Amount: small portion of the work appropriate for educational purpose
- Effect: no effect on the market for the work

Note that all four criteria must be addressed to satisfy the conditions for fair use. Kenneth Crews, the former director of the Copyright Advisory Office at the Columbia University Libraries, has developed a checklist that can be used to evaluate if a piece of copyrighted work meets the four criteria and thus is amenable to fair use.[12]

Although the law does not define what is a "small amount" of a work, it is sometimes defined by those looking to make use of fair use as 10 percent of a work.[13] However, this may be far too much of a work, especially if it is a commercial work. Stanford University's "Proposed Educational Guidelines on Fair Use" for students and faculty using commercial works in an educational capacity suggest a maximum of thirty seconds for music and lyrics and a maximum of three minutes for video and film works.[14] These numbers are an attempt to operationalize and provide guidance on the fair-use requirement of a "small amount."

Since courts ultimately make decisions on what is fair use and what is not, archives looking to employ fair use will never know if they are fully "in the clear." Thus, lawyers such as Briston who work in the archival domain advocate for a risk-management approach.[15] A risk-averse archive would want to avoid making available small amounts of commercial works or works that implicate litigious persons.

Materials such as recordings of noncommercial, noncreative events are safer opportunities for archives to try to exercise their fair use rights.

Many of the legal cases regarding fair use of copyrighted work have implicated university reserve systems, rather than copies made from archival material. For example, several publishers sued Georgia State University in 2008 for "'pervasive, flagrant and ongoing unauthorized distribution of copyrighted materials' through the library's e-reserve system."[16] Although the courts largely found that the university was within the bounds of fair use, the case took years to resolve, and appeals continue.[17] Fortunately, there are not such high-profile cases implicating archives. The downside of not having such court decisions in the archival domain is that the bounds of fair use have not been fully fleshed out.

Despite the opportunities opened up by fair use, there are some limitations that will be discussed in the following sections.

LAYERED RIGHTS

Moving image works and some audio works are notorious for having complicated rights, with much of the complication stemming from layered rights. Layered rights occur when a segment of audiovisual media implicates multiple rights holders.[18] Although a copyright owner may transfer his or her rights to an archives, there can be other rights embedded in the work that the donor does not have and cannot transfer.

Before attempting to distribute copies of a work, it is important to figure out if there are layered rights in the work. This includes both cases where the donor has signed a copyright transfer agreement and cases where the whole work is intended for online distribution or clips of a work are being used online. Hopefully, if there are copyrighted works within another work, the donor has transferred to the archives the paperwork that outlines the permissions to use these other works embedded in the donated work. If not, you may want to avoid providing digital access to works that include copyrighted songs or artworks if the permission clearances are not clearly outlined. For example, when putting together clips, it may be sensible to avoid parts of the work that use popular music or professional sports footage (which is often owned by corporations such as the National Football League).

EXAMPLE CASE: *EYE ON THE PRIZE*

One of the most infamous cases of complex layered rights—and the ability of this issue to stymie a work's use—is the film *Eye on the Prize,* one of the most comprehensive documentary films about the American civil rights experience, which was broadcast on PBS in 1987.[19] The film included 120 song titles, footage from 93 archives, and 275 still photographs. When the film was made, licenses for use of the material were negotiated for only five years. When the licensing agreements expired in the mid-1990s, the film became undistributable. Another notable rights issue relates to the ability to use the image of Dr. Martin Luther King Jr., which is controlled by his estate. The use of a celebrity's image does not implicate copyright law but rather publicity rights, which allow a person or his/her estate to control the use of his/her image in a commercial capacity.[20] Unlike privacy rights that end at death, personality rights carry on after death and can be controlled by an estate.

A segment of this film that illustrates the issue of layered rights occurs in the episode in which Dr. King's staff sings him the song "Happy Birthday." The song has only recently entered the public domain, and thus the copyright owner wanted payment for the use of the copyrighted work at the time the rights were being resecured.[21] Combined with the licensing of the archival footage and the rights for the use of Dr. King's image, a complex of layered rights needed to be overcome to rerelease the work. Fortunately—and through a massive fund-raising effort—the rights to the entire film were restored, and the film is distributed today.[22]

PRIVACY

Archives have the potential to enable the violation of individual privacy, such as when a researcher goes through boxes of videos on-site or browses content made available online through finding aids or other access tools. Privacy can be violated when an intentional intrusion into a person's seclusion or into private affairs causes psychological distress.[23] For example, assume party A donates a recording of a phone conversation between party A and party B, and party C listens to this recording that is available on-site at an archives. Party B finds out about this and feels distressed by the violation of his privacy, and could charge party A with violating his right to privacy.

When an archives puts information online, it is no longer acting as simply a keeper of other people's information, it is also acting as a publisher.[24] By putting information online, an archives could enable defamation, which is defined as having four elements: "(1) making a false and defamatory statement purporting to be fact about another person or entity, (2) by words or publication to a third person, (3) through the fault or negligence of the writer or speaker, (4) causing harm to the subject of the statement."[25] Although the archives is not making the defaming statement, it could involuntarily act as the "publication to a third person." It is not problematic to have recordings with defaming statements in an archives, but when the statements are published online, the archives could be interpreted as this third party. To complicate things further, when putting information online, an archives acts not only as a publisher but also as a global publisher, which exposes the archives to the laws of foreign countries.[26]

A related complication is not so much a legal issue but rather an ethical issue that presents itself because of the affordances of the web. When archives make audiovisual records available online, they often include basic metadata, such as the names of speakers included in videos. People have a tendency to Google themselves, and they may find records of themselves that they may have agreed to in the past—even signing donor agreements—but have since changed their minds about. These donors often make arguments related to the newfound availability of the records: "I never knew that these videos would be made available online—how was I to know that the Internet would exist in 1989?" In these cases, the donor is happy if the records remain in obscurity—in the archival equivalent of some basement or attic—but is less than comfortable with them a click away. This is a very valid argument, and it is more of an ethical issue than a legal one, because it assumes that the donor has signed over ownership and copyright to the archives. In cases such as this, it is best to just remove the offending video from the web as quickly as possible, and let the donor know. Alternatively, reaching out to donors (or their estates) proactively before putting materials online can help eliminate this issue.

EXAMPLE CASE: RECORDED INTERVIEWS

In my classes, I expose my students to a variety of legal and ethical issues through course projects that involve real collections. In one project, I had set up an opportunity for students to work with a dancer and dance journalist to establish a digital archive for her. This involved reformatting recorded interviews that were on compact audiocassette and creating an online presence for the digital archive. However, before this online presence could be created, a number of legal issues needed to be considered.

The dance journalist had interviewed dancers, creating audio recordings of their conversations. She then transcribed and edited the conversations and published them in dance magazines and books. As is common with journalists, she did not seek copyright transfer from the interviewee. Her ownership of the tapes on which the conversations were recorded was not in question. As she bought the tapes herself, she could transfer the ownership of the tapes to an archives. However, since the interviewees had not explicitly transferred the copyright of their interviews, the journalist could not transfer the copyright of such interviews to an archives or create copies of her own tapes for online distribution.

The students went ahead and digitized the tapes, noting that the tapes themselves were degrading and digitization was a preservation measure. Rather than putting the entire set of recordings online, the class decided to make small amounts of the interviews available online for educational and scholarly use (about 10 percent of the work).[27] For example, a sixty-minute recording would yield a six-minute clip that could be played on the web. The students reasoned that since the interviews had already been published in print, the interviewees' privacy would not be violated. Should researchers want to listen to full interviews, they could contact the journalist, and she could let them listen to her full copies.

In this case, students considered going back to original interviewees and securing copyright transfer forms. However, because of the time constraints, no copyright forms were secured. The website created by the students has been available online since 2011. In this time, it has not raised any objections from interviewees, and no interview clips have been removed. As with all applications of fair use, archivists can only say they are "in the clear" when the copyright lapses, which can take well over a hundred years. For this reason, there is always a possibility of a future "takedown" request. As a judge is the only person who can really say if you applied fair use correctly, you have to rely on your understanding of the law, past applications of fair use by other archives, and any outside legal assistance that you can obtain. The safest option is to offer not even small clips online, but this is also the least assertive use of an archives' rights.

DIGITAL MILLENNIUM COPYRIGHT ACT

Copyright law has been slow to change, and much of it is governed by a predigital understanding of how information, knowledge, and culture are circulated. Despite this, some legislation has been passed that acknowledges digital information, specifically the Digital Millennium Copyright Act (DMCA) of 1998.[28] The DMCA introduced several noteworthy elements for those managing moving image and sound collections in archives.

This law introduced the takedown notice or letter, which copyright owners can send to web hosts that are making their copyrighted work available online. As an archives, you can both send and receive such letters. You would send a takedown letter if a work that is copyrighted by the archives or parent institution is used in a way that violates the donor agreement. However, many archives do not go to great lengths to enforce their copyrights, as use is a primary objective of most archives. Archives may also receive takedown notices. When receiving such a notice, it is important to defend the work if it meets the conditions for fair use. If you determine that the way the work is used is not fair use (e.g., too much of the work is presented online), then the work should be removed from the web quickly and the copyright holder notified of the change.

The DMCA also introduced an important provision that disallows the circumvention of any encryption technology used to protect digital content. Many commercial works created on DVD or Blu-ray may use encryption. Fortunately, CDs do not have encryption technology built in, but other formats like MiniDiscs sometimes do have encryption enabled. Although hackers have since figured out the encryption keys for DVD and Blu-ray, making the decryption process relatively straightforward, it could be a violation of DMCA to decrypt an encrypted disk, even for preservation purposes.[29]

Whereas DMCA prevents all encryption tampering, exemptions for fair use—which must be applied for every three years to the librarian of Congress—has allowed decryption of DVDs and Blu-rays for this purpose.[30] Such decryption could include students' use of short clips in multimedia projects for educational purposes.

Despite this exemption, there is no explicit exemption for "ripping" a DVD or Blu-ray for preservation's sake. However, it is unlikely to be a very risky activity as long as the "ripped content" follows the logic of section 108 of the Copyright Act: the disc was ripped because a replacement copy could not be obtained in the market, and there are preservation issues with the original media (e.g., scratches to a DVD or Blu-ray that threaten its playability).

CREATIVE COMMONS

When a donor transfers to an archives the copyright of a work, one option to promote use of the work is to apply a Creative Commons license to it.[31] This allows individuals to use the work in ways that you set forth in the license without the need for the user to contact the archives and get written permission, thus streamlining the reuse process. Creative Commons licenses can dictate a variety of uses of the work, such as specifying that the work can be used in any noncommercial use as long as the creator is attributed. For works that have layered rights—where not all rights may have been secured by the archive or parent institution—archivists should avoid applying such a license, or at least conduct a risk analysis before doing so, because the archives or parent body only has the legal authority to license rights that it clearly owns.

DOWNLOADING MEDIA AND TERMS OF SERVICE

Sometimes institutional records such as videos are made available online through social media sites like YouTube, and the original recording media is then lost, making the copy on the social media site the only one available. In these cases, it may make sense to try to download the videos. If the username and password for the YouTube uploader can be retrieved, it is possible in most cases to download the compressed version of the video from YouTube. However, in cases where the username and password cannot be retrieved, it is possible to use extensions for web browsers like Firefox or Chrome that allow downloading of media from social media sites. Tools for doing so are discussed in chapter 10, "Digital Video Collections."

Despite the ability to download, it is against the terms of service of most social media sites. For example, the YouTube Terms of Service say "You shall not download any Content unless you see a 'download' or similar link displayed by YouTube on the Service for that Content," meaning that all media must be streamed (or controlled) through their service.[32] This of course makes sense for commercial social media sites because this allows them to package advertising to users and collect data on video use, which would be impossible if the videos were downloaded for offline viewing. However, if you or your parent institution is the copyright owner of the work, it is not very risky to attempt to download the work. Web 2.0 businesses are built around monetizing other people's copyrighted work by running advertisements with them, and because their business depends so much on other people's contributions, it is unlikely that they will be so stringent with legitimate copyright holders. Despite this, violating terms of service should be a last recourse, not the first.

In the minds of many people, being able to download a work versus only being able to view or stream a work has copyright implications. However, this is an artificial distinction that the law does not make. Copyright is implicated anytime a copy is made, such as over a computer network, which for practical purposes is the same whether it is downloaded or streamed. Further, the copyright holder retains the exclusive right to perform and copy the work. Thus, whether the video is streamed and played in a web browser or downloaded and played as a computer file, it is the copyright holder's exclusive right to allow this activity. Downloading a video may be against a social media site's terms of service, but there is no distinction in copyright law for streaming versus downloading.

CONCLUSION

Legal and ethical issues pervade the work of archivists who manage moving image and sound collections. Issues such as copyright, privacy, layered rights, and terms of service both enable and inhibit ways that moving image and sound collections are preserved and made available. At a minimum, archivists must stay up to date on the latest court rulings, legislation, and activities that impact how archives can preserve and make records available to their users. Further, archivists are advised to follow a risk-management strategy, which acknowledges that all risks to the archives or parent institution will never be fully vanquished. It is recommended that archivists make choices around access and copying that are defensible, clearly documented, and within the bounds of accepted practice within the archival community.

NOTES

1. Menzi L. Behrnd-Klodt and Christopher J. Prom, eds., *Rights in the Digital Era* (Chicago: Society of American Archivists, 2015); Menzi L. Behrnd-Klodt, *Navigating Legal Issues in Archives* (Chicago: Society of American Archivists, 2008).

2. Heather Briston, "Understanding Copyright Law," module 4 in *Rights in the Digital Era,* ed. Menzi L. Behrnd-Klodt and Christopher J. Prom (Chicago: Society of American Archivists, 2015).

3. Peter B. Hirtle, "Copyright Term and the Public Domain in the United States," January 1, 2016, http://copyright.cornell.edu/resources/publicdomain.cfm, permalinked on April 21, 2016, at https://perma.cc/U4F8-2CEY.

4. Briston, "Understanding Copyright Law."

5. Ibid., 22.

6. June M. Besek, *Copyright and Related Issues Relevant to Digital Preservation and Dissemination of Unpublished Pre-1972 Sound Recordings by Libraries and Archives* (Washington, DC: Council on Library and Information Resources, 2009), http://www.clir.org/pubs/reports/pub144/pub144.pdf, permalinked on April 21, 2016, at https://perma.cc/U4F8-2CEY.

7. Hirtle, "Copyright Term."

8. Society of American Archivists, *Orphan Works: Statement of Best Practices,* January 12, 2009, rev. June 17, 2009, http://www2.archivists.org/sites/all/files/OrphanWorks-June2009.pdf, permalinked on April 21, 2016, at https://perma.cc/P3ZG-HHVF.

9. Howard Besser et al., *Video at Risk: Strategies for Preserving Commercial Video Collections in Libraries* (New York: New York University Libraries, 2012), http://www.nyu.edu/tisch/preservation/research/video-risk/VideoAtRisk_SECTION108_Guidelines_2013.pdf, permalinked on April 21, 2016, at https://perma.cc/F5CZ-4EQ6.

10. Ibid.

11. Ibid.

12. Kenneth Crews, "Fair Use Checklist," Copyright Advisory Office, Columbia University Libraries, https://copyright.columbia.edu/content/dam/copyright/Precedent%20Docs/fairusechecklist.pdf permalinked on April 21, 2016, at https://perma.cc/M692-PE6X/.

13. Stanford University Libraries, "Proposed Educational Guidelines on Fair Use," http://fairuse.stanford.edu/overview/academic-and-educational-permissions/proposed-fair-use-guidelines/, permalinked on April 21, 2016, at https://perma.cc/LAY9-8XPN.

14. Ibid.

15. Briston, "Understanding Copyright Law."

16. Laura Burtle, "Research Guides: GSU Library Copyright Lawsuit," Georgia State University Law Library, 2016, http://libguides.law.gsu.edu/gsucopyrightcase, permalinked on August 15, 2016, at https://perma.cc/7XET-EPT4.

17. Ibid.

18. Kathleen Maguire, Nan Rubin, and Kara Van Malssen, *Intellectual Property and Copyright Issues Relating to the Preservation and Future Accessibility of Digital Public Television Programs* (2010), http://www.thirteen.org/ptvdigitalarchive/files/2009/10/IP-Report-fin.pdf, permalinked on April 21, 2016, at https://perma.cc/3T2A-CYFD.

19. Ibid.

20. Briston, "Understanding Copyright Law."

21. Ben Sisario, "'Happy Birthday' Copyright Invalidated by Judge," *New York Times*, September 22, 2015, http://www.nytimes.com/2015/09/23/business/media/happy-birthday-copyright-invalidated-by-judge.html, permalinked on April 21, 2016, at https://perma.cc/7U49-8XTN.

22. Maguire, Rubin, and Van Malssen, *Intellectual Property.*

23. Menzi L. Behrnd-Klodt, "Balancing Access and Privacy in Manuscript Collections," module 5 in *Rights in the Digital Era*, ed. Menzi L. Behrnd-Klodt and Christopher J. Prom (Chicago: Society of American Archivists, 2015).

24. June M. Besek, *Copyright Issues Relevant to the Creation of a Digital Archive: A Preliminary Assessment* (Washington, DC: Council on Library and Information Resources, 2003), http://www.clir.org/pubs/reports/pub112/pub112.pdf, permalinked on April 21, 2016, at https://perma.cc/GW58-744Q.

25. Behrnd-Klodt, "Balancing Access and Privacy," 74.

26. Besek, *Copyright Issues Relevant to the Creation of a Digital Archive.*

27. Dance Dialogues, http://dancedialogues.prattsils.org/, permalinked on August 15, 2016, at https://perma.cc/REJ6-7JKT.

28. Briston, "Understanding Copyright Law."

29. Ibid.

30. Parker Higgins et al., "Victory for Users: Librarian of Congress Renews and Expands Protections for Fair Uses," Electronic Frontier Foundation, October 27, 2015, https://www.eff.org/deeplinks/2015/10/victory-users-librarian-congress-renews-and-expands-protections-fair-uses, permalinked on April 21, 2016, at https://perma.cc/47BX-JV5H.

31. Creative Commons, http://creativecommons.org/, permalinked on April 21, 2016, at https://perma.cc/9V5G-2ZMP.

32. "YouTube Terms of Service," November 10, 2015, https://www.youtube.com/static?template=terms, permalinked on April 21, 2016, at https://perma.cc/6RJS-ARF7.

CHAPTER 4

Digital Preservation of Digitized and Born-Digital Content

Digital preservation is essential for the persistence of digitized and born-digital moving image and sound content. Digital preservation is defined here as the activities and planning that help ensure that digital information of enduring value remains accessible and intellectually faithful to its original form over time.[1] This book argues for the digital reformatting of analog materials for preservation and access rather than relying on aging media carriers and obsolete playback equipment. For this reason, this chapter will assume that digitized content has been created through reformatting or migration—and now the major task is to ensure its long-term persistence. Note that reformatting to digital formats only makes sense as a preservation strategy when there is adequate digital preservation infrastructure in place.

Whereas large cultural heritage institutions have made significant headway in providing digital preservation for archival assets—for example, setting up geographically dispersed digital repositories— medium and small institutions have struggled to meet minimum digital preservation standards. A simple but demonstrative example of this problem is that digital preservation standards require that digital assets, when accessioned into an archives, be incorporated into an enterprise storage system.[2] Many small cultural heritage institutions often do not have such systems and instead rely on consumer hard drives available for purchase at retailers or free storage from sites such as the Internet Archive. The discrepancy between digital preservation standards and the ability of small and medium cultural heritage institutions to meet those standards has prompted researchers to investigate how this chasm can be closed. This is best highlighted by the POWRR (Preserving [Digital] Objects with Restricted Resources) project—funded by the US Institute of Museum and Library Services—which is studying strategies for medium and small institutions to provide long-term preservation of digital assets.[3]

In the spirit of the POWRR project, this chapter will discuss some strategies for enacting basic digital preservation measures at small and medium archives. These strategies may diverge somewhat from what is possible at major cultural institutions, governments, and universities, which may be able to support sophisticated infrastructures and staffing.

MODELS OF DIGITAL PRESERVATION

In the digital preservation community, two models have developed to ensure the persistence of digital information. This chapter will focus primarily on the centralized model, but the other model, called the distributed model, may be worth exploring for some archives. The distributed model copies digital information across a network of institutions, and if a failure occurs somewhere in the network, then information can be restored from copies kept at other institutions. This model is best captured by the LOCKSS (Lots of Copies Keeps Stuff Safe) project and CLOCKSS (Controlled LOCKSS), which is used as a dark archive of published materials.[4] It also informs the MetaArchive Cooperative, which is a LOCKSS network of fifty institutions that keep copies of other institutions' content with permanent value.[5] This model may be unappealing to archives that steward content that needs to be restricted for some predetermined number of years (e.g., available to researchers twenty years after creation). Also, since this model depends on the Internet to synchronize network copies, it may be difficult to implement with moving image and sound materials, whose file sizes tend to be massive and do not lend themselves to easy transfer over the Internet.

The option that will be discussed more thoroughly here is the centralized option, where the institution commits to the digital preservation of assets with permanent value through its own efforts and resources. The centralized digital preservation solution that has gained steady traction over the last decade is what is known as a trusted digital repository, where the organization, resources, and technology of an organization are carefully orchestrated to ensure the persistence of digital information.[6] A process for certifying that repositories are indeed trustworthy has also been established, and the Society of American Archivists has published a book with the ambitious title *Becoming a Trusted Digital Repository*.[7]

This chapter will not attempt to impart all of the important ideas and standards that have been developed within the digital preservation community, but it will outline some basic steps that small and medium institutions can take to move forward with preserving digital or digitized audiovisual materials.

STORAGE TECHNOLOGIES

The most important step to take in promoting digital preservation is to have more than one copy of your data and to understand the strengths and limitations of the storage technologies that you are using. The basic building blocks for creating storage systems are discussed in the following sections.

RAID Systems

The best option for building a repository infrastructure is to use RAID (Redundant Array of Independent Disks) systems. RAIDs chain together two or more hard disks; should one disk fail, the rest of the array will be able to take over and keep all data intact. However, not all RAID drives keep redundant copies. Some RAID systems are designed to promote the speed of the array rather than data redundancy. Therefore, you will have to become familiar with the specific configuration of the RAID and assess either existing units or new ones to be purchased.

A simple RAID configuration is RAID 1, in which every hard drive in the array has a mirrored hard drive. Should a hard drive in the array fail, its mirror will take over and effectively keep any data from being lost. Figure 4-1 shows how the data blocks for "FILM" are spread across two disks in a mirrored fashion. An advantage of RAID 1 is that it can be achieved with only two hard disks. Other RAIDs that provide redundancy include RAID 5, where if one drive fails the data will remain intact.[8] RAID 0 should be avoided since it does not provide any data redundancy but rather is meant to promote array speed.

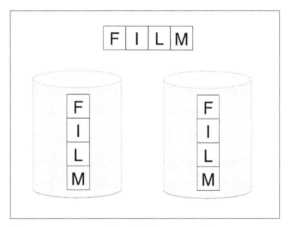

Figure 4-1. "FILM" data blocks are spread across two disks in a mirrored fashion using RAID 1.

Although RAID 1 is a great start, an even better RAID configuration is one in which two hard drives can fail and no information is lost. The best example of this is RAID 6. As figure 4-2 shows, the data blocks are spread across the four disks so that should one hard drive fail, the information can be rebuilt from what is known as "parity" information using mathematical operations. The disadvantage is that it requires at least four hard disks, and the time needed to spread the information across the array can slow read and write operations.

Like all systems, RAID systems should be purchased from reputable manufacturers. If a drive fails in a RAID system, the unit will start flashing red lights. Therefore, it is essential to check on RAID systems occasionally to make sure that no drives have failed, especially if they are stored in a closet where you do not normally see them. If one has failed, you can usually replace the drive with a new one without having to power down the unit and experience downtime. If RAID systems are stored in a nonsecured area, it is best to secure them to furniture with a locking device.

Although there is no definitive age when a hard drive must be replaced, research has indicated that their failure rate increases somewhat with age.[9] For this reason, hard drives within RAIDs should be refreshed at least every five to seven years.

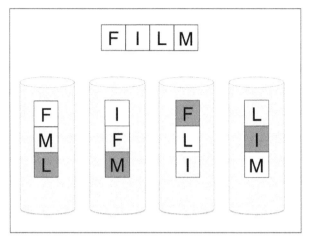

Figure 4-2. RAID 6 spreads information across at least four hard disks, so that if two disk drives fail, no information is lost.

While a RAID device is a great start, creating a secondary copy is essential, and tertiary copies are recommended.[10] Ideally, the copies should be dispersed into areas that face different disaster threats. For example, you would not want all of your copies stored in basements along a coastline with a history of hurricane flood damage. Creating copies can involve distribution over the Internet, wide-area networks, and offline by using parcel carriers. Because of the large file sizes and network requirements for sending moving image and sound records, offline carriers sending hard drives or data tapes may be a good option. For example, the digital art repository of the Museum of Modern Art synchronizes data from Manhattan to Long Island City over a wide-area network and sends offline copies on LTO tapes to an inland art storage facility.[11]

Independent Hard Disks

Although RAID devices are the best storage option for archives since they have redundancy built in, they can cost more than independent hard disks; independent hard disks may therefore be the only viable option for small archives. Independent hard disks are available as solid-state drives (no moving parts) and more traditional hard disks with spinning platters. Independent hard disks have no data redundancy; if a drive fails, all data may be lost. Although there are data recovery specialists, their services tend to be quite expensive, so it is imperative to have additional copies in case of failure. Despite the lack of built-in data redundancy, creating multiple copies using inexpensive independent hard disks is an option for the most resource-constrained archives.

Hard disks with spinning platters that are not routinely powered on can suffer from stiction, where the mechanism's lubrication fails and the disk head cannot move across the disk.[12] Therefore, it is recommended that hard disks be turned on at least yearly and the data skipped through (e.g., by playing some videos). Although solid-state hard drives have no moving parts and will not suffer from stiction, it is also a good idea to power them on yearly, which may bring to light other kinds of failures that are not yet known.

Because independent hard disks have no built-in data redundancy, creating multiple copies is especially important. Two copies are absolutely essential, but three is *highly* recommended. As with RAID devices, storing the drives in areas with different geographic threats is a worthwhile goal. In small archives that have only a single facility with no off-site storage options, archivists can bring their tertiary copies home with them or partner with a trusted institution to store each other's copies. Copies can be stored in acid-free boxes in a dry and cool environment away from activity that may damage them.

Like the RAID devices discussed, hard drives should be replaced every five to seven years, and all drives—including copies—should be powered on and skipped through yearly.

LTO Tapes

Although hard disks and RAIDs can be a great way to store information—especially if they are supported by multiple copies—the downside is that they can get quite costly, especially as storage needs increase. Because the file sizes of moving image and sound records can overwhelm a repository based on hard disks, several archives of large moving image and sound records have begun to use magnetic data tapes. The most popular of these are LTO (Linear Tape-Open) tapes; options include LTO 5, LTO 6, and LTO 7, with each successive version providing more storage capacity. The advantage of these tapes is that the tapes themselves often cost under $30 and feature extensive storage capacities. (See figure 4-3.) Unlike hard disks that can "randomly access" a file, tapes require sequential access, meaning that you would need to fast-forward through an entire tape to access data at the end of the tape.

LTO Tape Type	Capacity
LTO 4	800 GB
LTO 5	1.5 TB
LTO 6	2.5 TB
LTO 7	6 TB
LTO 8 (expected)	12.8 TB
LTO 9 (expected)	26 TB
LTO 10 (expected)	48 TB

Figure 4-3. Capacity of existing and expected LTO tapes.[13]

LTO tapes are used by the Library of Congress's Packard Campus of the National Audio-Visual Conservation Center for storing digitized video in their collections, as well as by other audiovisual archives, such as CUNY TV.[14] At CUNY TV, two copies of the entire video library are stored in separate LTO tape libraries, and when a specific video is needed, the tape is pulled off the shelf and loaded up on the tape reader.[15] For collections that have more extensive resources and need automation, tape robots are available that use mechanical arms to load the appropriate tape for the desired content.

Since LTO tapes can take a while to queue up the requested files, one option is to use RAID storage for mezzanine and/or access copies and to put master files on LTO tapes that are rarely accessed. If the master file is needed, it can be pulled from the tape.

One downside of LTO tapes is that files cannot be called up until the tape is loaded into the player, and it can be difficult to perform routine file fixity monitoring compared to data on hard disks. File fixity monitoring will be further discussed in the next section.

FILE FIXITY MONITORING

Keeping multiple copies on high-quality storage devices is an important first step. A laudable second step is monitoring file fixity, which allows an archives to verify that a file has not changed since it was ingested into a repository because of bit rot, bit flipping, hardware or software failure, or deliberate tampering.

We have all likely encountered some form of bit rot. This is most often manifested when we try to open a file and find that it has become corrupted and cannot be opened for some unexplainable reason. Although a software program could have made an error in its last write to the file, thus corrupting the file, it is also possible that bit corruption occurred in which the information unexpectedly changed. All digital information is written as electromagnetic signals into physical substances such as metals, those metals have imperfections, and like all human activity, manufacturing processes are not perfect. With that said, if bit rot or bit corruption happened routinely, we would never have adopted computers in such a widespread way. However, bit rot does occur often enough that we need to take some precautions.

Research has demonstrated that bit rot, bit flipping, or silent data corruptions occur in all storage systems, and that a way to demonstrate that this has occurred is through file fixity checks.[16] For example, Lakshmi N. Bairavasundaram and colleagues studied 1.5×10^6 hard drives over a period of 41 months and discovered 4×10^5 silent data corruption incidents. Similarly, David S. H. Rosenthal notes a study of data storage at CERN (the European Organization for Nuclear Research), where 1.2×10^{-9} of the data written to CERN's storage was permanently corrupted within six months.[17] In libraries and archives, bit rot has proven to be a persistent problem. Staff at Stanford University's Special Collections found that in donated media from the Stop AIDS Project, only 8 percent of CDs, 60 percent of 3.5-inch floppy disks, and 96 percent of Zip disks were successfully imaged, all as a result of some form of data corruption.[18] Fortunately, through engaging in file fixity monitoring and maintaining multiple copies of data, the problem of bit rot or bit corruption can be significantly mitigated.

File fixity monitoring depends on the idea of the checksum. In its simplest form, a checksum creates a sum of some intrinsic aspect of a file. As we all know, computer files are made up of binary data, and a simple checksum may add up all the 1s or 0s in a file. For example, assume we had an ASCII text file with my first name in it, as shown in figure 4-4:

01100001	01101110	01110100	01101000	01101111	01101110	01111001
a	n	t	h	o	n	y

Figure 4-4. A simple text file in binary format.

A simple checksum for this file could be the number 31, which sums together all the 1s in the file.

The limitation of this way of doing checksum is that it is possible for the checksum itself to be corrupted, not just the file. For example, if the number 31 is changed to 32, and another 1 is added to the file, then the file and the checksum match. To address this issue, more sophisticated algorithms for creating checksums have been developed that make use of mathematical properties such as prime numbers. The most popular algorithms used today are MD5 (Message Digest Algorithm) and SHA-256 (Secure Hash Algorithm), which can be run across files and generate hashes or checksums. With these algorithms, if the file should change in any way, the hash or checksum will change dramatically.[19] This is illustrated in figure 4-5, which shows how a tiny difference in a file's contents creates radically different checksums.

	Example A	Example B
Source File:	I hope you are enjoying this book.	I hope you are enjoying this book
MD5 Hash:	94249a5e0b9067d2a20e46c834ba2f80	beb488a3a2fbc96f98582cadedd3022f
SHA-256 Hash:	a54191824d6724f0e31cf327b6159a6f ea237a18232ca9f19903c00c12248df8	82972818c20c4f666e58a45f7e07c242 972ff937a9ae62a1b5415a386f5a611f

Figure 4-5. MD5 and SHA-256 hashes for a simple text file. Note that while there is only one difference between the files (the presence/absence of a period), the hashes are totally different.

With fixity monitoring, when files are ingested into a repository, the hashes are created and stored. Thereafter, the files are routinely scanned to make sure that the hashes and the files are still in sync. If a file's hash does not match what was ingested into a repository, this could indicate that a hardware failure has occurred or even that the files have been tampered with in some way. In this case, it is best to restore the copy from a secondary or tertiary copy.

Ideally, fixity monitoring would not have to be done manually by an archivist but would be done with repository software. Several repository softwares that provide functionality for monitoring file fixity are DSpace Direct, DuraCloud, Fedora3/Islandora7, OCLC Digital Archive, Preservica, and Rosetta.[20] However, if an archive is not using repository software, there are some free options for monitoring file fixity. One option is to use the BagIt packaging format created by the Library of Congress.[21] In this scenario, once files are ready for long-term storage, you put them in a "bag," which is a metadata envelope that includes file fixity information for all files, as well as directory information. When it comes time to make sure that nothing has happened to the files in the bag—resulting in a holey bag—then you just validate that the bag is intact. The Bagger software offers an easy-to-use tool for creating and validating bags.[22] Other free tools for monitoring file fixity include AVPreserve's Fixity and my own FixityBerry, among other pieces of software.[23]

In the previous section, it was noted that hard drives should be powered on at least yearly to prevent stiction. If file fixity information has been created using a tool like Bagger, it is recommended that fixity validation also occur at this time. If you find that there is a validation error, in which a file's fixity information no longer matches, then you can restore that file from a secondary or tertiary copy.

One challenge of monitoring file fixity on moving image records is that the files are very large, and thus it can take the monitoring tool a long time to read through every bit of the file. For this reason, archivists who monitor file fixity may want to perform checks less frequently (perhaps as infrequently as once a year) so that equipment is not tied up performing fixity checks.

FORMAT OBSOLESCENCE

In addition to making sure that multiple copies of data are stored and that file fixity is monitored, it is also important to monitor file formats for obsolescence. This is an especially important issue for video, which has layers of possible obsolescence issues. Open formats, such as ones that are openly documented, and formats that are easily decoded (e.g., text-based formats such as XML) are preferable to proprietary formats that are not openly documented.[24] One option is to keep a registry of file formats that are stored in given collections so that if a format becomes endangered, the location of files in that format can be easily identified. If open formats do not exist for a particular file format, or if the migration to an open format is not entirely successful, then the original software can be preserved so that files can be opened using that software. This preserved software, although potentially unable to run on future computers, could be run in emulated environments (e.g., a modern computer emulating Windows 3.1).[25]

For a discussion of format obsolescence, particularly as it pertains to video, see chapter 9, "Analog Video Collections," and chapter 10, "Digital Video Collections." For more discussion of emulation of software-based records, see chapter 11, "Complex Media."

IMAGING AND MIGRATING MEDIA

Throughout this book, the approach to preserving moving image and sound records—except in select cases—is to digitize analog media when possible. For born-digital media, the approach is to migrate digital media into an institution's repository, which at a minimum should have multiple copies of the data and ideally regular fixity checks of files. For each specific media type in the book, migration and imaging options are discussed. Please refer to the specific chapters in this book for guidance on handling specific kinds of media.

TRUSTED DIGITAL REPOSITORIES

If your repository is able to achieve geographical redundancy and perform file fixity checks, then the repository starts to look more like a trusted digital repository (TDR). As the name states, TDRs are a framework for ensuring that digital repositories are trustworthy, meaning that they will not randomly fail and render inaccessible the content being stewarded by them. The TDR framework grew out of the recognition that digital repositories were prone to failure if not carefully managed and supported. Influential in building the TDR framework was the earlier work by a consortium of space agencies looking to ensure that digital information was accessible for the long term, resulting in the Open Archival Information System model (OAIS).[26] Since then, it has been adopted as a best practice in preserving digital information from a wide variety of institutions, including libraries and archives within colleges, universities, and governments.[27] The model necessitates the creation of SIPs (Submission Information Packages), AIPs (Archival Information Packages), and DIPs (Dissemination Information Packages), among other elements.[28] The SIP is the version of the information package that is transferred from the creator to the OAIS; the AIP is the version of the information package that is stored and preserved by the OAIS; the DIP is the version of the information package delivered to the researcher in response to an access request.[29]

How does this work in practice? Assume, for example, that you take in a collection that includes a small batch of electronic records. Most of the electronic records are PDFs, which according to your repository's policy is an acceptable access and preservation format. However, you encounter a few sound recordings that are saved as ".band" files, which you realize are Garage Band files. You recognize that Garage Band is a proprietary format created by Apple that does not have good preservation prospects (e.g., new versions of the software do not necessarily even open files created by older versions).

This collection of files—including the Garage Band files—is part of the SIP (Submission Information Package) because they represent what was submitted to the archives by the creator. However, to enable digital preservation, those Garage Band files need to be normalized to formats well suited for preservation and access. In OAIS, there should be a set of repository policies that outlines what the preservation and access formats should be for each given file format included in the SIP. Using this policy, you export the Garage Band files as Microsoft WAV files for preservation and MP3 for access, which—as discussed in chapter 7, "Audio Collections"—are good formats for preservation and access, respectively.[30] These normalized files, in addition to the SIP files, are included in the AIP, which is the package that gets preserved. When a user requests access to the sound recording, you consult the DIP (Dissemination Information Package) and supply him or her with the MP3. Should MP3 files be rendered obsolete, you can create a new access file based on the preservation WAV file.

The TDR framework builds upon the OAIS model by describing the elements needed to make a repository trustworthy.[31] This includes aspects related to technology, resources, and the host organization.[32] The criteria for trustworthiness are further articulated in the Trusted Repositories Audit and Criteria (TRAC) report, which makes the elements needed to ensure trustworthiness even more explicit.[33]

Although creating a certifiable TDR may be a worthy goal, many small institutions struggle with creating a basic level of digital preservation infrastructure. For example, Ben Goldman contends that while OAIS and TDR may be worthy long-term goals for manuscript and special collection repositories, the requirements may be too great, and such organizations may be better served by starting small with something as simple as network file storage.[34] Other initiatives have looked to simplify digital preservation more generally, such as through the National Digital Stewardship Alliance's levels of digital preservation, which provide simplified criteria for ensuring the trustworthiness of a repository.[35] And lastly, several softwares have been developed to help create trustworthy repositories that support OAIS, such as Artefactual Systems' Archivematica, Tessela's Preservica, and OCLC's CONTENTdm.[36]

WORKING WITH IT DEPARTMENTS

If your archives has an IT department, they may already have storage set up on RAID devices. It is important for archivists to be able to ask and get answers to questions about storage technologies. For example, is the RAID being backed up? Is the data on RAID 5, RAID 6, or even redundant? Are the backups being tested? It is also important to be able to talk to IT about your data storage needs. For example, if over the next year you plan to digitize 10 hours of analog video and you know that 10-bit uncompressed video takes 100 GB per hour, they need to know you need to store a terabyte of additional data. IT may balk at the data storage needs of digitized video and may not be familiar with LTO technology. Therefore, you may need to be the one to present this option to your IT department. It is also essential to develop a strong working relationship with members of the IT department, because IT will form the backbone of all digital preservation activities.

REFRESHING EQUIPMENT

When purchasing digital repository infrastructure, it is important to remember that the hardware should be refreshed and all the content migrated regularly. Although there is no hard and fast rule for how long hard drives can be used, I have recommended in this book that hard drives be refreshed every five to seven years. As with all machines, they get less reliable as they age. Although some hard drives may continue to function perfectly for decades, it is more risky to use old equipment. Therefore, when making five-year plans, it is important to budget for equipment refreshes. Fortunately, storage capacities increase each year, and thus the storage cost of one TB today will likely be less in 2020, 2025, and 2030.

CLOUD STORAGE OPTIONS

Although it is recommended that primary copies of your archival assets remain on-site, the cloud may be an option for storing secondary or tertiary copies of data. Services that are designed to store archival assets, such as DuraCloud, can be especially useful because they are designed for this explicit purpose, unlike generic storage services that are meant for other uses (e.g., Dropbox).[37] When selecting a cloud provider, it is important to have a good estimate of current and expected data storage needs, because the cost of the service often increases with data storage requirements. Keep in mind that cloud services require you to upload your data over the Internet, which can "hog" an institution's broadband connection. For this reason, doing some tests with a provider before committing to it is recommended. This test could include evaluating the speed at which assets can be transferred and its impact on the institution's broadband connection.

Is cloud storage secure? There are a number of security concerns. The first concern is that when transmitting data over the Internet to the cloud, there is an opportunity for the data to be intercepted. At a minimum, you would want the connection between your host machine and the cloud service to be encrypted, which most cloud services either have as an option or require. Examples of unencrypted connections include standard FTP, which sends the username and passwords over an unencrypted channel as well as all the data, which can be intercepted. Secure FTP, which encrypts data, or some other method that uses encryption is highly recommended. Once the data is on the cloud service, staff at the service who have access to the machine or storage systems can access your data. However, as huge companies rely on cloud providers like Amazon and Rackspace, among others, for cloud storage and services, there have not been any widely reported cases of such companies misusing the information that has been entrusted to them. Further, there is no conclusive evidence that cloud company data centers are any less secure than data centers operated by institutions. For this reason, cloud storage is a compelling option for maintaining secondary or tertiary copies of data.

EXAMPLES FROM ARCHIVAL PRACTICE

In the following sections, examples are provided of how medium and small cultural heritage institutions have engaged in digital preservation, especially with respect to their moving image and sound records. The first two examples are based on personal work; the last two are based on interviews with practicing archivists and illustrate a range of environments and solutions devised to address digital preservation needs of audiovisual records.

Medium-Sized Art Museum
USA

In 2013–14, I worked as an electronic records consultant for an electronic records startup grant to a medium-sized art museum. During this project, our goal was to set up an electronic records repository that adhered to at least level 1 of the NDSA Level of Digital Preservation for storing the backlog of records needing appraisal, arrangement, and description.[38] Such records can include moving image and sound records, including born-digital video. To accomplish this, we needed at least two copies of our data that were not co-located, and we also needed to create file fixity information. This was accomplished by working closely with the IT department and setting up a RAID 6 storage device (also called network-attached storage or NAS) made by the manufacturer Synology[39] in the server room at the museum's offices. To provide geographic redundancy, the data was synchronized using the Linux program RSync over a wide-area network to an identical Synology device in another museum facility in another part of the city. File fixity was checked using the program AceAudit, which can monitor directories for changes in file fixity information.[40] AceAudit checks files daily and sends an email report to the archives.

Although the museum uses data mirroring technologies for a variety of applications to keep information in sync between locations, the method used here avoided mirroring but kept independent copies of data that were synced on a fixed interval. Automated mirroring systems should be avoided because accidentally deleted files, or files that become corrupt through hardware or software failure, need to be restored from the secondary copy. If an automatic mirroring system is used, meaning both copies are always identical, restoring from a secondary copy would not be an option.

In addition to setting up this repository, an obsolete media workstation was assembled that would be able to create disk images of all media that were found in the archives, such as Jaz drives, Zip disks, 3.5-inch floppy disks, Blu-ray, and DVDs, among other formats.

Lesbian Herstory Archives
Brooklyn, New York

As a more resource-constrained example, I offer the case of the Lesbian Herstory Archives (LHA), which operates with an all-volunteer staff and is one of the oldest LGBT archives in the United States, having celebrated its fortieth anniversary in 2015. My classes have been digitizing analog audio and video for the LHA since 2010 and making it available to the public at http://herstories.prattinfoschool.nyc. The website features access copies of digitized media, such as MP3s and MP4s of audio and video. The master audio files (in Microsoft WAV format) and the master video files, amounting to 1.2 TB, need to be stored, as well. LHA does not have an IT department or a server room. After students digitize content, LHA maintains a copy on a hard drive, as do I. The copies I keep on the hard drive are connected to a Raspberry Pi computer, which is powered on weekly using a power timer and which checks the files for fixity errors using the program FixityBerry.[41] When the check is complete, an email is sent letting me know if there are any fixity errors. The hard drives are replaced every five to seven years. Although this process is far from perfect (e.g., it would be better if a RAID were used, and if the copies at LHA were also monitored), having more than one copy and separating the copies geographically does provide some protection to the data. LHA is pursuing options to enhance its digital preservation capabilities, such as investing in a RAID storage device that can be stored on-site.

Marist Archives, Society of Mary
Wellington, New Zealand

Elizabeth Charlton, archivist for the Society of Mary, New Zealand, was interviewed on November 28, 2016, via telephone. Her work highlights a strategy that incorporates vendor-supported reformatting of audiovisual media with on-site digital preservation of resulting digitized records.

The Marist Archives document the activities of the Society of Mary in New Zealand and its contribution to the Roman Catholic Church. Charlton—as the sole archivist with some volunteer help—became interested in addressing the accessibility and preservation of audiovisual materials in the collection. These include oral histories recorded on compact audiocassette from the 1980s, most of which were not transcribed, as well as recorded events, such as jubilee masses, lectures on reel-to-reel tape from the 1950s and 1960s, and films depicting indigenous groups, among other types of audiovisual material. Charlton recognized that the environmental conditions for storing the original media were not ideal, and she was interested in media reformatting as a means for preservation and access to the material. She notes that the "Cost of Inaction" calculator created by AVPreserve, which is used to analyze the cost of not engaging in reformatting of audiovisual materials, was influential in prioritizing the need to reformat audiovisual material.[42]

Before engaging in reformatting, she identified all audiovisual materials in the archives and separated them from other material. As equipment for reformatting of audio, video, and film was not available on-site, and the specifics of which equipment and what formats were best were not entirely clear, vendor support and expertise were necessary. Charlton prioritized reformatting the oral history collection for its importance to the work of the society and reached out to vendors in New Zealand, Australia, and the United States for quotes on the cost. She found that with currency conversion and shipping costs, the total costs were approximately the same. With respect to other audiovisual materials, she found that some films in the collection were suffering from vinegar syndrome, and she plans to use a standard freezer to wrap and freeze them to slow down their degradation. Eventually, she hopes to reformat the films to digital formats for access.

Whereas the reformatting is planned to occur off-site, the resulting digitized files will be stored in-house. A primary copy will be stored on a server in one facility, and another copy will be stored in another facility with some geographic separation. Further, copies on independent hard disks are also maintained. Digital storage space needs to be planned and advocated for as the newly digitized assets have extensive space needs. The digitized audiovisual materials will be sharing the storage space with born-digital records, such as textual records, that have recently been accessioned into the archives.

Charlton notes that the need for reformatting or migration from obsolete media carriers has only now started to become recognized in New Zealand. Overall, she finds that it is taking a long time to change the mindset of "if I have got the artifact, I have the material," and she feels that digital preservation is "a different skill set that needs to be integrated into an archivist's toolkit."

Archives of the Great American Songbook Foundation
Carmel, Indiana

Lisa Lobdell, archivist at the Great American Songbook Foundation, was interviewed on November 29, 2016, via telephone. Her work highlights a strategy that uses vendor-supported reformatting with a collaborative approach to ensure preservation and access.

The library and archives of the Great American Songbook Foundation preserve the published and unpublished materials related to the "Great American Songbook," such as materials related to the "standards" from Meredith Willson (*The Music Man*), Johnny Burke ("Pennies from Heaven"), and Hy Zaret ("Unchained Melody"). Situated within the Carmel Center for the Performing Arts in Carmel, IN, and founded by songbook supporter and performer Michael Feinstein, the archives holds a variety of audiovisual materials, including antique formats such as glass and aluminum discs coated with lacquer from the 1930s through the 1950s.

With funding from the Grammy Foundation, the archives was able to undertake a preservation assessment in 2012 and 2013 to identify and prioritize recordings for digitization. Funds from this foundation as well as from family foundations were raised to digitize recordings; digitization was done by George Blood LP, a provider of archival audiovisual digitization services based in Philadelphia. In addition to the lacquer discs, nearly every format of audiovisual media was identified in the archives, including 2-inch Quadruplex videotape and Super 8 and 16 mm films, among other formats. The media feature a variety of content, including musical recordings made in and out of studios, television recordings, and home movies. Lobdell found that establishing a relationship with George Blood was beneficial not only for the expertise he and his company brought to the digitization but also for the relationship itself. This meant she could ask for advice as needed and could send him images of media for identification.

Lobdell found that creating a digital repository for the archives would be too costly to create and maintain. She decided that a collaborative approach would be necessary. She partnered with the Libraries of Indiana University, Bloomington, to host the archives' digitized content in their repository. IU Bloomington houses a substantial film archives and has significant expertise in the area of audiovisual archives and digital preservation. The IU repository will enable digital preservation functions like file fixity monitoring, while the access system allows Lobdell to grant researchers access to digitized items and control how long they have access to the item.

CONCLUSION

This chapter agrees with the POWRR project, which explores digital preservation for small and medium cultural institutions, that "it is time to embrace a 'good enough' approach to digital preservation."[43] Whereas creating certifiably trustworthy digital repositories may be a worthy long-term goal, many small and medium cultural institutions struggle to secure basic infrastructure. For this reason, such institutions may be better served by working with IT staff to build out basic components, such as setting up network storage (e.g., RAID 6 systems) and creating some redundancy (e.g., making a secondary copy and storing it off-site). Further, for large video collections, repositories may want to explore LTO tape options as a cost-effective way of maintaining digitized masters. Once these components are in place, exploring other facets of digital preservation, such as file fixity monitoring, is a worthwhile goal. As the POWRR project staff note, "digital preservation is an incremental process."[44] Therefore, it is a capacity that can be built up over time and become more robust—and even more trustworthy—as infrastructure and know-how are developed. The chapter concluded with several examples of repositories that are building out their digital preservation infrastructure—some supported by IT departments, others requiring collaboration with external institutions.

NOTES

[1] This definition is consistent with the definition from the Association for Library Collections & Technical Services, Preservation and Reformatting Section, Working Group on Defining Digital Preservation, American Library Association. See http://www.ala.org/alcts/resources/preserv/defdigpres0408, permalinked on April 21, 2016, at https://perma.cc/V4MS-7ZFQ.

[2] See, for example, National Digital Stewardship Alliance's Level of Digital Preservation, http://www.digitalpreservation.gov/ndsa/activities/levels.html, permalinked on April 21, 2016, at https://perma.cc/GJK5-STEV.

[3] Amanda Kay Rinehart, Patrice-Andre Prud'homme, and Andrew Reid Huot, "Overwhelmed to Action: Digital Preservation Challenges at the Under-resourced Institution," *OCLC Systems & Services* 30, no. 1 (2014): 28–42.

[4] LOCKSS, http://www.lockss.org/, permalinked on April 21, 2016, at https://perma.cc/JUE2-MGJ9; CLOCKSS, https://www.clockss.org/, permalinked on April 21, 2016, at https://perma.cc/RN5U-LG8E.

[5] MetaArchive Cooperative, https://www.metaarchive.org/, permalinked on April 21, 2016, at https://perma.cc/D4TN-VNJB.

[6] *Digital Preservation Management: Implementing Short-Term Strategies for Long-Term Solutions*, online tutorial developed for the Digital Preservation Management workshop, developed and maintained by Cornell University Library, 2003–6; extended and maintained by ICPSR, 2007–12; and since 2012 extended and maintained by MIT Libraries, http://www.dpworkshop.org/, permalinked on April 21, 2016, at https://perma.cc/36JB-Z886.

[7] Center for Research Libraries, *Trustworthy Repositories Audit and Certification: Criteria and Checklist* (Chicago and Dublin, OH: CRL and OCLC, 2007), http://www.crl.edu/sites/default/files/attachments/pages/trac_0.pdf, permalinked on April 21, 2016, at https://perma.cc/8U6C-6MR2; Steve Marks, *Becoming a Trusted Digital Repository* (Chicago: Society of American Archivists, 2015).

[8] LSI Storage, "Simply Storage: RAID," YouTube video, https://www.youtube.com/watch?v=t5X7jhAMatw, permalinked on April 21, 2016, at https://perma.cc/3MNK-S2AB. Note that this video inspired figures 4-1 and 4-2.

[9] Eduardo Pinheiro, Wolf-Dietrich Weber, and Luiz Andre Barroso, "Failure Trends in a Large Disk Drive Population," in *Proceedings of the 5th USENIX Conference on File and Storage Technologies (FAST '07)*, San Jose, CA, February 13–16, 2007.

[10] Based on advice from the National Digital Stewardship Alliance's Level of Digital Preservation, http://www.digitalpreservation.gov/ndsa/activities/levels.html, permalinked on April 21, 2016, at https://perma.cc/6PGB-SVAV.

[11] Ben Fino-Radin, "MoMA's Digital Art Vault," *Inside/Out: A MoMA/MoMA PS1 Blog*, April 14, 2015, http://www.moma.org/explore/inside_out/2015/04/14/momas-digital-art-vault, permalinked on April 21, 2016, at https://perma.cc/A9YF-T7FV.

[12] Gordon F. Hughes and Joseph F. Murray, "Reliability and Security of RAID Storage Systems and D2D Archives Using SATA Disk Drives," *ACM Transactions on Storage* 1, no. 1 (2004): 95–107; Anthony Cocciolo, "FixityBerry: Environmentally Sustainable Digital Preservation for Very Low Resourced Cultural Heritage Institutions" (paper presented at iConference 2015, Newport Beach, CA, March 24–27, 2015), http://www.thinkingprojects.org/fixity_berry_iconf_final.pdf, permalinked on April 21, 2016, at https://perma.cc/58W9-NEX2.

[13] "Linear Tape Open," *Wikipedia*, https://en.wikipedia.org/wiki/Linear_Tape-Open, permalinked on April 21, 2016, at https://perma.cc/8N53-MLHD.

[14] James Snyder, "The Basics and Challenges of Media Archiving" (paper presented at SMPTE Bits by the Bay 2014, Chesapeake Beach, MD, May 19–21, 2014), https://www.smpte.org/sites/default/files/section-files/BBTB%20101%20Fundamentals%20of%20Archiving%20pt1%20-%20James%20Snyder.pdf, permalinked on April 21, 2016, at https://perma.cc/XT2R-6C52; Dinah Handel, "Archival Workflows and Media Micro-services at CUNY Television" (paper presented at the annual meeting of the Association of Moving Image Archivists, Portland, OR, November 18–21, 2015), http://ndsr.nycdigital.org/wp-content/uploads/2015/11/DHandelAMIAPoster.pdf, permalinked on April 21, 2016, at https://perma.cc/Y2P2-5595.

[15] Ibid.

[16] David S. H. Rosenthal, "Bit Preservation: A Solved Problem?," *International Journal of Digital Curation* 5, no. 1 (2010): 134–48; Lakshmi N. Bairavasundaram et al., "An Analysis of Data Corruption in the Storage Stack," *ACM Transactions on Storage* 4, no. 3 (2008).

[17] Péter Kelemen, "Silent Corruptions," Eighth Annual Workshop on Linux Clusters for Super Computing, https://www.nsc.liu.se/lcsc2007/presentations/LCSC_2007-kelemen.pdf, permalinked on April 21, 2016, at https://perma.cc/97HF-H67F.

[18] Laura Wilsey et al., "Capturing and Processing Born-Digital Files in the STOP AIDS Project Records: A Case Study," *Journal of Western Archives* 4, no. 1 (2013): 1–22.

[19] "MD5," *Wikipedia*, https://en.wikipedia.org/wiki/MD5, permalinked on April 21, 2016, at https://perma.cc/XHQ3-BSGS; "SHA-2," *Wikipedia*, https://en.wikipedia.org/wiki/SHA-2, permalinked on April 21, 2016, at https://perma.cc/TZ67-MZFS.

[20] Excerpted from POWRR project's list of repository software or hosted solutions that provide file monitoring, http://digitalpowrr.niu.edu/tool-grid/, permalinked on April 21, 2016, at https://perma.cc/N6F4-92SQ.

[21] "BagIt," *Wikipedia*, https://en.wikipedia.org/wiki/BagIt, permalinked on April 21, 2016, at https://perma.cc/Y8UE-R65N.

22 See http://sourceforge.net/projects/loc-xferutils/files/loc-bagger/, permalinked on April 21, 2016, at https://perma .cc/575N-PHM3.

23 Fixity, https://www.avpreserve.com/tools/fixity/, permalinked on April 21, 2016, at https://perma.cc/H9TD-25QG; FixityBerry, https://github.com/acocciolo/fixityberry, permalinked on April 21, 2016, at https://perma.cc/S3T7-RHQR.

24 Consultative Committee for Space Data Systems (CCSDS), *Reference Model for an Open Archival Information System* (OAIS) (Washington, DC: CCSDS, 2002).

25 Stewart Granger, "Emulation as a Digital Preservation Strategy," *D-Lib Magazine* 6, no. 10 (2010), http://www.dlib.org/dlib /october00/granger/10granger.html, permalinked on April 21, 2016, at https://perma.cc/8VKB-9D2N.

26 Ibid.

27 Brian F. Lavoie, *The Open Archival Information System Reference Model: Introductory Guide*, 2nd ed. (Dublin, OH: OCLC Office of Research, 2012), http://dx.doi.org/10.7207/twr14-02, permalinked on April 21, 2016, at https://perma. cc/7KVK-D5JM.

28 Erin O'Meara and Kate Stratton, "Preserving Digital Objects," in *Digital Preservation Essentials*, ed. Christopher J. Prom (Chicago: Society of American Archivists, 2016).

29 Lavoie, *The Open Archival Information System Reference Model*.

30 This assumes that the WAV files are created using a sample rate and bit depth that are the same or better than the recordings included in the Garage Band file. More information on this issue is provided in chapter 7, "Audio Collections."

31 RLG and OCLC, *Trusted Digital Repositories: Attributes and Responsibilities* (Mountain View, CA: RLG, 2002), http://www .oclc.org/content/dam/research/activities/trustedrep/repositories.pdf, permalinked on April 24, 2016, at https://perma.cc /5XNF-JDWS.

32 *Digital Preservation Management* tutorial.

33 OCLC and CRL, *Trustworthy Repositories Audit and Certification: Criteria and Checklist* (Chicago: CRL and Dublin, OH: OCLC, 2007), http://www.crl.edu/sites/default/files/attachments/pages/trac_0.pdf, permalinked on April 21, 2016, at https://perma.cc/5ETG-2CNQ.

34 Ben Goldman, "Bridging the Gap: Taking Practical Steps Toward Managing Born-Digital Collections in Manuscript Repositories," *RBM: A Journal of Rare Books, Manuscripts, and Cultural Heritage* 12, no. 1 (2012): 11–24.

35 National Digital Stewardship Alliance's Level of Digital Preservation, http://www.digitalpreservation.gov/ndsa/activities /levels.html, permalinked on April 21, 2016, at https://perma.cc/9974-3D9C.

36 Archivematica, https://www.archivematica.org, permalinked on April 21, 2016, at https://perma.cc/B7A3-8RR7; Tessela's Preservica, http://preservica.com/, permalinked on April 21, 2016, at https://perma.cc/Q2VQ-T7GU; OCLC CONTENTdm, http://www.oclc.org/contentdm.en.html, permalinked on April 21, 2016, at https://perma.cc/FP26-67M8.

37 DuraCloud, http://www.duracloud.org/, permalinked on April 21, 2016, at https://perma.cc/S5EK-R6NK.

38 National Digital Stewardship Alliance's Level of Digital Preservation, http://www.digitalpreservation.gov/ndsa/activities /levels.html, permalinked on April 21, 2016, at https://perma.cc/H28Y-NABN.

39 Synology, https://www.synology.com/en-us/, permalinked on April 21, 2016, at https://perma.cc/Q2MA-F2HV.

40 AceAudit, https://wiki.umiacs.umd.edu/adapt/index.php/Ace:Main, permalinked on April 21, 2016, at https://perma .cc/AW8F-EMA6.

41 FixityBerry, https://github.com/acocciolo/fixityberry, permalinked on April 21, 2016, at https://perma.cc/9F29-JEWH.

42 AVPreserve, "Cost of Inaction Calculator," https://coi.avpreserve.com/, permalinked on December 1, 2016, at https://perma .cc/H6P2-EL2Y.

43 Jaime Schumacher, Lynne M. Thomas, and Drew VandeCreek, *From Theory to Action: "Good Enough" Digital Preservation Solutions for Under-Resourced Cultural Heritage Institutions* (2014), 15, http://commons.lib.niu.edu/bitstream/handle /10843/13610/FromTheoryToAction_POWRR_WhitePaper.pdf, permalinked on April 21, 2016, at https://perma.cc /3CWG-CW5S.

44 Ibid.

CHAPTER   5

Access and Outreach

OVERVIEW

Traditionally, archives provide access to archival collections via reading rooms, where call slips are issued for boxes that are retrieved and made available to researchers in a loosely supervised environment. Screener copies or even the archival master of the media on tape or disc are handed to the user, who watches or listens to them in the reading room and then returns them. For electronic records, especially records with privacy concerns, archives are increasingly making laptops available to researchers with copies of the records on them, often with the Internet and USB ports disabled so that records cannot be copied in bulk.[1] This chapter explores some additional ways to make moving image and sound records available to users, especially online, and discusses some outreach strategies that take advantage of these media.

MEDIA EXHIBITION ONLINE: BRIEF HISTORY

Increasingly, digitized and born-digital moving image records are contributed to online repositories with a public access component. However, online access has been slow to develop, and other forms of recorded information such as still images and text are better represented in online collections. For example, if you search for your favorite subject in the Digital Public Library of America, which is an aggregator of library and archival records available digitally in the United States, you will notice that there are typically few or no moving image and sound records available, especially compared to other types of records. This is because there has been relatively little work in digitizing moving image records compared to still image records.[2] Barriers include issues discussed in this book, such as technical challenges in digitizing and storing media, but also rights issues that complicate public access.

Making high-quality moving image and sound records available online has been a challenge until recently. Sound records are more likely to be digitized than video records because they can be more easily digitized and presented online. The advent of the MP3 audio encoder significantly enabled distribution of sound over the Internet. MP3 uses a perceptual encoder to remove sounds that the listener should not be able to hear or notice, thus drastically reducing file sizes.[3] Because these files can be transmitted in a low-bandwidth environment, high-quality sound files could be transmitted over the Internet by the late 1990s, and MP3 ushered in an era of illegal file sharing that still persists today.[4]

Compared to sound, exhibiting high-quality video reproductions online has been difficult, and it did not become a reality until this decade. In the late 1990s and early 2000s, low-quality videos could be streamed online through a combination of streaming servers and client software. For example, streaming servers with client components such as Real Player, Apple QuickTime, Windows Media Player, and Macromedia Flash (now owned by Adobe) were commonplace ways to stream video online.[5] Setting up streaming video using these options tended to be quite complicated because you needed to purchase and install the streaming server, or orchestrate the use of someone else's streaming server.

YouTube rocketed to fame in 2005 by providing a means for people to easily share videos with their friends, families, and colleagues.[6] The model was imitated by a number of competitors, such as Google Video, which was absorbed into YouTube after Google's purchase of YouTube in 2006. Today, YouTube allows any user to upload video, and it is an increasingly common distribution platform for commercial media assets, such as television programs, music videos, and other commercial content. With this commercialization of YouTube has come the growth of advertising, which is often required viewing—at least for a few seconds—before a video can be watched.

Today, once popular Flash video has been superseded by HTML5 video, and commercial video websites such as YouTube continue to attract billons of viewers.[7] For most archives interested in streaming their video and sound, the two most salient methods are hosting the video or sound content yourself using HTML5 distribution methods (which will be discussed below), uploading it to a noncommercial repository such as the Internet Archive, or using a commercial platform such as YouTube or Vimeo. Although I am an advocate for the first two options, some archives may want to use the commercial options because of their larger user base and the ability to play back video on a wide variety of devices (e.g., mobile devices, televisions, etc.).

HTML5 DISTRIBUTION OF VIDEO

Development of HTML5 began in the late 2000s, with the standard adopted in 2014.[8] Although it is a complex standard well beyond the scope of this book, its media elements are particularly relevant for archives looking to make moving image and sound records available. Particularly salient is the introduction of the video tag, which allows videos to be featured in a web page with HTML code like the following:

```
<video src="oralhistory1.mp4" width="320" height="240" controls></video>
```

The decoding and playback of the video is handled directly by the web browser—thus, there is no need for external players like QuickTime or Windows Media Player.

The best way to take advantage of HTML5 video is to use repository software that supports it. Simple repository software, like Omeka, allows for videos to be played back in this fashion. For example, my students selected Omeka for use in oral history digitization projects for the Lesbian Herstory Archives, with HTML5 playback options shown in figure 5-1.

Figure 5-1. Omeka with HTML5 plugin simplifies playback of video.

Despite the ease with which the video tag can be called up in HTML5 web pages, there are some issues to consider when preparing videos for playback. The video tag is not able to play back all forms of video. Further, some forms of video do not lend themselves to easy playback over the Internet. For example, you would want to use formats designed for Internet playback, such as formats that allow the video to start playing as soon as enough information has been downloaded, rather than having to wait for the entire file to download.

When distributing copies of video over the web, it is necessary to create web-optimized access copies of the videos. To create the access copies, you can use master copies of the video, or mezzanine copies, which are high-quality copies. The HandBrake program is particularly easy to use to compress videos for web distribution.[9] It is an open-source program that works on both Mac and PC, and it has a user-friendly user interface, shown in figure 5-2.

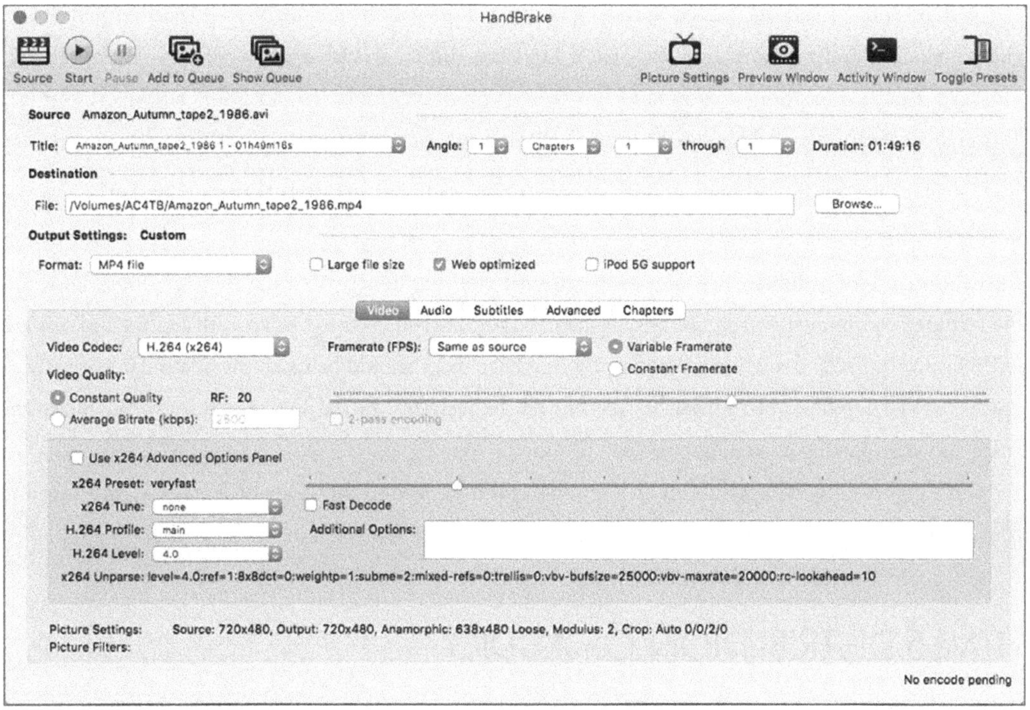

Figure 5-2. HandBrake can be used to compress videos for web distribution.

To create access copies of analog video, useful options include the following:

Container	MP4
Web Optimized	Yes
Large File Size	No
Video Codec	H.264
Framerate	Same as source
Audio	(leave as defaults, which should follow the source)

Figure 5-3. Setting for HandBrake for creating access copies of videos.

The H.264 video encoder is widely used for encoding video over the Internet. For example, it is used by YouTube and Vimeo, as well as on Blu-ray discs.[10] For a discussion of video encoders, see chapter 9, "Analog Video Collections," and chapter 10, "Digital Video Collections."

The "web optimized" setting is important, as it ensures that metadata is placed in the front of the file, so that it knows how much data needs to be downloaded before the video can start playing. This ensures that the video plays back as quickly as possible.

One way to speed up video playback is to shrink the dimensions of the video, which reduces the overall file size. For analog video that originates on VHS, reducing the video dimensions to 320 by 240 pixels can help achieve this.[11] Since VHS is a fairly low-resolution format and is estimated to have only that much resolution inherently, this is a suitable dimension.[12] For a discussion of resolutions and other issues in video, see the aforementioned chapters about video.

Other tools for resizing and compressing videos include FFmpeg, which is a powerful open-source video encoding and manipulation package.[13] However, unlike HandBrake, which has a graphic user interface, FFmpeg has only a command line–based interface, similar to old DOS systems. Using the Terminal application on a Macintosh computer, you can issue commands such as the following:

```
for i in *.mp4; do ffmpeg -i "${i}" -vcodec h264 -s 320x240 -movflags faststart "320_${i}";
done
```

This command loops through all files in the current working directory (using the "for" loop) and runs the FFmpeg command on each file, with specific flags that re-encode the video with H.264 and resize it to 320 by 240 pixels. It also specifies that the "faststart" flags should be used; this is similar to the "web optimized" setting described earlier, which puts all the technical metadata in the front of the file so the video can start playing as soon as possible.

Although issuing commands via the command line is beyond the scope of this book, you can find help on using these tools online.[14]

HTML5 DISTRIBUTION OF AUDIO

As with video, HTML5 brought the introduction of the audio tag, which can readily play back audio in a web browser using code such as the following:

```
<audio src="mabel_hampton_07.mp3" width="350" controls></audio>
```

In this example, the MP3 file can be played back using standard playback controls (e.g., play, stop, fast-forward, etc.). As with video, not all file formats are well suited for playback over the Internet. For example, the Microsoft WAV file makes a great preservation master but is poorly suited for Internet playback because of large file sizes and because the entire file needs to be downloaded before it can be played. MP3 files are suitable for playback because they are so widely supported and easy for most modern web browsers to play back. MP3 has been succeeded by Advanced Audio Coding (AAC), which often has the file extension M4A.[15] Today, both MP3 and M4A files provide suitable access to most sound records.

There are many tools for converting WAV files to MP3 files. For example, on Macintosh the application Switch is easy to use and has a graphic user interface.[16] However, command-line tools can also be used. The advantage of command-line tools is that you can keep a text file with all your frequently used commands; when you need to apply a transformation (e.g., convert a WAV to an MP3), you can just copy and paste the command into the command-line prompt. One particularly useful command-line tool is called LAME, which is an MP3 encoder.[17] For example, you can convert a WAV file to an MP3 file by issuing the following simple command via the command line:

```
lame oral_history1.wav oral_history2.mp3
```

This command can be combined with the "for" loop as in the earlier example, allowing you to batch-convert a large number of WAV files to MP3. For help getting set up with LAME, see the resource in the endnotes.[18]

ACCESS ISSUES AND HTML5

Despite the easy playback that HTML5 affords, one issue may be troubling to some archives. Because the MP3 or MP4 files simply reside on the web server, it is fairly easy for a user to download the files directly to a desktop computer. For example, assume a user views the source of a web page and sees the following:

```
<video src="oralhistory1.mp4" width="320" height="240" controls></video>
```

He or she can simply type the following in the address bar of the web browser:

```
http://yourhost.edu/yourdirectory/oralhistory1.mp4
```

By using the "File ➔ Save Page" option in the browser, the MP4 file will be directly downloaded to the computer. This may not be a problem for many archives: being able to download media for later viewing may be perfectly acceptable. However, some institutions may feel uncomfortable with downloading versus streaming, and HTML5 does nothing to prevent downloading.

Essentially, anything that can be listened to or watched via the Internet can be downloaded with varying degrees of effort. For example, video—even offered through streaming services—can be captured using video capture tools, and audio can be relatively easily rerecorded during playback. Thus, if an archive insists that in no way can media be downloaded, then it is best to not offer remote access to such content over the Internet. Requiring researchers to use controlled workstations in a reading room is the only real way to prevent downloaded copies from being made.

SOCIAL MEDIA FEATURES FOR USER ENGAGEMENT

In addition to making a video or sound element easily playable, there are other ways to engage users online. These include features for users to leave comments on video and audio, which can sometimes help fill holes in the metadata. Providing affordances for users to easily share content via social media sites such as Twitter and Facebook can help spur discussion about a particular person, event, or interview. Repositories like Omeka have plugins for easily activating all of these features.

NONCOMMERCIAL REPOSITORIES

The Internet Archive (IA) allows the upload and playback of video and audio, with an increasingly sophisticated search, discovery, and playback interface that easily rivals that of commercial media.[19] Beyond playback, IA also provides options for downloading alternative forms of the media, such as Torrent files or alternative encodings. The advantage of the Internet Archive is that it is both a nonprofit and a library, so playback is not infused with the advertisements that are growing increasingly prevalent on commercial video platforms. The only notable disadvantage of using the Internet Archive as a distribution platform is that you cannot regulate access; access is granted to the entire Internet or to no one. Some repositories may need to make select video or audio available on-site or available upon request via a link out of privacy or copyright concerns.

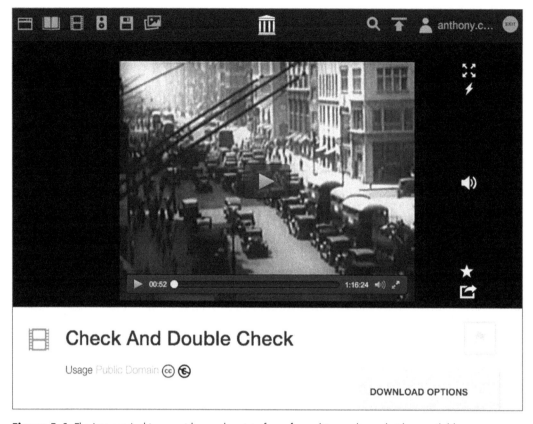

Figure 5-4. The Internet Archive provides modern interfaces for making audio and video available.

COMMERCIAL PLATFORMS

Commercial platforms such as YouTube for video or SoundCloud for audio can be a compelling option for archives because they include features beyond HTML5 playback, have large user communities, and work well with a variety of devices. These platforms often have easy-to-use interfaces that streamline content contribution. Despite these advantages, a notable disadvantage is that the user must consent to the service's terms and conditions, which archivists should be aware of before committing themselves and their institution.

YouTube

Although not onerous, YouTube's Terms of Service have some aspects that an archives and its parent institution should be aware of.[20] The most notable issue is the rights that content contributors give to YouTube. Although copyright owners do not transfer their copyright and ownership to YouTube, they do "grant a worldwide, non-exclusive, royalty-free, sublicensable and transferable license to use, reproduce, distribute, prepare derivative works of, display, and perform the Content in connection with the Service and YouTube's (and its successors' and affiliates') business. . . ."[21] For example, YouTube, its parent company, Google, and its successors can use the media contributed in its own promotional material, without any say from the owner about how the content is used. Also, since that right is transferable, YouTube could theoretically sell these rights in the future. An archivist should also consider that although he or she may "delete" content from YouTube, YouTube "may retain, but not display, distribute, or perform, server copies of your videos that have been removed or deleted."[22] Therefore, although the content may be deleted from the public side of YouTube, the video may still remain on company servers.

Another issue to consider is YouTube's "right to remove Content without prior notice."[23] Therefore, any content can be removed for any reason at the sole discretion of YouTube. Lastly, YouTube's Terms of Service state that children under thirteen are "not to use the Service," which may be an issue for some archives.

In addition to the Terms of Service, users must consent to the Community Guidelines and Privacy Policy. The Community Guidelines should not present any major issues to archives, as they ask for simple things like no pornography, hate speech, or extreme violence. However, the privacy policy could present some issues to some archives. For example, information like search queries and location data are recorded and used for more effective advertising.[24] Archivists may not want to subject their own personal information to targeted advertising or subject patrons to such activity.

The last issue with the Terms of Service is that "YouTube may, in its sole discretion, modify or revise these Terms of Service and policies at any time, and you agree to be bound by such modifications or revisions."[25] This is a somewhat troubling statement, as users must agree to all changes to the terms without knowing what those changes might be.

SoundCloud

Whereas YouTube has become the most well-known commercial video hosting website, SoundCloud has become a popular audio sharing service. Searching SoundCloud for "oral history" indicates that this site has been used extensively for making this form of recorded sound available. SoundCloud's Terms of Use are similar to YouTube's, with some notable distinctions. First, by uploading content to SoundCloud, you "grant a limited, worldwide, non-exclusive, royalty-free, full paid up, license to other users of the Platform, and to operators and users of any other websites, apps and/or platforms to which Your Content has been shared or embedded using the Services ("Linked Services"), to use, copy, repost, transmit or otherwise distribute, publicly display, publicly perform, adapt, prepare derivative works of, compile, make available and otherwise communicate to the public . . . ."[26] This is very expansive: not only are certain rights given to the hosted platform, rights are also given to all downstream users of that platform, such as the right to "copy" and "prepare derivative works." For some archives, this may be consistent with policies, but for others this may go beyond what they are willing to part with.

Unlike YouTube, when users delete content from the SoundCloud service, that will "result in the deletion of the relevant files from SoundCloud's systems and servers."[27]

FEDERATED OPTIONS

Most often, libraries and archives have built web-accessible digital libraries and archives to allow users to access their content. By doing so, content becomes discoverable through commercial search engines such as Google and Bing. However, it has become increasingly clear that commercial engines prioritize "fresh" content, or content that is regularly updated, over static content in the ranking of their search results.[28] This can be problematic for archives, which provide access to content that may be decades—or even centuries—old. An emerging option for archives to make their content available is through aggregators like the Digital Public Library of America (DPLA), which provides a portal to millions of items of content from libraries, archives, and museums in the United States. Europeana in Europe and Trove in Australia perform a similar function.

Archives cannot directly upload an item or even upload a feed of their metadata into DPLA. Rather, archives can provide a feed of their metadata to a DPLA service hub, which is a regional aggregator of content that is automatically fed into DPLA.[29] For example, New York State has the Empire State Digital Network (ESDN) hosted by Metropolitan New York Library Council (METRO), which aggregates content from New York and is fed automatically into DPLA. If you are interested in getting your content into DPLA, contact the service hub for your state or region.[30] Note that DPLA does not host the content; archives are responsible for hosting their own content, using one of the methods described earlier. DPLA provides a search interface whose results link back to this hosted content.

ACCESSIBILITY TO THE HEARING-IMPAIRED AND VISUALLY IMPAIRED

US institutions that receive federal funds, such as student aid dollars, are required to make their websites accessible to the hearing-impaired and visually impaired.[31] For the visually impaired, websites should be accessible to screen readers like JAWS, which reads the contents of web pages to users.[32] When websites are read to users, the content of the web page and the navigation options should be clear. Images, videos, and audio should have "alternate" tags that describe what is in the image, video, or audio. In the following example, screen readers would read the ALT tag rather than attempt to play the video:

> <audio src="oral_history1.mp3" alt="Edwin Lopez interview 2015 March 3, transcript available to the hearing impaired by request"></video>

Ideally, transcripts for all audio and video would exist. However, since this is a labor-intensive and expensive prospect, it may be necessary to have in place options for on-demand transcription creation. Another option is to build in user-contributed transcription options, which has seen some recent successes such as at the Smithsonian Transcription Center.[33] User-generated transcription tools include Omeka's Scripto plugin.[34] For video content, having closed-caption options available is ideal.

Engaging individuals who are hearing-impaired or visually impaired, or at least working with those with expertise in providing services to these communities, is the best way to ensure that websites are functioning optimally. Recently, a hearing-impaired student enrolled in my course Projects in Digital Archives, where our task was to digitize oral history recordings from the Center for Puerto Rican Studies and make them available via a website. Although the student could not create descriptive metadata for these oral histories, the student's participation made everyone in the class (and the instructor!) remember how important the descriptive metadata and transcripts are for such projects.

DIGITIZATION ON DEMAND

This book has argued for digital reformatting for preservation of and access to analog recordings. However, how should digitization be prioritized? One option that archivists are increasingly adopting is digitization on demand. This option allows a researcher to request a media item and access a digitized copy—either on-site or online—rather than handling the original item, with the risk of it failing and possibly being ruined. There are many possible variations on this theme. For example, some archives may create copies that are good enough for access and not create preservation masters, thus relying on the original as the preservation master. Others may create preservation masters from which the access copies are derived. Some archives may charge for this service, whereas others may view it as an integral part of their preservation and access commitments and do so free of charge.

For example, the Hammerstein Archives of Recorded Sound at the New York Public Library notes that users "never directly handle sound recordings; this helps to protect rare and fragile items."[35] Some recordings are played back and directly "piped into specially designed listening and viewing booths," while others require "preservation reformatting prior to auditioning" and being piped into the booth.[36] NYPL does not charge for listening to the recording, even if the request prompted a preservation reformatting. However, they charge for making copies that can be taken home.[37]

Other archives have similarly adopted costs for providing copies of audiovisual recordings, which can help offset the costs of preservation reformatting. For example, the Southern Folklife Collection at the University of North Carolina, Chapel Hill, prices items already digitized differently from those needing digitization: $25 for an audio item that has not been digitized yet, and $8.25 for an item that has already been digitized, both of which are delivered as MP3 or WAV files.[38] The Center for Popular Music at Middle Tennessee State University charges $80 per hour with a half-hour minimum for audio copies, billed in fifteen-minute increments, with a 50 percent discount to students, faculty, and staff of the university.[39]

In the three examples above, media reformatting labs and professional staff support this work. Digitization on demand usually requires setting up equipment needed to do the reformatting on-site. Can digitization be done on demand without dedicated staff? Although dedicated staff and lab space are ideal, there are ways to work around this in reduced-resource contexts. In reformatting, the major labor-intensive task that requires dedicated staff is the need to watch or listen to the entire recording as it is captured. In reference to video oral histories, Scott Pennington and Dean Rehberger argue that while this is ideal, there may be other options:

> The captured video should also always be viewed. Best practice is for trained video professionals to monitor and check the file-creation process. To save funds and expert time on projects we have asked non-specialists who may be part of the project, volunteers, or in some cases clerical staff to watch the video for problems. Personnel can be given access to down-sampled versions of the files, and by watching may spot problems in the digitization workflow. Specialists involved in the analog-to-digital conversion process should always view the first few files completely.[40]

Thus, Pennington and Rehberger argue that while watching is ideal, it can be expensive and time-consuming; there are ways to distribute the quality control process across multiple staff, and viewing emphasis should be on "the first few files." Because of the labor involved, organizations such as the Bay Area Video Coalition have created software tools for identifying media reformatting problems, such as issues that may occur with video reformatting.[41] Some archives such as the Library of Congress's Packard Campus of the National Audio-Visual Conservation Center use videotape "robots" to digitize recordings.[42] In cases such as this, automated tools for monitoring reformatting issues grow increasingly important.

The approach that I most often use for reformatting I call the "concurrence" strategy, which involves some listening and watching during reformatting but also doing other work at the same time. The general workflow includes the following. First, I watch or listen to the beginning of every recording as it is being digitized. During this time, I ensure that the sound and image (in the case of video) are entirely consistent with the analog playback and make adjustments as needed. (See the "playback" sections of relevant chapters for more on making such adjustments.) Then, I set an alarm on my smartphone for the maximum time of the recording. For example, if I am digitizing a sixty-minute audiocassette tape on side A, I will set my alarm for thirty minutes. When the alarm goes off, I return my full attention to the reformatting station and ensure that the tape has stopped playback and has reached its end. I play back the last minute of the digitized recording to ensure that its end was logical. If the ending does not seem right, I check to ensure that the analog and digitized endings match up. Once the endings check out, I do a quick visual inspection of the sound wave throughout the digitized recording to ensure consistency. Any excess digitized white space will be deleted from the end of the recording. I use a similar process for videotape, except the excess video frames are trimmed off the end and the middle frames are skimmed through to ensure that they look and sound as expected.

Although professional organizations such as the International Association of Sound and Audiovisual Archives (IASA) and Association for Recorded Sound Collections (ARSC) recommend more attention to playback than my "concurrence" strategy allows, I have found that it works well for cassette-based formats (e.g., compact audiocassette, VHS, U-matic) and has not proven problematic. Despite this, additional empirical research is needed on the occurrence of errors introduced by using the "concurrent" strategy. This strategy may be better suited for the creation of access copies and less well-suited for the creation of new preservation masters.

When using the concurrent strategy during digitization—or even when not using such a strategy—it is best to offer downstream users the ability to report any perceived problems with the digitized recording. These inquires can prompt further checks between the digitized copy and the original media item.

If a recording is going to be listened to or watched in its entirety during digitization, it is recommended that this opportunity be used to improve metadata for records that are minimally described, such as creating item-level records where ones do not exist, or fleshing out metadata fields that are lacking such descriptions. As the listener or watcher should be able to develop a good understanding of the media item's contents, it would be a shame to not capture this knowledge.

Some digitization-on-demand requests are easier to fulfill than others. For example, a digitization-on-demand service may work well for a researcher who wants to watch a couple of videotapes, but less well for a researcher who needs to fast-forward through a large collection looking for specific footage. Rather than adopting a single strategy for providing access to collections, it may be necessary to have multiple approaches based on researcher needs and available resources.

Lastly, digitization-on-demand statistics and experiences can influence other digitization decisions. For example, if digitization on demand has prompted chunks of a collection to be digitized, indicating researcher demand, then it may influence a decision to digitize the rest of the collection.

REFORMATTING WITH VOLUNTEER ASSISTANCE

Another option to consider—one that has been woefully under-researched—is the possibility of using volunteers, including students and researchers, to digitize recordings. This requires that workflows for digitization are worked out in advance, sufficient equipment is in place, and the volunteer is properly trained to perform the workflow. This option can work well if the volunteer is interested in the content and there are incentives in place for the researcher to do the digitization, such as allowing him to keep copies of the digitized material. Also, using volunteers only makes sense if the scope of the digitization is enough to offset the time investment in providing training.

For certain collections, it is possible to connect the value of reformatting to public or local history, thus making this work attractive for community service reasons. There is some evidence that engaging students in reformatting work, such as for oral histories, can lead them to be more engaged in historical aspects and issues implicated in the work.[43] Thus, for the right collection, it could be possible to work with educators such as middle school or high school history teachers, or even after-school programs, to involve students in reformatting by tying this work into learning about local history. Although it may be easier to simply outsource reformatting to a vendor, reformatting does offer an opportunity for individuals to learn about a collection and its contents, and it does not necessarily have to be a ghastly repetitive process if the fruits of the labor will be used in some meaningful way.

Figure 5-5. Video display station with headphones at the Museum of the Moving Image, Queens, New York.

EXHIBITION

In addition to making moving image and sound collections available via reading rooms and websites, exhibition in galleries is a way to make such records known and meaningful to patrons. Increasingly, archivists find themselves in positions to curate exhibitions or participate in curation activities. There are several ways that most moving image and sound records can be exhibited. The first way is through controlled playback, which could include the media being played in a loop, or—for longer works—to begin playback at some predefined time (e.g., video exhibition begins every half hour). Because of the high cost of film prints and the relative rarity of film projectors that can play on a loop, most moving image records are converted to some form of video. Typically, exhibition organizers use a DVD or Blu-ray player that can be put on an automatically repeating mode. With this option, headphones can be used (see figure 5-5) or sound can play openly over speakers. If headphones are not used, the volume will have an impact on the entire exhibition experience, since the sound will travel. An alternative is to carve out some kind of alcove or minitheater, where visitors can walk in or even sit and watch. Some visitors would rather not put on public headphones because of germs, so low-volume playback may be a good option for many galleries.

Other options are to provide a more interactive viewing experience by providing play, pause, fast-forward, and rewind options using a dedicated player or a digital kiosk. For example, the Andy Warhol Museum in Pittsburgh has the entire corpus of Warhol's films available via digital kiosks with headphones that can pull up any digitized film or video for viewing.[44] Similarly, at the Museum of the Moving Image in Queens, visitors can listen to film scores from an interactive kiosk called the Composer Jukebox.

For longer works that require sustained attention, exhibition in a theater space may be the most appropriate option. However, this can be a challenge for libraries and archives that do not have dedicated theater or film exhibition space.

As video technology continues to progress with increasingly high resolutions, a particularly compelling method to exhibit vintage analog video is to use television sets from the period, which provide a more authentic viewing experience than new screens. Vintage CRT television sets can be purchased

Figure 5-6. Visitors can listen to film scores from the Composer Jukebox at the Museum of the Moving Image, Queens, New York.

readily from eBay and other resellers, and digital-to-analog signal converters needed to show digitized content can still be purchased new. Although the sets themselves may be a bit more finicky than their modern counterparts and can fail unpredictably because of their age, they add a realistic dimension that visitors may appreciate. For example, in the New-York Historical Society's 2013 exhibition *AIDS in New York: The First Five Years*, the use of period television sets, with their glowing quality, added to the overall exhibition experience.

EDUCATIONAL OUTREACH: OVERVIEW

In addition to making moving image and sound collections available via reading rooms, websites, and galleries, more extensive outreach is becoming more common. In archives based at higher education institutions, archivist Marcus Robyns advocates for archivists to play a more active role in outreach, making an archives a learning laboratory and the archivist more of an educator.[45] Although he notes that some archivists may be hesitant to do this, fearing that it may compromise their objectivity, it does offer a way for archives to reach out to new communities and positively affect the overall educational process. Some options for engaging in outreach are discussed below.

EDUCATIONAL OUTREACH: OUTREACH TO YOUTH

Much of the research on archival outreach has focused on paper-based materials. For example, of the wide variety of excellent archival outreach projects included in the edited volume *Past or Portal? Enhancing Undergraduate Learning through Special Collections and Archives*, none specifically mentions moving image and sound materials.[46] Despite the lack of published cases, there is plenty of opportunity to make use of these materials. Through partnership with professors or other educators, archivists have opportunities to create exciting programs that bring collections to life.

When working with professors or educators, it is important to delineate what the learning outcomes of the project will be. When developing an educational program, it is useful to state, "by the end of this program/workshop/course, students will be able to . . . " followed by a few bullet points of what students will have learned.

One option for engaging students with archives is to have students curate exhibitions online or in a physical setting. As discussed in this book, the lack of digitized moving image and sound records inhibit them from being accessed and used in curation projects. However, a digitization project can be followed up with partnerships with professors or educators, in which students create exhibitions using digitized materials. In the context of an MSLIS program, I have had students both digitize materials and curate exhibits using the digitized materials.[47] In doing this work, I have found that the process of digitizing a collection and curating it online accelerates the development of students' historical knowledge of the topic.[48]

Another way to involve students is to have them engage in media projects, such as creating their own short documentary films; they can use archival footage such as oral histories, recordings of events, and other moving image and sound records. This could best be accomplished in collaboration with a professor who works with students on media projects.

These options discussed with respect to undergraduate students can also be used with high school students. Although archives are not a part of most high school campuses, pioneering archives like the Brooklyn Historical Society bring in students from the community to work on exhibition curation through after-school programs.[49] High schools may have media production facilities that independent archives do not. Therefore, these types of partnerships require some back-and-forth between high school and archival facilities. Other programs, such as the Brooklyn Public Library's Brooklyn Connections, bring in public high school students to work on projects that make use of rare archival material and tie into Common Core standards.[50] This project includes lesson plans that can be adapted for other collections and contexts.

Archivists interested in using their archives' materials in educational outreach projects may want to learn more about Common Core standards. These standards were developed by educators in the United States to describe what students should know by the end of a given grade. Archives have the potential for enhancing learning around Common Core standards, specifically those in the social studies area that require primary source engagement. For example, the following standards for students in grades six through eight illustrate the need for students to learn about things that archives are well suited to provide in partnership with educators:[51]

> Analyze the relationship between a primary and secondary source on the same topic.
>
> Cite specific textual evidence to support analysis of primary and secondary sources.
>
> Determine the central ideas or information of a primary or secondary source; provide an accurate summary of the source distinct from prior knowledge or opinions.

EDUCATIONAL OUTREACH: FILM SCREENING WITH DISCUSSION

Educational outreach can also be accomplished through film screenings followed by discussion. Documentary film can be an effective educational tool. For example, in studying the outcomes of 425 film screenings at public libraries from a community engagement initiative of the PBS program *POV*, researchers found that "the screening of socially and culturally significant documentaries at public libraries, combined with post-screening discussions, can positively impact library patrons' interest in becoming more civically engaged and foster a greater understanding of the issues raised by the films."[52]

An example of using film screenings in tandem with collecting moving image records comes from Brooklyn College, where the Archives and Special Collections acquired the raw footage from Shola Lynch's 2004 film *Chisholm '72: Unbought and Unbossed*. Shirley Chisholm was the first African American to run for president and first woman to run for the Democratic Party nomination. She was an alumna of Brooklyn College, which made the interviews conducted by Lynch an excellent addition to the collection.[53] A whole program of educational activities around Chisholm was presented, including two film screenings and discussions with the filmmaker.[54]

Not all post-screening discussions require the filmmaker or record creator to be present. For example, the *POV* program mentioned earlier required all film screenings to be followed by a post-screening discussion. That discussion could mean inviting a local expert for a question-and-answer session or having a librarian facilitate a discussion using a discussion guide available from *POV*.[55] Every *POV* film has a discussion guide available to provide practical examples of how to hold a discussion and the types of questions to ask.[56]

Another project that used documentary film for education is Teaching the Levees, which used Spike Lee's 2006 film, *When the Levees Broke: A Requiem in Four Acts*, as an opportunity to spur democratic dialogue in communities throughout the country.[57] The curriculum was designed to support democratic dialogue, defined as "structured discussions designed to tackle tough issues."[58] Project planners asserted that when such a dialogue is finished, "participants should leave feeling that they better understand the issues, better understand the points of view of those with whom they disagree, and, perhaps most importantly, can better articulate their own viewpoint."[59] The project culminated with sending thirty thousand copies of the film to schools, libraries, and community centers across the country.[60] This example illustrates that the use of documentary films, which are often filled with archival footage, offers many exciting opportunities to become an "archivist as educator."

CONCLUSION

Enhancing access to moving image and sound records can begin with making them more available on the web using tools such as HTML5 media elements. However, expanded access is only a beginning. Archivists can consider more expansive outreach efforts, such as exhibitions, collaborations with professors and other instructors on course projects, and becoming an archivist as educator.

NOTES

1. For example, this is the case with Susan Sontag's electronic records at the UCLA Special Collections. For a discussion of the researcher experience, see Benjamin Moser, "In the Sontag Archives," *New Yorker* (January 30, 2014), http://www.newyorker.com/books/page-turner/in-the-sontag-archives, permalinked on April 21, 2016, at https://perma.cc/8MT7-8XCG.

2. Karen F. Gracy, "Distribution and Consumption Patterns of Archival Moving Images in Online Environments," *American Archivist* 75, no.2 (2012): 422–55.

3. Jonathan Sterne, *MP3: The Meaning of a Format* (Durham, NC: Duke University Press, 2012).

4. Ibid.

5. Bruce Lawson and Remy Shary, *Introducing HTML5* (Berkeley, CA: New Riders, 2011).

6. Jean Burgess and Joshua Green, *YouTube: Online Video and Participatory Culture* (Cambridge: Polity Press, 2009).

7. "YouTube Statistics," https://www.youtube.com/yt/press/statistics.html, permalinked on April 21, 2016, at https://perma.cc/FWA7-BVCA.

8. "HTML5," *Wikipedia,* https://en.wikipedia.org/wiki/HTML5, permalinked on April 21, 2016, at https://perma.cc/C9X7-YZQC.

9. HandBrake, https://handbrake.fr/, permalinked on April 21, 2016, at https://perma.cc/6AN5-8AVX.

10. "H.264/MPEG-4 AVC," *Wikipedia,* https://en.wikipedia.org/wiki/H.264/MPEG-4_AVC, permalinked on April 21, 2016, at https://perma.cc/KE3H-CAPA.

11. Assumes a standard 4:3 aspect ratio.

12. Jim Taylor, *DVD Demystified* (New York: McGraw Hill, 1998).

13. FFmpeg, https://www.ffmpeg.org/, permalinked on April 21, 2016, at https://perma.cc/WT8U-S78N.

14. Anthony Cocciolo, "Unix Commands and Batch Processing for the Reluctant Librarian or Archivist," *Code4Lib Journal* 23 (2014), http://journal.code4lib.org/articles/9158, permalinked on April 21, 2016, at https://perma.cc/255L-BUU4.

15. "Advanced Audio Coding," *Wikipedia,* https://en.wikipedia.org/wiki/Advanced_Audio_Coding, permalinked on April 21, 2016, at https://perma.cc/D77D-P57Q.

16. Switch, http://switch-mac.en.softonic.com/mac, permalinked on April 21, 2016, at https://perma.cc/227C-PFHA.

17. LAME, http://lame.sourceforge.net/, permalinked on April 21, 2016, at https://perma.cc/HSU2-KHRF.

18. Cocciolo, "Unix Commands."

19. Internet Archive, http://archive.org, permalinked on April 21, 2016, at https://perma.cc/HA2V-FLN4.

20. "YouTube Terms of Service," https://www.youtube.com/t/terms, permalinked on April 21, 2016, at https://perma.cc/3UQT-EZNL.

21. Ibid.

22. Ibid.

23. Ibid.

24. "Google Privacy Policy," https://www.google.com/intl/en/policies/privacy/, permalinked on April 21, 2016, at https://perma.cc/JGJ2-55J4.

25. "YouTube Terms of Service."

26. "SoundCloud Terms of Use," https://soundcloud.com/terms-of-use, permalinked on April 21, 2016, at https://perma.cc/7LTR-KR3N.

27. Ibid.

28. Kenning Arlitsch and Patrick S. O'Brien, *Improving the Visibility and Use of Digital Repositories through SEO* (Chicago: ALA TechSource, 2013), 74.

29. DPLA Hubs, http://dp.la/info/hubs/, permalinked on April 21, 2016, at https://perma.cc/Z6JE-NZVG.

30. Ibid.

31. For more information, see "Library Services for People with Disabilities Policy," American Library Association, http://www.ala.org/ascla/asclaissues/libraryservices, permalinked on April 21, 2016, at https://perma.cc/A2GY-SXK5.

32. JAWS, http://www.freedomscientific.com/Products/Blindness/JAWS, permalinked on April 21, 2016, at https://perma.cc/F33E-TSBC.

33. Smithsonian Transcription Center, https://transcription.si.edu/, permalinked on April 21, 2016, at https://perma.cc/8PJX-XUSH.

34. Omeka plugin Scripto 2.0, http://omeka.org/codex/Plugins/Scripto_2.0, permalinked on April 21, 2016, at https://perma.cc/3K55-HG98.

35. New York Public Library, "Using the Archives of Recorded Sound: Avenues of Access," https://www.nypl.org/about/divisions/rodgers-and-hammerstein-archives-recorded-sound/access, permalinked on September 6, 2016, at https://perma.cc/6C6H-4DJU.

36　Ibid.

37　Ibid.

38　University of North Carolina, Chapel Hill, "Southern Folklife Collection: How to Order," http://library.unc.edu/wilson /sfc/how-to-order/, permalinked on September 6, 2016, at https://perma.cc/CP2U-MJWY.

39　Middle Tennessee State University Center for Popular Music, "Fees and Services," http://www.mtsu.edu/popmusic/fees .php#audiorepro, permalinked on September 6, 2016, at https://perma.cc/JR9P-EU4V.

40　Scott Pennington and Dean Rehberger, "The Preservation of Analog Video through Digitization," in *Oral History in the Digital Age*, ed. Doug Boyd et al. (Washington, DC: Institute of Museum and Library Services, 2012), http://ohda.matrix. msu.edu/2012/06/preservation-of-analog-video-through-digitization/, permalinked on September 6, 2016, at https://perma .cc/Z6JP-T7PB.

41　Bay Area Video Coalition, "Preservation Tools: QC Tools," https://www.bavc.org/preserve-media/preservation-tools, permalinked on September 6, 2016, at https://perma.cc/A6BA-Y3FU.

42　"Jim Linder: Archive Automator," *Time*, http://content.time.com/time/specials/packages/arti-cle/0,28804,2091589_2092033_2098414,00.html, permalinked on January 27, 2017, at https://perma.cc/5723-ARMX.

43　Anthony Cocciolo, "Learning History through Digital Preservation: Student Experiences in a LGBT Archive," *Preservation, Digital Technology & Culture* 42, no. 3 (2013): 129–36.

44　Warhol Museum Film and Video Collection, http://www.warhol.org/collection/filmandvideo/, permalinked on April 21, 2016, at https://perma.cc/YA33-4T43.

45　Marcus C. Robyns, "The Archivist as Educator: Integrating Critical Thinking Skills into Historical Research Methods Instruction," *American Archivist* 64, no. 2 (2001), 363–84.

46　Eleanor Mitchell, Peggy Seiden, and Suzy Taraba, *Past or Portal? Enhancing Undergraduate Learning through Special Collections and Archives* (Chicago: Association of College & Research Libraries, 2012).

47　Anthony Cocciolo, "Situating Student Learning in Rich Contexts: A Constructionist Approach to Digital Archives Education," *Evidence Based Library and Information Practice* 6, no. 3 (2011): 4–15.

48　Cocciolo, "Situating Student Learning."

49　Brooklyn Historical Society, "After School and Collaborative Programs," http://www.brooklynhistory.org/education/after. html, permalinked on April 21, 2016, at https://perma.cc/UA6R-C7PC.

50　Brooklyn Connections, Brooklyn Public Library, http://www.bklynlibrary.org/brooklyncollection/connections, permalinked on April 21, 2016, at https://perma.cc/BUE6-J6LP.

51　Common Core State Standards Initiative, "English Language Arts Standards: History/Social Studies: Grade 6–8," http:// www.corestandards.org/ELA-Literacy/RH/6-8/, permalinked on April 21, 2016, at https://perma.cc/7YNL-5BS7.

52　Anthony Cocciolo, "Public Libraries and PBS Partnering to Enhance Civic Engagement: A Study of a Nationwide Initiative," *Public Library Quarterly* 32, no. 1 (2013): 1–20.

53　Shirley Chisholm Project of Brooklyn Women's Activism from 1945 to the Present, http://depthome.brooklyn.cuny.edu /womens/studies/chisholm-project/The_Shirley_Chisholm_Project/Archive_%26_Oral_History_Collection.html, permalinked on April 21, 2016, at https://perma.cc/E67R-G3U2.

54　"Shirley Chisholm Day, November 30, Celebrated at the Late Congresswoman's Brooklyn College Alma Mater," press release, 2013, Brooklyn College, http://www.brooklyn.cuny.edu/bc/spotlite/news/?link=112005#, permalinked on April 21, 2016, at https://perma.cc/U9JG-TGXC.

55　Cocciolo, "Public Libraries and PBS."

56　For example, see the "Discussion Guide" option on *POV* film web pages, such as those available at http://www.pbs.org/pov /aiweiwei/, permalinked on April 21, 2016, at https://perma.cc/J8R3-N9GJ.

57　Margaret Crocco Smith, "Introduction," in *Teaching the Levees: A Curriculum for Democratic Dialogue and Civic Engagement*, ed. Margaret Crocco Smith (New York: Teachers College Press), 1–5.

58　Ibid., 2.

59　Ibid., 2.

60　Hui Soo Chae et al., "Teaching the Levees: Creating an Online Resource to Facilitate Democratic Discourse and Civic Engagement" (paper presented at the annual meeting of the American Educational Research Association, New York, NY, April 9–13, 2007), available at http://www.thinkingprojects.org/ttl_aera.doc, permalinked on April 21, 2016, at https:// perma.cc/H9A9-DE8E.

CHAPTER 6

Interactions with Moving Image and Sound Producers

Moving image and sound producers create a wide variety of products, from simple recordings of meetings, interviews, and events to oral history projects, documentary films, independent films, television programs, and feature-length motion pictures. Although most general archives are much more likely to find and accession recordings of events than the original source material of feature-length motion pictures, you never know what opportunities may be presented.

This chapter provides an overview of the relationship between archivists and producers of moving image and sound records, such as documentary filmmakers who may record dozens of interviews for a given project. This chapter will discuss opportunities for archivists to collaborate with producers to ensure that they are engaged in digital preservation of their own work. Finally, this chapter offers advice on encouraging producers to donate their work to nonprofit archives, as well as steps to consider when taking in a collection from a producer.

MOVING IMAGE AND SOUND PRODUCERS AND NONPROFIT ARCHIVES

Individuals who produce moving image and sound works, such as those who produce independent films including documentaries, are generally unaware that nonprofit audiovisual archives can serve as the final home for their work. In the landmark study *The Digital Dilemma 2: Perspectives from Independent Filmmakers, Documentarians and Nonprofit Audiovisual Archives (DD2)*, researchers found that many filmmakers do not engage in long-term preservation actions for their work, such as migrating from obsolete media or file formats or storing material in climate-controlled rooms.[1]

DD2 notes the personal experience of filmmaker Tom Quinn, who faced a worst-case scenario when working on a project with born-digital technology. He explains, "I shot a film that took seven years and screened it once for family and friends. A week after the screening my hard drive crashed so the only complete copy I ever made was a highly compressed DVD."[2] This was a huge loss because it prevented him from having the film screened at film festivals and picked up by a distributor. For his new film shot in standard definition, he explains that his digital preservation strategy is to create two tapes on HDCAM, two Blu-rays, and two hard drives of the film in uncompressed QuickTime format—one for him and one for his producer. He plans to "put the tapes in a Tupperware container in a closet in his house that has the most consistent room temperature."[3] He believes that this strategy will "keep him above the technology curve for ten to fifteen years."[4] Although it is admirable that filmmakers such as Quinn are starting to seriously engage in digital preservation activities, the story highlights the somewhat resource-constrained contexts many filmmakers are working in. Unfortunately, Tupperware is not a trusted digital repository.

Despite this, many nonprofit archives are not able to offer much more than Quinn's Tupperware solution. According to a recent study from moving image archives researcher Karen Gracy, many archives are ill-equipped to engage in digital reformatting of obsolete media or to store digitized or born-digital material in trustworthy repositories because of resource constraints and gaps in expertise.[5]

If archives can surmount the digital reformatting challenge and provide some basic digital preservation, they have an opportunity to take in very interesting moving image and sound collections. Despite this opportunity, archivists need to understand that many moving image and sound producers—even those who create works like educational films for public broadcast—are still interested in monetizing their assets for as long as possible. Collecting monies on existing works, even ones that are quite old, helps fund new projects. Therefore, a work is most likely to be donated to a nonprofit archives when the financial viability of the asset drops to a very low level.

In addition to working with creators of commercial works, archivists have ample opportunity to work with creators whose works may have tremendous historical and local community value but little or no commercial value, and whose content is within the archives' collecting scope. These works are indeed worthy of the archivist's attention. The creators can include individual or family donors who have home movies, politicians who have campaign ads and speeches, and members of an academic community who may have a wide variety of records (e.g., lectures, campus radio station recordings, oral histories, etc.). In cases where the works have no clear monetary value, it is best to get ownership and copyright transferred using donor agreements like the one presented in figure 3-1 in chapter 3, "Legal and Ethical Issues," and to do it sooner rather than later if the records are in a suboptimal storage environment.

For commercial works, getting creators to transfer copyright can be more challenging. To encourage creators to donate, one option—rather than seeking outright copyright of the work—is to seek a bequest, which allows the ownership and copyright to be transferred at death. A more appealing and easier to implement option is to use a licensing approach. For example, Christopher J. Prom of the University of Illinois Archives notes that an option they currently use is having copyright "transferred to the archives, but the donor is provided either an exclusive or nonexclusive right to use the materials for commercial use during his or her lifetime. This allows the archives to make it available, and allow other uses, while the donor can continue to use it during his or her lifetime, including for sale." This approach allows "both the donation and the continued commercial exploitation by the creator or owner of copyright."[6]

Works captured in standard-definition video may be declining in financial value. At a panel on "Archival and Survival" at the NYC DocFest, a gathering of documentary filmmakers, panelists noted that licensing high-definition footage is increasingly valued over standard-definition footage.[7] Therefore, it is possible that the huge amounts of work in standard-definition video may have declined in value in favor of higher-resolution works, such as those in HD, 2K, and 4K resolutions, because of viewer preferences for images that take full advantage of their high-resolution television sets.

An archives may not want to seek donation of a film and its copyright, but rather the raw collection of moving image and sound material that went into the creation of the film. When a documentary filmmaker produces a film, there is often a large amount of unused footage, like interviews, that may make an excellent addition to a collection. For example, Brooklyn College's Archives and Special Collections acquired the raw footage from Shola Lynch's 2004 film *Chisholm '72: Unbought and Unbossed*. Shirley Chisholm was the first African American to run for president and the first woman to run for the Democratic Party nomination, and she was an alumna of Brooklyn College, which makes the interviews conducted by Lynch an excellent addition to the collection.[8]

A last opportunity to consider is creating proactive partnerships with filmmakers by establishing an understanding that even before a work is begun, or soon after, the raw material—such as oral histories—will reside in the nonprofit archives. For example, Jim Hubbard and Sarah Schulman's film *United in Anger: A History of ACT UP* (2012) relied heavily on material from the ACT UP Oral History Project, which they created and have since donated to the Harvard College Library.[9] Although in this case the donation came after the oral histories were created, it illustrates how a dynamic can be developed where documentary films, oral histories, and archives can work together to sustain collective memory. This approach was used with the Lesbian Herstory Archives' Daughters of Bilitis (DOB) Oral History Project, which combined oral histories and the imperative to archive them, culminating in the creation of a documentary film. (The DOB was the first lesbian social and political organization, created by Del Martin and Phyllis Lyon in San Francisco in 1956.[10]) Unfortunately, the documentary film was never completed. The unfinished and unreleased film, as well as the oral histories, are kept together and made available online.[11]

DIGITAL PRESERVATION FOR THE PRODUCER

Since donation to archives may happen decades after moving image and sound records are created, it is important that filmmakers themselves engage in digital preservation so that they have something to donate when the time comes. Archivists have opportunities to provide digital preservation advice to filmmakers, which is quite similar to the advice that they should follow themselves.

The following is the recommended advice that archivists could provide to makers of moving image and sound records. First, when producers buy a hard drive that will store their work, they should clearly label it with the date the drive went into service. This allows them to know when the data should be migrated to a new device. If acquired by an archive, this will also be useful for digital preservation purposes. Although there is no hard-and-fast rule for how old a drive should be before it is replaced, I would recommend five to seven years. This is especially true for hard drives with spinning platters and moving parts, which are likely more susceptible to the ravages of time than solid-state hard disks that do not have moving parts. You can tell which is which by listening closely for sound coming out of the drive.

Solid-state drives make no noise, whereas most hard drives with spinning disks produce a low hum, subtle clicking, and slight vibrations that can be felt when touched.

In addition, the producer should clearly label the drive with the contents (e.g., "Master .AVI of *X* film in uncompressed 10-bit"), in addition to the date.

Next, the producer should make multiple copies. Three copies are recommended, and at least two are absolutely essential. I recommend using storage technologies with built-in redundancy such as RAID (which are discussed in more detail in chapter 4, "Digital Preservation"), although they tend to be far more expensive than stand-alone drives. Also, when preparing the three copies, I recommend that the producer not buy three of the exact same model of hard drive. If that particular model or even that particular subset of machines is prone to failure, this will help ameliorate that problem. Further, I recommend that purchased drives come from well-known manufacturers, which include Seagate, Western Digital (WD), Samsung, Toshiba, HP, SanDisk, G-Technology, and LaCie, among others.

If a producer intends to donate materials to the archives, the archives may want to keep a third or fourth copy as a service to the producer. Although I am not aware of any archives providing this service, this kind of collaboration could help preservation efforts and build relationships that could lead to future donations.

Additionally, copies should be distributed. For example, a producer can leave a copy at her studio or workplace and a copy at home, and give a copy to someone else, such as a distributor or other associate. Ideally, the three copies would be distributed such that they would not be subject to the same geographic disaster threats. For example, you would not want your three copies in basements spread across Lower Manhattan during a disaster similar to Hurricane Sandy in 2012. When the drives age out and need to be replaced, all three copies should be refreshed. The hard drives should be stored in as cool and dry an environment as possible, and away from activity that could damage the drives. Putting the drives in an acid-free box to keep away dust is also recommended.

Lastly, all three sets should be powered on at least once a year and the files skimmed through. As described in chapter 4, "Digital Preservation," hard disks with spinning platters can suffer from stiction, where the lubrication fails and the disk head cannot move to the proper place. Powering on also helps ensure that other forms of failure have not occurred, such as format obsolescence. Although solid-state hard drives have grown in popularity and should be more resilient to the ravages of time since there are no moving parts, they should also be checked at least once a year. The producer should put it on the calendar for some predetermined date each year and email the keeper of the third copy to do the same. If one of the copies fails, it can be restored from another copy.

To aid the producer's memory, put a printout of the directory contents in the acid-free box to help ensure that the contents of the disk are what was originally stored.

PERSUADING PRODUCERS TO DONATE

Recent events have indicated that moving image and sound works are susceptible to the orphan works phenomenon, such as where a work persists on film but the owner cannot be found. This is best illustrated in the closing down of DuArt's photochemical division in New York; DuArt was the premier place for independent filmmakers to have their film developed, duplicated, and stored, but it has since moved away from photochemical film as the profession has switched to digital technology.[12] For this reason, the *New York Times* reported in 2014 that there were "thousands of unclaimed films" at DuArt, left there by filmmakers who passed on, forgot about them, or were simply unable to be reached. This has resulted in the formation of IndieCollect, which aims to create an index of independent films with the location of the master materials, including the orphaned films from DuArt.[13] Whereas a 16 mm film stored in a cold and dry environment can persist for decades, it is unlikely that the original source material for today's digital films will persist as well as the films stored at DuArt, thus necessitating more active collaboration between archives and producers of moving image and sound works.

As discussed in chapter 3, "Legal and Ethical Issues," it is recommended that archives seek not only physical ownership of moving image and sound records but also copyright. This greatly simplifies providing access to the collection and allowing it to be shared over electronic networks. However, many producers of moving image works have been taught—wisely enough—that it is important to retain their copyrights so that they can control the work and be compensated for providing access to the work (e.g., through distribution agreements with streaming services like Netflix, film screenings at cinemas, etc.). However, there are some arguments that an archivist can use to induce artists, documentarians, and others to transfer their copyright. First, it is useful to remind artists of the public, nonprofit function that archives play by facilitating access to information, knowledge, and culture for the betterment of society. Second, donors can deduct the fair market value of their donation on their taxes (for donations with market values over $5,000, an independent appraiser is needed).[14] Archivists should never offer monetary appraisals on the fair market value of a donation.[15]

Donors can be motivated to donate a work because of the preservation functions your archives can offer. Preservation functions include the storage environment available at your facility. For example, if you have an archival storage room that is controlled and monitored to remain cold and dry throughout the year, this can be a positive inducement. Further, being able to perform format migrations to preservation-worthy formats, such as from Betamax to uncompressed 10-bit digital video, can be a significant advantage.

A donor can be further induced to make a contribution by being able to discuss possible public programming or access functions that your archive can provide. This can be as simple as providing access copies to the work, such as on DVD or Blu-ray. It can also include other types of programming around the work, such as film screenings with discussions, gallery exhibitions, and other types of public promotion of the work.

TAKING IN A COLLECTION

When taking in a collection from a moving image and sound producer, first ensure that all of the boxes and media are properly labeled. If they are not, you can sit down with the donor and work on labeling together. Adhesive labels are not always necessary, but if they are used, consider archival-quality labels that are more resistant to drying out and falling off. Such labels can be found from archival retailers like Gaylord, Talas, Hollinger Metal Edge, and University Products, among others. Alternatives include putting media in acid-free envelopes and labeling the envelope with pencil.

It is also useful to determine the approximate age and obsolescence issues with the media you have acquired so that you can prioritize migration efforts. For example, with hard disks, although manufacturers often do not print dates of manufacture on disks, clues include the storage capacity of the drive. It is generally true that hard drive capacity has increased over time, although capacity does not always indicate age (e.g., sometimes people want to buy smaller hard drives for specific reasons, hence these options remain). Storage capacity of a drive should be noted in an accession's condition note because it is a clue to the disk's age. Figure 6-1 maps hard drive capacities to the years that those disk capacities were available in retail stores, as well as expected capacities based on manufacturer statements. Note that the capacities are approximate; early adopters willing to spend more money will likely have access to higher capacity drives sooner than others.

Year	Hard drive capacity
1995	250 MB to 2.9 GB
2000	10 GB to 82 GB
2005	160 GB to 250 GB
2010	500 GB to 2 TB
2015	500 GB to 12 TB
2020	up to 20 TB
2025	up to 100 TB

Figure 6-1. Hard disk capacities by year. See notes for methodology.[16]

Also worth noting is the interface for the drive, such as USB, FireWire, Thunderbolt, SCSI, or other interface. Drives that look old and unfamiliar likely are and should be prioritized for migration. Once popular interfaces, like SCSI (pronounced "scuzzy"), shown in figure 6-2, have been superseded by USB, FireWire, and Thunderbolt. Information like interface type should also be entered into an accession record's condition note, which can help in planning migration efforts.

Figure 6-2. Sample SCSI interfaces. Creative Commons image courtesy of https://commons.wikimedia.org /wiki/File:Scsi-connectors.jpg.

CONCLUSION

In sum, there are opportunities for collaboration between producers of moving image and sound works, such as documentary filmmakers, and archivists. Producers of moving image and sound works are generally unaware that archives can serve as the final repository for their work, and thus many films are never donated and simply remain in storage unclaimed. This signals an opportunity for archives to engage in more active outreach to producers who may have accumulated materials that align well with their collection scope, such as Brooklyn College's acquisition of the Shirley Chisholm materials. Other opportunities for collaboration include providing advice and assistance in a producer's digital preservation efforts, which could both enhance overall preservation efforts and result in an eventual donation.

NOTES

[1] Science and Technology Council of the Academy of Motion Picture Arts and Sciences, *The Digital Dilemma 2: Perspectives from Independent Filmmakers, Documentarians and Nonprofit Audiovisual Archives* (2012), https://www.oscars.org/science-technology/sci-tech-projects/digital-dilemma-2, permalinked on September 15, 2016, at https://perma.cc/3NET-TGZC.

[2] Jason Guerrasio, "Continuing Dilemma," *Filmmaker Magazine*, Winter 2010, http://www.filmmakermagazine.com/archives/issues/winter2010/reports-continuing-dilemma.php, permalinked on April 21, 2016, at https://perma.cc/W9U7-DBPS.

[3] Ibid.

[4] Ibid.

[5] Karen Gracy, "Ambition and Ambivalence: A Study of Professional Attitudes toward Digital Distribution of Archival Moving Images," *American Archivist* 76, no. 2 (2013): 346–73.

[6] Christopher J. Prom, personal communication, August 30, 2016.

[7] Jessica Berman-Bogdan, Domenick Propati, Mick Reed, Jill Drew, and Thom Powers (facilitator), "Monetize Your Outtakes," panel discussion, NYC DOC Fest Insiders Conference: Archival and Survival, New York, NY, November 17, 2015.

[8] Shirley Chisholm Project of Brooklyn Women's Activism from 1945 to the Present, http://depthome.brooklyn.cuny.edu/womens/studies/chisholm-project/The_Shirley_Chisholm_Project/Archive_%26_Oral_History_Collection.html, permalinked on April 21, 2016, at https://perma.cc/KNV2-RWF8.

[9] Sarah Schulman, *The Gentrification of the Mind: Witness to a Lost Imagination* (Berkeley: University of California Press, 2012).

[10] Marcia M. Gallo, *Different Daughters: A History of the Daughters of Bilitis and the Rise of the Lesbian Rights Movement* (New York: Carroll & Graf, 2006).

[11] Morgan Gwenwald, Manuela Soares, and Sara Yager, "Lesbian Herstory Archives Daughters of Bilitis Video Project," video recordings, 1988, Herstories: Audio/Visual Collections, http://herstories.prattsils.org/omeka/collections/show/36, permalinked on April 21, 2016, at https://perma.cc/7XNS-2HRJ.

[12] John Anderson, "The Movie Crypt at the Top of the Stairs: At DuArt, Thousands of Unclaimed Films," *New York Times*, August 20, 2014, http://www.nytimes.com/2014/08/24/movies/at-duart-thousands-of-unclaimed-films.html, permalinked on April 21, 2016, at https://perma.cc/9KHP-PFZH.

[13] IndieCollect, http://indiecollect.org/, permalinked on April 21, 2016, at https://perma.cc/D9GT-EVKD.

[14] Aaron Purcell, *Donors and Archives: A Guidebook for Successful Programs* (Lanham, MD: Rowman & Littlefield, 2015).

[15] Ibid.

[16] Data for the years 1995 to 2010 are based on calculated averages from open data, assembled by Rufus Pollock from the Little Tech Shoppe website (http://data.okfn.org/data/rgrp/hard-drive-prices, permalinked on April 21, 2016, at https://perma.cc/X3DY-EU9H); 2015 data is based on an investigation of external hard drives available on the Best Buy website by the author. The 2020 and 2025 figures are based on the following articles about manufacturer expectations: Lucas Mearian, "Seagate to Produce 5TB Hard Drive Next Year, 20TB by 2020," *Computer World*, September 9, 2013, http://www.computerworld.com/article/2484814/data-center/seagate-to-produce-5tb-hard-drive-next-year--20tb-by-2020.html, permalinked on April 21, 2016, at https://perma.cc/AQC9-BM8L; Lucas Mearian, "Want a 100TB Disk Drive? You'll Have to Wait 'til 2025," *Computer World*, November 25, 2015, http://www.computerworld.com/article/2852233/want-a-100tb-disk-drive-youll-have-to-wait-til-2025.html, permalinked on April 21, 2016, at https://perma.cc/EG7U-WNTK.

PART II

FORMAT-SPECIFIC GUIDANCE

CHAPTER 7

Audio Collections

Audio media, including both analog and digital audio, are frequently found in archival collections. Analog audio always appear on specialized carriers, such as compact audiocassettes, vinyl records, or open-reel tapes. Digital audio can appear on specialized carriers (e.g., DAT or digital audio tape) but can also appear as computer files (e.g., MP3s, WAVs, etc.) on nonspecialized digital carriers such as hard drives. The best practice in maintaining audio collections for long-term preservation is to migrate the content to digital files that are stored in a trustworthy digital repository.[1] (For a discussion about establishing a trustworthy digital repository, see chapter 4, "Digital Preservation.") Acknowledging that digitization and migration are expensive, time-consuming, and labor-intensive projects, this chapter discusses ways that the work can be delayed as well as steps for beginning to do the work. However, before format migration is discussed, some basic background on audio is necessary.

BRIEF HISTORICAL BACKGROUND

Recorded sound dates from Thomas Edison's invention of the tinfoil cylinder in Menlo Park, NJ, in 1877.[2] Cylinders began to be used commercially with the introduction of the wax cylinder by North American Phonograph Company in 1889 and by Edison's National Phonograph in 1896.[3] Cylinders gave way to flat discs beginning with the introduction of Gramophone records in 1893. The adoption of flat-disc recordings grew with the introduction of the Victrola in 1906 by Victor Talking Machine Company, which was eventually absorbed by RCA.[4] This era was notable in that it relied solely on acoustics such as large horns to produce sound.[5]

In 1925, horns gave way to electrically amplified sound, which had the distinct advantage over acoustic phonographs of having volume control.[6] At this point, records were played typically at 78 rpm (rotations per minute). Because of the high speed of the spinning disc, the largest disc (12 inches) could play only about three and a half minutes of recorded sound.[7] In 1948, Columbia Records introduced the LP (long-playing disc) that rotated at 33 1/3 rpm and could play up to twenty-two minutes of recorded sound.[8] In 1949, RCA Victor rolled out 45 rpm records, which eventually made 78 rpm records obsolete; they were used for distributing song singles.[9] Both 33 1/3 rpm and 45 rpm records use microgroove technology, which features smaller grooves than earlier discs with coarse grooves, thus allowing more recorded sound onto a single disc.[10] In 1958, LPs became available in stereo, which featured an independent recording for the left ear and the right ear.[11]

Grooved discs were the dominant format for recorded sound until the invention of magnetic recording. In the United States, magnetic recordings first appeared between 1920 and 1945; the recordings were made onto steel tape or wire.[12] Steel is both expensive and prone to breaking, especially compared to what replaced it as the dominant way of making magnetic recordings: coated magnetic tape. Introduced in 1935, the German Magnetophon recorded sound onto cellulose acetate tape coated with magnetic particles and was used largely for dictation, military field applications, and radio.[13] The advantage of magnetic recording over disc recording is that the tape could be erased and recorded over; thus, it was useful for records with short-term value like dictation.

Based on Magnetophons recovered in Germany at the end of the war, the US company Ampex created their first tape recorders.[14] By 1948, magnetic tape was in widespread commercial use.[15] By the 1950s, "magnetic audio recording had completely revolutionized the record and broadcasting industry," where "all records were mastered on tape, and radio broadcasters were exclusively using tape as a time-delay and programming tool."[16]

In the 1950s, magnetic tape reached the consumer market through open-reel tape recorders, especially adopted by those interested in making their own recordings, and was used in homes alongside vinyl records.[17] Consumers further adopted magnetic tape in the 1960s and 1970s with the introduction of cartridge-based tape, especially the eight-track tape and the compact audiocassette.[18] Compact audiocassettes reached high levels of popularity through devices such as portable tape players—especially the Sony Walkman and the "boom box"—home stereo systems, and telephone answering machines.[19]

All forms of analog audio were disrupted by the introduction of digital audio, especially the compact disc (CD).[20] The CD was introduced in 1982 and was the first commercially successful form of digital audio, allowing 79.8 minutes of audio recording onto a single side of a disc.[21] CDs remained dominant until music distribution was challenged by Internet distribution, first by MP3 files over copyright-infringing file sharing systems like Napster, then by distribution through Apple's iTunes, which was introduced in 2003.[22] The general recent trend has been the movement from physical media to web-based distribution of sound, with subscription services such as Spotify, Pandora, Google Music, and Apple Music gaining a significant foothold.[23] Despite this trend, new recordings on vinyl disc, compact audiocassette, and CD persist alongside web-based distribution of sound recordings.[24]

TECHNICAL DIMENSIONS OF ANALOG AND DIGITAL AUDIO

Cylinder and disc recordings, like all analog audio devices that came after them, attempt to imprint a representation of the sound wave onto some physical medium.[25] Disturbing air with pressure creates sound waves, resulting in vibrations that travel through the air in a wavelike pattern. [26] Thumping one's chest several times will create a low-frequency sound wave, resulting from (in large part) the vibrations of the muscles and bones in the chest.

The earliest analog recording technology imprinted a representation of a sound wave between the grooves of a disc or cylinder.[27] As the record or cylinder plays, a needle or stylus picks up the pressure disturbance encoded in the imprinted wave. If one scans a vinyl disc using a flatbed scanner at high resolution (2400 pixels per inch, or ppi) and zooms in on the resulting image, one can see the sound wave imprinted between the grooves of the disc. (See figure 7-1.)

Figure 7-1. Zoomed-in view of vinyl disc containing Pyotr Tchaikovsky's *Swan Lake*.

Figure 7-2. A portion of the optical sound track to the left of an actor, from the trailer for the film *All the King's Men* (2006).

In a somewhat similar fashion, many films shown in theaters before the widespread use of digital sound used what is known as an optical sound track, where the sound wave is visually imprinted onto the piece of film. During playback, twenty-four photographic frames per second are projected onto a screen, creating the illusion of a moving image. As those frames are projected, light is pushed though the optical sound track, which is converted into an electromagnetic signal and then back into sound.[28] For an illustration of motion picture film with the optical sound track alongside the photographic element, see figure 7-2.

Converting a range of electromagnetic signals into sound reached its zenith with magnetic audiotape, which "encode[s] the shape of the sound wave as magnetic pulses onto metal."[29] The tapes are often composed of a piece of plastic (or some other substrate like acetate) and a layer of iron oxide (known popularly as rust) that is painted or glued onto the plastic. Magnets encode the signal onto the metal rust. During playback, the electromagnetic signal is converted back into a sound wave.

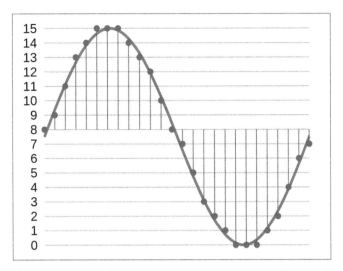

Figure 7-3. A sound wave is mapped onto numbers in a 4-bit sound universe. Creative Commons image courtesy of https://en.wikipedia .org/wiki/Pulse-code_modulation#/media/File:Pcm.svg.

In analog audio, a fluid representation of the sound wave is encoded onto the medium (e.g., as an optical representation of a wide range of electromagnetic signals representing the sound wave); in digital audio, information is imprinted in bits (zeros and ones) into the medium. The bits encode large numbers that correspond to sounds. In a simple case, the numbers are packed together in sequence, the numbers are read, and the corresponding sound is played.

As an example, assume that we want to digitize a recording using a 4-bit computer. Figure 7-3 illustrates how the sound wave is mapped onto the 4-bit sound universe. In this case, the 4 bits are known as the bit depth of the recording. Realistically, no one would use so few bits since they can only encode 16 different sounds (as shown in figure 7-4), but the concept applies to greater bit depths. For example, the popular CD uses a bit depth of 16, which can represent up to 65,536 sounds. The possible range of values can be computed using the formula $2^{bit\text{-}depth}$. Digital recordings with a bit depth of 24 can represent 16,777,216 different sounds, which is the same as 2^{24}.

#	Bits	#	Bits	#	Bits	#	Bits
0	0000	4	0100	8	1000	12	1100
1	0001	5	0101	9	1001	13	1101
2	0010	6	0110	10	1010	14	1110
3	0011	7	0111	11	1011	15	1111

Figure 7-4. Four bits can represent only up to sixteen different sounds.

In general, the larger the bit depth, the greater possible dynamic range between the faintest sound and the loudest sound. Also, a larger bit depth provides for a more accurate representation of the analog sound. However, after a certain point, it ceases to matter because the human ear and brain cannot distinguish between so many millions of different sounds. For encoding sound over the telephone, 8 bits are used; 16 bits are used for CDs; and 24 bits are often used for high-quality digitization of analog audio.[30]

For digital audio quality, the sample rate is as important as bit depth. The sample rate corresponds to how frequently the analog signal's digital value is noted and recorded. In the example from figure 7-3, if each of those twenty-six samples were collected over the course of one second, we would say the recording has a sample rate of twenty-six times per second.

Much like bit depth, the frequency with which an audio signal is sampled translates to better quality representation of the analog sound. However, much like bit depth again, the human ear and brain cannot make such infinitesimally small distinctions. Thus, CDs sample the analog signal 44,100 times per second, also known as 44.1 kHz. High-quality digitization may sample up to 96,000 times per second, or 96 kHz. As you probably noted, Hz and kHz are used to measure wave cycles and can easily be converted to a rate of "times per second." For example, in our earlier example of 26 samples per second, we would say the sample rate is 26 Hz, or .026 kHz.

STORAGE AND OTHER PRESERVATION CONSIDERATIONS

Not long ago, the best practice in preservation and access to analog audio recordings was reformatting them onto new analog audio recordings.[31] However, today the best practice in maintaining sound collections is to maintain computer files in trustworthy repositories.[32] Thus, analog content should be digitized as computer files, and digital content should be migrated off carriers and ingested into trustworthy repositories. As this can be a daunting challenge, especially for smaller repositories, some actions can be pursued to delay digitization or migration.

The first action is to ensure that the physical storage environment is adequate. The *ARSC Guide to Audio Preservation* notes that long-term storage environments for all audio carriers should have temperatures between 46°F and 53°F, with 25–35 percent relative humidity.[33] The International Association of Sound and Audiovisual Archives (IASA) recommends the same temperature and humidity figures.[34] Audio carriers should never be kept in freezing temperatures. If climate control is not available, archivists should strive to keep the material in as cool and as dry an environment as possible, using portable air conditioners and dehumidifiers where possible, and attempting to keep temperature and humidity fluctuations to a minimum. Inexpensive digital hydro-thermometers can be purchased that report temperature and humidity, with maximum and minimum values for each. More sophisticated and expensive devices can be purchased that log temperature and humidity over time. These are often referred to as preservation environment monitors (PEM).

For analog material, digital reformatting decisions should be guided by a number of factors. An important consideration is the significance of the collection, such as its relevance to historical research and scholarship as well as the institution's collecting policy and mission. Further, the existing uses should be considered as well. Is this collection frequently consulted? Are users accessing the master copies or duplicates? If access is frequent, and the master is used for access, this should certainly motivate digitization. The age of the materials is also worth considering, particularly the age of the carriers. For example, materials on 1970s vintage open-reel tapes are better candidates for digitization than materials from the 2000s on compact audiocassettes because of a variety of issues that aging tapes face. However, age alone should not be a deciding factor. In the *ARSC Guide to Audio Preservation*, Carla Arton notes that "some formats are more stable than others" and that "vinyl long-playing discs (LPs) and shellac discs are typically more chemically stable than lacquer discs or magnetic audio tape."[35]

In some cases, migrating born-digital audio recordings to computer files should be prioritized. Recent research has indicated that digital material burnt onto consumer recordable CDs have suffered bit rot or corruption, making them very poor carriers of content for long-term storage.[36] Further, some digital formats make use of digital rights management (DRM) technology that makes retrieving the audio as computer files difficult. For example, I recently had a class attempt to retrieve recordings of interviews with dancers on Sony MiniDisc recorded by a dance journalist. The Sony MiniDisc is a born-digital audio recording technology that began production in the early 1990s, with vendor support for the format ending in 2013.[37] The MiniDisc had a USB interface, creating the impression that files could be downloaded as computer files; depending on how they were recorded, sometimes they could be. However, because these recordings were created using Sony's DRM technology, they could only be played back and not copied as files. Although Sony had produced dozens of models of MiniDisc, only the final model produced (the RH1) fully disabled the DRM protection and allowed all MiniDisc content to be transferred as computer files. The one model that allowed for this continues to command a high price through resale sites like eBay. The class resorted to a suboptimal solution: playing back the recording and digitizing it, which was the best we could do.

PRESERVATION REFORMATTING: ANALOG

The best practice in digitizing analog audio is to create a preservation master file, which samples the sound 96,000 times a second (96 kHz), with each sample comprised of 24 bits of data.[38] From this master file, a variety of derivatives can be created, including versions to be streamed on the web. Although some recent research indicates that most typical users cannot tell the difference between a 24-bit/96 kHz recording and a 16-bit/44.1 kHz recording, there can be a loss of some fine details in choosing the lower sampling rate and bit depth.[39] These details can include things such as background activities or noise in recordings, which later may prove to be valuable context. File sizes based on different sampling rates and bit depths are shown in figure 7-5.

Note that most modern recordings are recorded in stereo, meaning that there is an independent recording maintained for the left ear and the right ear. Thus, when digitizing a stereo recording, two

Sampling Rate	Bit Depth	Minimum File Size for an Hour of Audio[40]	Usage	Mono or Stereo
8 kHz	8 bits	28.8 MB	Telephone	Mono
44.1 kHz	16 bits	635.04 MB	Compact disc	Stereo
48 kHz	24 bits	1.04 GB	Jackson's recommended minimum for analog audio digitization	Stereo
96 kHz	24 bits	2.07 GB	Recommended analog audio digitization resolution, aka IASA-TC04 standard	Stereo

Figure 7-5. Disk space for digitized audio with varying sampling rates and bit depths.

independent streams should be digitized for the left ear and the right ear; both get packed into a single file. Recordings that are not in stereo are referred to as mono recordings.

If one were to search the web for digitization equipment for compact audiocassette, vinyl record, or other analog audio, one would find a wide variety of devices. However, most of these devices will not sample at the best-practice audio digitization rate of 24-bit/96 kHz. Most of these devices only digitize at a CD rate of 16-bit/44.1 kHz. These devices may work for creating access copies, which are needed so that masters are less frequently accessed. But copies made using 16-bit equipment should be considered just access copies and less-than-optimal stand-ins for the original recording.

Derek Jay Jackson, an audio preservation consultant, notes that for some formats like the compact audiocassette, a 24-bit/48 kHz rate should be adequate for creating preservation masters.[41] However, as mentioned earlier, many of the inexpensive, consumer-grade devices offer resolutions of only 16-bit/44.1 kHz, thus still requiring the purchase of more expensive hardware that can produce audio digitization at that resolution.

To create digital masters, a device to convert analog sound to digital sound is required. In my classroom at Pratt Institute, we purchased several analog-to-digital converters, specifically Benchmark Systems ADC1 USB devices.[42] These devices take an analog audio input and output the sound via a USB cable to the computer. Open-source audio recording tools like Audacity can be used to capture the digitized signal, then save the master files as 24-bit Microsoft WAV files.[43] The benefit of having an analog-to-digital converter is that a wide variety of analog signals can be connected to it (e.g., compact audiocassette tapes, turntables, reel-to-reel players, etc.), and it will reliably convert that analog signal to digital information. The downside is that the devices themselves are fairly expensive.[44]

Figure 7-6. An open-reel tape deck purchased on eBay, which has worked reliably for several years.

Also required are players for each analog media. The best practice is to purchase professional play-back equipment.[45] Of course, for many formats, such as open-reel tapes, the equipment is no longer manufactured and needs to be purchased through a reseller. I have purchased several playback devices in the past from sites like eBay and have generally had good experiences. Devices that have been cleaned and restored by reputable sellers are the best option. Reviews of sellers should be read in depth, their websites studied, and photographs of the device closely inspected. It is a good idea to purchase devices that can be returned if needed. Another option is to try to collect devices from donors, who may be able to provide an ownership history and point out uses and idiosyncrasies of the device.

Before playing back any media for digitization, especially on a device that you have never used or that has not been used in a while, it is always a good idea to use a test tape or disc first. This ensures that the device is working properly and that if the device should fail in some serious way, it will damage the test media and not the archival item.

When digitizing an analog medium, it is important to ensure that the digital output corresponds exactly to the analog input. It is best to check this in a quiet environment using high-quality headphones.[46] In addition to an auditory check, it is necessary to check the visual waveform produced during the digital capture. Figure 7-7 shows the digitization in Audacity of an analog audio

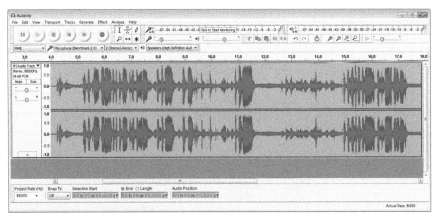

Figure 7-7. Audio digitization in Audacity. Note that it is being digitized in stereo, 24-bit/96 kHz.

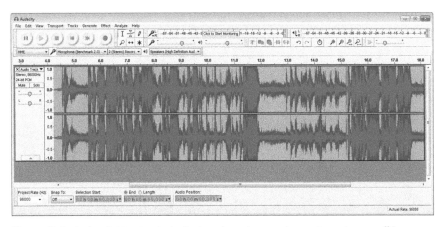

Figure 7-8. Audio digitization in Audacity, where the sound wave is getting cut off because the microphone volume is too loud.

recording on compact audiocassette from the Archives of the Center for Puerto Rican Studies. With recordings of spoken language, one should see gaps between words and between sentences. Also, note how the sound wave fits comfortably within the limits of the digital recording range. Figure 7-8 illustrates the same sound recording being digitized, where part of the wave is getting cut off because the microphone volume is set too loud. This can be corrected by lowering the volume to produce the wave shown in figure 7-7.

For audiotapes like compact audiocassettes, many audio engineers recommend using tape players that allow you to adjust the tape azimuth. Azimuth refers to the angle of the recording and playback head relative to the magnetic tape. For optimal playback, tape heads on the playback device should have the same azimuth as the recording device. Because tapes are recorded on a wide variety of devices by different manufacturers, there are slight variations between models; adjustment of the azimuth compensates for this. Because it is difficult to illustrate azimuth adjustment in print form, I refer the reader to some useful YouTube videos cited in the notes.[47] Note that many audiocassette players do not have azimuth adjustment; it is a feature more commonly found on higher-end machines.

When digitizing audio that is rerecordable, and the media supports a write-protection tab, it is recommended that the tab be enabled to prevent the recording from being accidentally recorded over. For example, on the popular compact audiocassette, there are two write-protection tabs that can be popped out using a minispatula to prevent the recording from being recorded over. (See figure 7-9.)

PRESERVATION REFORMATTING: DIGITAL

With born-digital audio recordings, it is best to transfer the audio off media carriers as computer files and ingest them in trusted digital repositories. Once the computer files have been retrieved, the only consideration is if the format is well suited for long-term preservation. The best formats for long-term

Figure 7-9. Before digitizing, enable the media's write-protection options, such as popping out the write-protection tabs on compact audiocassettes.

preservation are those that are openly documented, widely used, and simple to decode. Formats such as Broadcast Wave (BWF) and Microsoft Wave (WAV) are suitable formats since they use a simple encoding scheme, pulse-code modulation (PCM), which encodes the bits sampled in linear fashion.[48] The Library of Congress maintains a list of digital (including audio) formats and their sustainability, which can be consulted when assessing if a format is in danger of not being supported.[49] Formats not well suited for long-term preservation are those that are proprietary, not openly documented, and not widely used; in these cases, media should be migrated to formats with better long-term sustainability. When performing a format migration, the file should not need to be played back and redigitized. Redigitization of content that is already stored digitally should be a final recourse, as it will likely result in a generation loss, which means some audio information may be lost in the digital-to-analog and back-to-digital conversion process. The digital conversion process should not discard any information, such as subjecting the original recording to lossy compression, or otherwise reducing the bit depth and sampling rate. Further, if a file is migrated to a new format, the original format should be retained in addition to the migrated version.

COMMONLY ENCOUNTERED FORMATS

The formats that archivists are likely to encounter include the compact audiocassette and the CD. The first is analog, and the second is digital.

CDs, although looking much alike, come in three different types, and these distinctions matter a great deal for preservation reasons. The first type is pressed discs, which were the first kind of CD and were usually created by professional disc pressing operations. This is the type of disc that was sold in music stores (before they closed), and the back side shines silver. Binary information is imprinted into

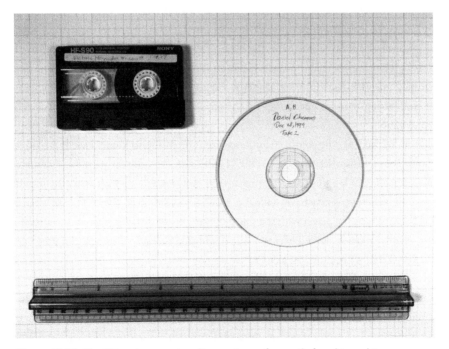

Figure 7-10. The CD and compact audiocassette are frequently found in archives.

the plastic of these discs, hence the information is optical, or visible (although only with a microscope). Although these discs are susceptible to deterioration, they are more robust than the burnable CDs that came after them.[50]

CD-Rs burn impressions into dyes, and once data is written to a disc it cannot be rewritten. Like dyes in clothing, the dyes can fade over time. The *ARSC Guide to Audio Preservation* references research that finds that the "dye layer is sensitive to ultraviolet radiation; exposure to sunlight for several days can render them unreadable."[51] Further, a report from UNESCO found a wide variety of reasons these formats are ill suited for long-term preservation, including the deterioration of the dyes.[52] Audio contained in this format should be prioritized for migration to digital WAV files (or similar format) stored in trusted digital repositories. The back side of these discs tends to shine purple when compared to pressed discs.

CD-RWs allow for data to be rewritten to them through storing information on metal alloys. Studies of the persistence of information recorded in this format, specifically studies of DVD±RW, which uses a similar technology to CD-RW, indicate that this format is less stable than burning impressions into dyes as used in CD-R and DVD±R.[53] Thus, audio recordings on this media should be transferred to trustworthy digital repositories as WAV files (or similar format).

It is worth noting that CDs can be created with file systems as well as audio streams. Thus, CDs do not necessarily contain audio information; they can be generic carriers for digital information. CDs that contain files or computer programs are often referred to as CD-ROMs, which are discussed at length in chapter 11, "Complex Media." At any rate, they are unreliable media and should not be trusted for long-term storage.

If the CD and its cousin the DVD are unreliable carriers of digital information, does this also apply to "gold" CDs and DVDs? Unfortunately, gold CDs and DVDs that have information written to them using CD and DVD burners should not be trusted. Like all CD-Rs and DVD±Rs, the information is recorded into dyes and not the gold itself.[54] Further, since every CD and DVD burner uses different lasers to burn the impression into the dyes, what one CD/DVD burner wrote may not be entirely compatible with the reader that is used in the future.[55] Although gold may be less corrosive than other metals, as the advertising for such products indicates, the coating of the disc is only one factor among several that play into the disc's future readability. For this reason, resources are better spent elsewhere, such as in establishing trusted repositories using some of the building blocks described in chapter 4, "Digital Preservation."

In addition to the CD, the compact audiocassette is often found in archives. It is a popular carrier for recordings like oral histories from the 1980s, 1990s, and even the early 2000s. Compact audiocassettes come in a variety of lengths (e.g., 90 minutes, 60 minutes, etc.), which is usually indicated on the label. These audiocassettes usually have a side A or side 1 and a side B or side 2. The sides can be accessed by inserting the tape into the player with the side you want to access facing out. If the tape label includes its duration, this duration is divided between side A and side B (e.g., 90 minutes on the label means 45 minutes on side A and 45 minutes on side B).

When digitizing audiotapes with two sides, it is useful to maintain each side of the tape as a separate file. People had to flip over the tape to continue a recording from side A to side B, and this contextual information is worth preserving. A side B with no audio information should be noted as such, so that it is clear that it was checked and was not overlooked. Lastly, the write-protection tabs should be popped out, which prevents the compact audiocassette from being accidentally recorded over.

ADDITIONAL AUDIO FORMATS

There are a variety of additional formats that archivists may well encounter in their processing, appraisal, and reappraisal. Some of these formats are pictured in figures 7-11 and 7-12.

The microcassette is a shrunken version of the analog compact audiocassette. It can be fairly easily digitized by connecting a microcassette player to an analog-to-digital audio converter.

The Sony MiniDisc is a born-digital audio recording technology, and its contents are best imported into trusted digital repositories as computer files using the Sony RH1 MiniDisc player, which disables the DRM protection that can be found on many MiniDiscs. The Sony MiniDisc has a write-protection tab that can be enabled, and the tab should be enabled when accessioned into an archives.

Open-reel magnetic tape is an analog recording format with tape widths that range from ¼ inch to 2 inches. Such tapes were used from 1945 through the 2000s.[56] A professional audio specialist who has experience with this format should handle any tapes that show signs of physical deterioration, such as warping or emitting substances. One issue sometimes found with this format is what is known as sticky shed syndrome, where moisture gets between the metal and the substrate (e.g., plastic), causing the metal to flake off.[57] One treatment for sticky shed syndrome is to bake the tapes, which causes the glue holding the metal to the substrate to function properly temporarily, and then digitize the tapes. Only experienced persons should attempt this. Carrier deterioration is signaled by metal oxide left on the tape heads during playback; in these cases, the playback should be stopped and an audio expert consulted.

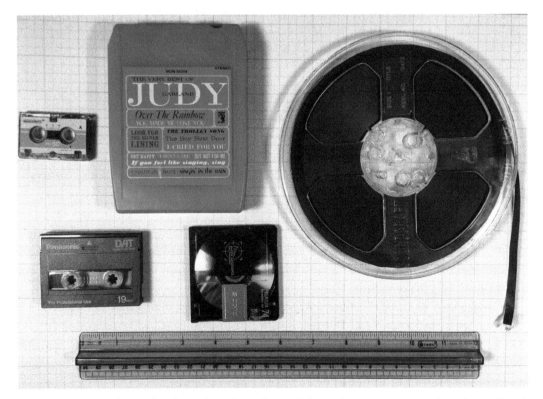

Figure 7-11. Some formats found in archives (top to bottom, left to right): microcassette, eight-track tape, ¼-inch open-reel magnetic tape, DAT tape, and MiniDisc.

Figure 7-12. More formats found in archives: disc-based formats, such as the vinyl disc (pictured is a long-playing disc, or LP).

The eight-track is an analog recording technology used between 1963 and 1982; it is similar to the compact audiocassette and open-reel tape.[58] This format can be digitized by connecting an eight-track player to an analog-to-digital audio converter. However, because of the age of this format, it may be best to consult an audio specialist.

A wide variety of analog disc-based formats exist, including vinyl discs, shellac discs, and lacquer discs (also known as acetate discs). Different discs are designed to be played at different speeds; frequently used speeds include 78 rpm, 45 rpm, and 33 1/3 rpm. An audio specialist should be consulted for digitizing these discs, as playback requires selecting the correct stylus (or needle) and making adjustments to the pressure applied to the needle.

Figure 7-13. Very uncommon formats found in archives, including magnetic wire (left) and cylinder recording (right).

UNCOMMON FORMATS

Uncommon formats found in archives include cylinders and magnetic wire recordings, both of which are older analog recording media (see figure 7-13). Cylinders predate disc recordings and were produced between 1898 and 1929; they encode the sound wave between the grooves of the cylinder.[59] An audio specialist who has experience with this format should be consulted for digitization. Magnetic wire, produced between 1939 and 1955, is similar to magnetic audiotape in that electronic magnetic signals are encoded into the metal.[60] Because of the rarity of this format, an audio specialist who has experience with this format should be consulted.

NONSPECIALIZED CARRIERS OF DIGITAL CONTENT

Although perhaps somewhat obvious, it is useful to note that audio collections can be contained on any digital carrier saved as computer files, such as Microsoft WAV files, MP3 files, and other file formats. Files saved on these carriers are best ingested into trusted digital repositories. Like the other media discussed, born-digital media is also best stored in cold, dry environments. Storage devices such as 3.5-inch and 5.25-inch floppy disks, although only storing around 1 MB of digital information, can contain short, low-quality recordings. Larger format digital storage devices, such as Zip drives, Jaz drives,

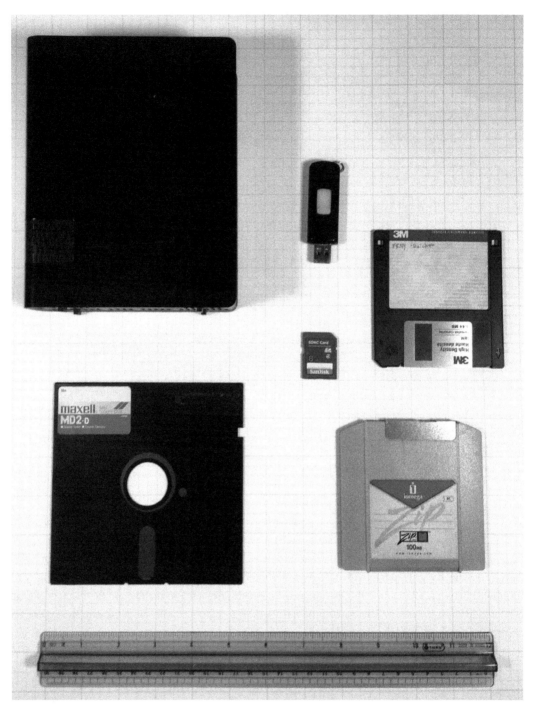

Figure 7-14. Audio can be held on nonspecialized digital carriers, such as (top to bottom, left to right): USB spinning-disk hard drive, USB solid-state thumb drive, solid-state memory card, 3.5-inch floppy disk, 5.25-inch floppy disk, and Iomega Zip drive.

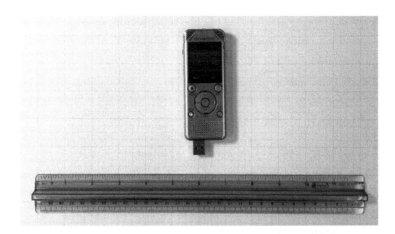

Figure 7-15. A wide variety of digital recording devices, like this Olympus Digital Voice Recorder WS-801, can contain audio recordings that can be transferred via USB.

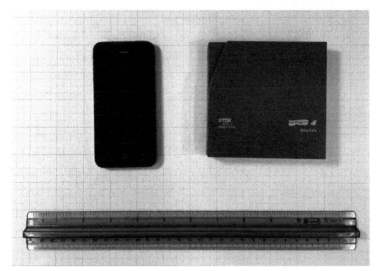

Figure 7-16. Audio collections can be contained on digital carriers like LTO tapes (right) and the Apple iPhone 4 (left).

spinning-disk hard drives, solid-state hard drives, DVDs, Blu-rays, and memory cards can store larger collections of audio recordings (some of this media is pictured in figure 7-14). Audio recordings can also be found on specialized audio recording devices, such as the Olympus voice recorder pictured in figure 7-15. Smartphones, such as the Apple iPhone pictured in figure 7-16, are growing in popularity for recording meetings and interviews. Figure 7-16 also includes an image of an LTO (linear tape-open) 4 tape, which can contain audio collections and other digital information.

PRESERVATION REFORMATTING: MANAGEMENT CONSIDERATIONS

Some formats can be digitized in-house, while other formats are best outsourced. Rare formats, such as cylinders and magnetic wire recordings, are best outsourced to audio specialists since the playback equipment and necessary expertise are quite rare. Recordings on grooved disc are also best outsourced to audio specialists since the correct stylus or needle must be chosen for playback to avoid causing damage to the disc.[61] Any media showing signs of physical deterioration, such as warped tapes or tapes emitting substances, are best left to audio specialists. Formats that may be good candidates for in-house digitization include more recent formats, such as cartridge-based audiocassettes. However, even then, outsourcing may make more sense. If the collection to be digitized is small, it may be best to outsource it because the resources necessary to assemble an audio digitization setup can cost at least a few thousand dollars. However, if you wish to routinely digitize audio recordings and possibly offer use of the setup to people within the community, then it may make sense to assemble a workstation. The workstation needs to include an analog-to-digital audio converter, a computer, high-quality headphones, and playback equipment for each type of media that needs to be digitized, all set up in a quiet space.

For in-house digitization, resources such as the *ARSC Guide to Audio Preservation* recommend trained personnel, physical space, time, and funding, which are all beyond the initial equipment cost.[62] Consult this guide for further guidance on assembling an analog audio digitization program.

Outsourcing digitization involves writing a request for proposals (RFP), selecting a vendor, and ensuring the quality of the work completed by the vendor. The purpose of an RFP is to get vendors to submit cost estimates on completing the digitization work so that you can select the vendor that provides the best work within your budget. In assembling the RFP, at a minimum you would want to quantify the number of media that are being digitized, the type of media, and the total estimated duration. For more assistance on creating an RFP, especially related to audio collections, AVPreserve's *Guide to Developing a Request for Proposal for the Digitization of Audio* is recommended.[63]

An easy way to meet a wide variety of vendors to send the RFP to is to attend a gathering like the annual meeting of the Society of American Archivists. The exhibition hall always features many digitization vendors. In an afternoon, you can get a thorough sense of the services offered by specific vendors, approximate costs, and transportation or shipping options. I also recommend having discussions with other archivists and librarians who have outsourced digitization to vendors and getting a thorough sense of their experiences. For example, some questions worth asking include:

- Did the vendor deliver the digitized materials on time and on budget?
- Did any original material come back damaged?
- Were any mistakes made, such as sides of tapes left undigitized or parts of audio cut off?
- Was the vendor responsive to inquiries once work began?

In the United States, grants are available for the digitization of materials, including audio, from federal, state, and local government sources. For example, in New York City, our regional library member organization—the Metropolitan New York Library Council—offers a digitization grant program.[64] On their website, they include examples of successful grant applications that can be used by others in preparing their grant applications. Based on my experience in preparing grant applications and in reviewing grants for this program and others, it is important to make clear to grant reviewers the significance of the collection being digitized. This can include statements from researchers who vouch for the collection's significance and the value the digitization will offer. Alternatively, citing usage statistics for frequently used collections can help make the argument. Lastly, discussing how the digitized material will be used in an educational capacity, such as in K–12 programs or undergraduate classrooms, can enhance the argument for significance. Funders want to avoid a situation where a collection is digitized and never used, thus providing no near-term benefit. Reviewers also want to ensure that digitization will make use of best practices, many of which have been discussed in this chapter. When preparing a grant proposal, ensure that a digital preservation plan is in place, so that grant reviewers do not have to worry about the newly digitized files being lost, deleted, or destroyed through neglect, indifference, or ignorance. Lastly, reviewers want to ensure that elements besides the digitization are suitable, which can include a clear plan for metadata creation, realistic cost figures, and sensible time frames.

Federal agencies that provide digitization grants include the National Historic Records and Preservation Commission (NHPRC), the Institute of Museum and Library Services (IMLS), and the National Endowment for the Humanities (NEH), among others. Funds can also be generated through individual donations—both small and large gifts—and private foundations.[65]

POST-DIGITIZATION

The final consideration is what to do with the original carrier after digitized masters have been created and the quality has been verified. Generally, keeping the original carrier is a good idea, unless significant storage pressures are present. If a carrier is to be disposed of, taking photographs of the media and making sure labels are clear is a recommended practice. These digital photographs can be maintained with the digitized audio files and help provide context and perspective to future researchers. If the media is to be kept, make sure that the fact that it has been digitized is clearly communicated to individuals who may encounter the media. For media stored in a box, this can be as simple as filing a piece of bond paper that lists the media, the resulting digitized files, and the date of digitization. Alternatively, place the media in an acid-free envelope and label it as digitized. For media kept on a shelf, write on a piece of bond paper that the media was digitized on *X* date and the resulting file names, and slip that into the case, which will help make it clear that the media has been digitized and the digital versions should be consulted. Avoid using adhesive labels or stickers that inevitably fall off.

CONCLUSION

This chapter has recommended that analog audio be digitized and born-digital audio be migrated off carriers, and both incorporated into trustworthy repositories. As this is a daunting challenge, this process can be delayed to some extent by storing carriers in cool and dry environments. However, it is best to begin thinking about digitization and migration, especially for material with significant value or content on carriers with noted preservation issues. This can include getting a realistic sense of the quantity of audio media to digitize, including those that need digitization sooner as well as those that can be delayed, and exploring options for funding a digitization operation.

NOTES

[1] William Chase, "Preservation Reformatting," in *ARSC Guide to Audio Preservation,* ed. Sam Brylawski et al., (Washington, DC, and Eugene, OR: ARSC, CLIR, and Library of Congress, 2015), 110–26.

[2] Harrison Behl, "Audio Formats: Characteristics and Deterioration," in *ARSC Guide to Audio Preservation,* 14–36; IASA Technical Committee, *Guidelines on the Production and Preservation of Digital Audio Objects,* 2nd ed., ed. Kevin Bradley (Aarhus, Denmark: IASA, 2009).

[3] Curtis Peoples and Marsha Maguire, "Preserving Audio," in *ARSC Guide to Audio Preservation,* 1–13.

[4] Roland Gelatt, *The Fabulous Phonograph, 1877–1977,* 2nd ed. (New York: Macmillan, 1977).

[5] Andre Millard, *America on Record: A History of Recorded Sound* (Cambridge: Cambridge University Press, 1995).

[6] Ibid.

[7] Walter L. Welch and Leah Burt, *From Tinfoil to Stereo* (Gainesville: University Press of Florida, 1994).

[8] Millard, *America on Record.*

[9] Ibid.

[10] Behl, "Audio Formats."

[11] Ibid.

[12] Mark H. Clark, "Steel Tape and Wire Recorders," in *Magnetic Recording: The First 100 Years*, ed. Eric D. Daniel, C. Denis Mee, and Mark H. Clark (Piscataway, NJ: IEEE Press, 1999), 30–46.

[13] Friedrich K. Engle, "The Introduction of the Magnetophon," in *Magnetic Recording: The First 100 Years*, 47–71.

[14] Beverley R. Gooch, "Building on the Magnetophon," in *Magnetic Recording: The First 100 Years*, 72–91.

[15] Peoples and Maguire, "Preserving Audio."

[16] Gooch, "Building on the Magnetophon," 90.

[17] Mark H. Clark, "Product Diversification," in *Magnetic Recording: The First 100 Years*, 92–109.

[18] Ibid.

[19] Ibid.

[20] Peoples and Maguire, "Preserving Audio."

[21] Behl, "Audio Formats."

[22] Jonathan Sterne, *MP3: The Meaning of a Format* (Durham, NC: Duke University Press, 2012).

[23] Hannah Karp, "Era of Free Digital Music Wanes," *Wall Street Journal,* November 13, 2014, http://www.wsj.com/articles /era-of-free-digital-music-wanes-1415839234, permalinked on April 21, 2016, at https://perma.cc/KCV9-XLMU.

[24] Lauren Rudser, "Miss the Hiss? Fanatics Flip for Tunes on Cassette Tapes," *Wall Street Journal,* October 20, 2011, http:// www.wsj.com/articles/SB10001424052970204002304576631361693349974, permalinked on April 21, 2016, at https:// perma.cc/3U94-LT5E; Ellen Huet, "Resurgence in Vinyl Records Means Booming Business—And Growing Pains—for Factories," *Forbes,* July 8, 2015, http://www.forbes.com/sites/ellenhuet/2015/07/08/resurgence-in-vinyl-records-means-booming-business-and-growing-pains-for-factories/#2715e4857a0b585d60057419, permalinked on April 21, 2016, at https://perma.cc/FRU4-B5KS; Jesse Cannon, "How CDs Keep Clinging on to Life," *Alternative Press,* June 23, 2015, http:// www.altpress.com/features/entry/how_cds_keep_clinging_on_to_life, permalinked on April 21, 2016, at https://perma.cc /DE4S-H767.

[25] Stanley R. Alten, *Audio in Media,* 10th ed. (Boston, MA: Wadsworth, 2014).

[26] Ibid.

[27] Behl, "Audio Formats."

[28] Raymond Fielding, *A Technological History of Motion Pictures and Television* (Berkeley, CA: University of California Press, 1967).

[29] Behl, "Audio Formats," 22.

[30] Alten, *Audio in Media.*

[31] Christopher Ann Patton, "Preservation Re-Recording of Audio Recordings in Archives: Problems, Priorities, Technologies, and Recommendations," *American Archivist* 61, no. 1 (1998): 188–219.

[32] IASA, *Guidelines on the Production and Preservation of Digital Audio Objects.*

[33] Carla Arton, "Care and Maintenance," in *ARSC Guide to Audio Preservation*, 59.

[34] Dietrich Schüller and Albrecht Häfner, eds., *Handling and Storage of Audio and Video Carriers: Technical Committee Standards, Recommended Practices, and Strategies* (London: International Association of Sound and Audiovisual Archives, 2014).

[35] Arton, "Care and Maintenance," 54.

[36] Kevin Bradley, *Risks Associated with the Use of Recordable CDs and DVDs as Reliable Storage Media in Archival Collections—Strategies and Alternatives* (Paris: UNESCO, 2006); Laura Wilsey et al., "Capturing and Processing Born-Digital Files in the STOP AIDS Project Records: A Case Study," *Journal of Western Archives* 4, no. 1 (2013): 1–22.

[37] Matt Peckham, "The Ides of March: Farewell, Sony MiniDisc Player," *Time*, February 4, 2013, http://techland.time.com/2013/02/04/the-ides-of-march-farewell-sony-minidisc-player/, permalinked on April 21, 2016, at https://perma.cc/9PBV-CVJF.

[38] Chase, "Preservation Reformatting," 112; IASA Technical Committee, *Guidelines on the Production and Preservation of Digital Audio Objects*.

[39] Anthony Cocciolo, "Digitizing Oral History: Can You Hear the Difference?," *OCLC Systems & Services* 31, no. 3 (2015): 125–33.

[40] Assumes lossless compression encoded with pulse-code modulation (PCM).

[41] Derek Jay Jackson, "Defining Minimum Standards for the Digitization of Speech Recordings on Audio Compact Cassettes," *Preservation, Digital Technology & Culture* 42, no. 2 (2013), 87–98.

[42] Benchmark Media Systems, http://benchmarkmedia.com/, permalinked on April 21, 2016, at https://perma.cc/8J3W-JW32.

[43] Audacity, http://audacityteam.org/, permalinked on April 21, 2016, at https://perma.cc/U79K-WHSU.

[44] At the time of purchase in 2012, the devices retailed for $1,800.

[45] Arton, "Care and Maintenance," 73.

[46] Mike Casey and Bruce Gordon, *Sound Directions: Best Practices for Audio Preservation* (Bloomington, IN, and Cambridge, MA: Indiana University and Harvard University, 2007).

[47] Simon Spiers, "Cassette Azimuth Adjustment," YouTube video, https://www.youtube.com/watch?v=YhvqOtWwQ1E, permalinked on April 21, 2016, at https://perma.cc/Y45Y-4NYX.

[48] Behl, "Audio Formats," 33.

[49] Sustainability of Digital Formats: Planning for Library of Congress Collections website, http://www.digitalpreservation.gov/formats/index.shtml, permalinked on April 21, 2016, at https://perma.cc/7N6J-CK4Z.

[50] Behl, "Audio Formats," 29.

[51] Behl, "Audio Formats," 30.

[52] Bradley, *Risks Associated with the Use of Recordable CDs*.

[53] Joe Iraci, "The Stability of DVD Optical Disc Formats," *Restaurator* 32, no. 1 (2011): 39–59.

[54] Bradley, *Risks Associated with the Use of Recordable CDs*.

[55] Ibid.

[56] Behl, "Audio Formats," 24.

[57] Ibid.

[58] Behl, "Audio Formats," 25.

[59] Behl, "Audio Formats," 16.

[60] Behl, "Audio Formats," 22.

[61] Arton, "Care and Maintenance," 73.

[62] Chase, "Preservation Reformatting," 119–23.

[63] Chris Lacinak, *Guide to Developing a Request for Proposal for the Digitization of Audio* (AVPreserve, 2015), https://www.avpreserve.com/wp-content/uploads/2015/05/AVPS_Audio_Digitization_RFP_Guide.pdf, permalinked on December 6, 2016, at https://perma.cc/R9L8-UFP5.

[64] See http://metro.org/digitization-grant-program/, permalinked on April 21, 2016, at https://perma.cc/64EK-EC3U.

[65] The Foundation Center provides a database of grants; see http://foundationcenter.org/, permalinked on April 21, 2016, at https://perma.cc/5ZWX-4BEN.

CHAPTER 8

Film Collections

The most long-standing moving image technology is film, which acts as a capture, exhibition, and preservation medium. Unlike many of the audio and video formats discussed in this book, film is unique in that there will never come a time when someone discovers a film and cannot figure out how to decode it. By virtue of being able to hold a film up to a light source and see the succession of images, it is free from some of the technological obsolescence challenges that face many digital and analog formats.[1] Despite the longevity of film, it is not without its challenges. As movie theaters have transitioned to born-digital cinema projection, and several companies that make, develop, and digitize film have gone out of business or transitioned to other activities, the future of film is endangered.[2] This chapter provides a brief overview of the history of the medium, along with the film formats that archivists may encounter, as well as some preservation concerns. It also discusses storage environments for enhancing the preservation of film and explores digital reformatting as a preservation option.

BRIEF HISTORICAL OVERVIEW

Although film is one of the oldest moving image technologies, there were some antecedents. These include the kineograph (see figure 8-1), which is a simple flip-book, and the zoetrope, which shows images in quick succession through small openings, creating the illusion of a moving image (see figure 8-2).[3]

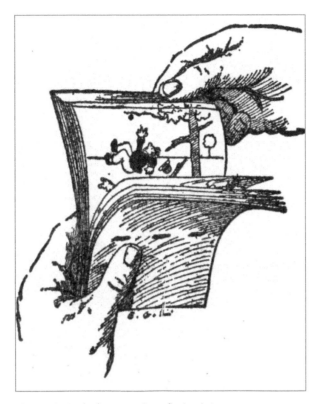

Figure 8-1. The kineograph, or flip-book.[4]

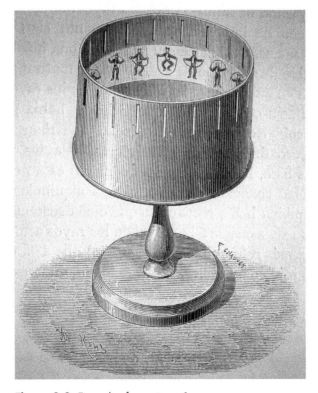

Figure 8-2. Example of a zoetrope.[5]

Figure 8-3. Mutoscope.[6]

Late nineteenth-century devices that could animate short sequences were often used in entertainment settings such as carnivals and circuses.[7] For example, the Mutoscope (figure 8-3) allowed a viewer to crank a flip-book and see an animated sequence.

Beyond these simple optical-illusion devices created in the late nineteenth century, recent archaeological research indicates that human interest in creating moving images dates back far longer. Discovered in the mid-1990s, the paintings in Chauvet Cave in southeastern France were created between 32,000 and 26,000 BC and depict Paleolithic animals that appear animated when torchlight is moved across them.[8] In the panel of the painting in figure 8-4, the rhinoceros has been drawn with seven horns, which simulates movement when light moves across it. Humans would seem to have an innate need to document their experiences through moving images.

Thomas Edison developed motion picture film technology in the 1890s. Some simultaneous invention occurred in France and England, making motion pictures appear on both sides of the Atlantic around the same time.[9] Early films were short, with fictional films such as the inventive films of Georges Méliès the most popular.[10] A frame from his creative 1902 film *A Trip to the Moon* is shown in figure 8-5.

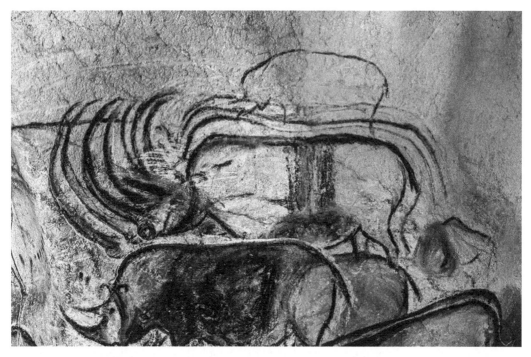

Figure 8-4. A panel from Chauvet Cave depicting a rhinoceros with seven horns.[11]

Figure 8-5. Frame from *A Trip to the Moon* (1902) by Georges Méliès.

After World War I, feature films, which typically lasted at least forty minutes, surpassed short films in popularity.[12] During this period, films were silent. This changed in 1927 with Warner Brothers' release of *The Jazz Singer*, which had a sound track that included singing and some spoken dialogue.[13] This signaled the end of the silent era and the beginning of "talkie" pictures.

The introduction of sound was followed by what is often referred to as the Golden Age of Hollywood cinema, which lasted from the 1930s through the 1950s.[14] Although Hollywood films often outshine other activities that make use of film, there was also an increasing use of film for documentary purposes; this was made more possible with the introduction of "safety film," which did not combust like nonsafety film. Before the introduction of video recording, film was also used to record early television through a device called the kinescope.[15] Beyond Hollywood, other countries—including France, England, India, Japan, Germany, and Mexico, among many others—had and continue to have vibrant film communities.[16]

Digital technology slowly impacted the filmmaking industry, with special effects being the first area affected.[17] In addition to special effects, analog sound in films eventually gave way to digital sound, made possible by sound systems by providers like Dolby and Sony.[18] As illustrated in figure 7-2 in chapter 7, "Audio Collections," digital sound elements were squeezed into 35 mm films using technology similar to QR codes.

By the 2000s, the editing process—which until that point had involved splicing together pieces of film using sticky tape—also became digital.[19] Under the old system, motion pictures were captured with film and required overnight film development to turn the negative into a film positive. The film positive could be loaded onto a projector and exhibited. On many film sets, crews watch the raw footage from the previous day, also known as "dailies." With the introduction of digital technology, the film is digitized (the product is also known as telecine), converting it to a video format that can be used by editing systems, such as those made by Avid.[20] With the introduction of digital editing systems, the film can be manipulated in other ways—for example, through a process known as digital intermediate (DI), which allows changes to the colors and other characteristics of the film's images.[21]

The last remaining elements of the film production process to give way to digital technology were capture and exhibition. Digital capture and exhibition were achieved with George Lucas's *Star Wars: Episode I, The Phantom Menace* in 1999. The film was captured digitally using HD cameras (today more commonly used for making television programs) and was projected digitally in two theaters in New York and Los Angeles.[22] Audience members who saw that film at other theaters saw film prints. By 2015, most major movie theaters in the United States had transitioned to digital projection, as many Hollywood studios had stopped shipping film prints to theaters.[23] In the years since *The Phantom Menace,* companies such as RED, ARRI, and Panavision have created digital cinema cameras for capture that far exceed HD image quality.

Today, use of photographic motion picture film for producing moving image and sound works has declined and is used by select Hollywood directors and artists.[24] Many film schools have moved students away from the use of film for their projects. For example, at my own institution, Pratt Institute, the Department of Film and Video transitioned from 8 mm film to digital filmmaking techniques as the primary tool used for student projects earlier this decade. Although some film schools continue to teach students on equipment such as 16 mm film cameras, and some students continue to be interested, it is becoming more of a specialized interest area rather than a required skill.

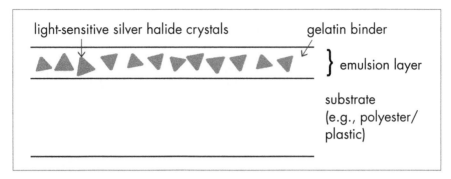

light-sensitive silver halide crystals   gelatin binder

} emulsion layer

substrate
(e.g., polyester/
plastic)

Figure 8-6. Simplified cross-section of motion picture film.

FILM AND ITS TECHNICAL DIMENSIONS

Film is made up of light-sensitive silver halide crystals or grains; when developed, they turn into silver metal, which are the particulates that make up the image (see figure 8-6). These silver particles are embedded in a gelatin binder, both of which form the emulsion. The emulsion is layered on top of a clear or semiclear substrate or base, such as plastic or polyester. The plastic has sprocket holes in it, so that the film can be wound around a reel, run through the projector, and loaded onto a take-up reel. A 16 mm film projector is illustrated in figure 8-7. In typical film projection, twenty-four photographic frames per second are shown with a very brief blackout between frames, creating the illusion of a moving image.[25]

Figure 8-7. A 16 mm film projector.

FILM FORMATS AND PRESERVATION ISSUES

Archivists can encounter all formats of film, including 35 mm, 16 mm, 8 mm, and Super 8 mm, which can include color and black-and-white film. The millimeter designation corresponds to the width of the film, or the film gauge. Each of these film formats is shown in figure 8-8.

Figure 8-8. Film formats (left to right): 8 mm, Super 8 mm, 16 mm, and 35 mm.

Figure 8-9. Technicolor film camera with three strips of film, Museum of the Moving Image, Queens, New York.

35 MM FILM

The 35 mm film format is one of the earliest film formats; it was used in Edison's first films.[26] Some films today are still shot on 35 mm film.[27] Because the amount of silver needed to create such large images requires significant expense, this format is typically reserved for widely released commercial works, such as Hollywood films, or films with significant financial backing.

The production of color films increased with the introduction of Technicolor, which required filming scenes with three strips of film representing the three primary colors: magenta, cyan, and yellow. When put together, they create a full-color image. Figure 8-9 shows a Technicolor camera with the three strips of film passing behind the camera lens.

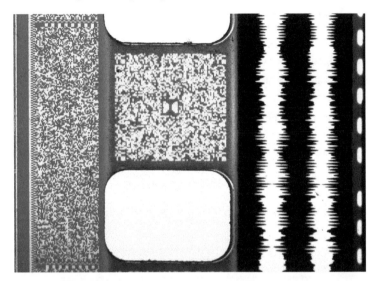

Figure 8-10. Sound elements on 35 mm film, including Sony SDDS sound (left), Dolby Digital (between sprocket holes), and optical sound track (right).[28]

As mentioned earlier, sound was introduced in Hollywood films in the late 1920s. Sound elements on motion picture film can include an optical sound track, as mentioned in chapter 7, and also digital sound (figure 8-10) or even a magnetic sound track (pictured in figure 8-11 on both sides of the leftmost film). These digital sound elements use similar technology to QR codes, where the digital information is encoded in the optical pattern and decoded during playback.

SMALL-GAUGE FILMS

The 16 mm film format was used extensively in the educational film market before the advent of VHS, as well as in documentaries and films with less commercial backing. The formats of 8 mm and Super 8 mm films were used for home movies before the advent of VHS, as well as in some films with less commercial backing (e.g., the work of amateur filmmakers, experimental art films, student films, etc.). Although both Super 8 and 8 mm films are about 8 mm wide, 8 mm films have larger sprocket holes. Because Super 8 films use smaller sprocket holes, the image area is more than 1 mm wider than on 8 mm film. Note that 8 mm, Super 8, and 16 mm films can have magnetic sound tracks or, if silent, no sound track. Magnetic sound tracks are usually a thin strip of rust-colored tape, similar to the tape found in compact audiocassettes. Films in the 16 mm format can also use an optical sound track similar to the one shown in figure 8-10.

It should be noted that filmmakers working with small-gauge formats often do not photograph the image onto a negative, which is typical of commercial works, but rather the image is captured onto the film as a positive image. This type of film is known as reversal film.[29] When reversal film is used in a camera and then processed, it can be loaded directly onto the projector and exhibited. This has significant cost savings because there is no need for printing onto a new roll of film. When appraising small-gauge films, it is important to note if the film is on reversal film, and if it is, then this is the original source material. You can identify a film as being reversal film if the edges of the film are black rather than clear, which is typical with film prints. Motion picture consultant Brian R. Pritchard provides a useful guide online for identifying reversal film, as well as other aspects related to 16 mm film.[30]

OTHER FILM GAUGES

Although the aforementioned film gauges are the ones most archivists will encounter, there are some other film gauges with limited use. For example, some Hollywood films have been shot and are exhibited on 70 mm film, which has twice the image size as 35 mm film. (For a comparison, see figure 8-11.) Recent 70 mm films include Quentin Tarantino's *The Hateful Eight* (2015) and Paul Thomas Anderson's *The Master* (2012).[31] Older major films that were shot on 70 mm include *Ben-Hur* (1959), *West Side Story* (1961), and *Hello Dolly!* (1969).[32] Because of the significant upfront cost of using this technique, 70 mm film will likely be reserved for the most significant films or most persistent directors. Other film formats include the 9.5 mm format, introduced in 1922, which is a small-gauge format more often found outside of the United States, including in Europe and the British Commonwealth countries.[33]

Figure 8-11. (Left) 70 mm film from *Indiana Jones: The Last Crusade* (1989) with magnetic sound track; (right) 35 mm film from *All the King's Men* (2006) with optical and digital sound tracks.

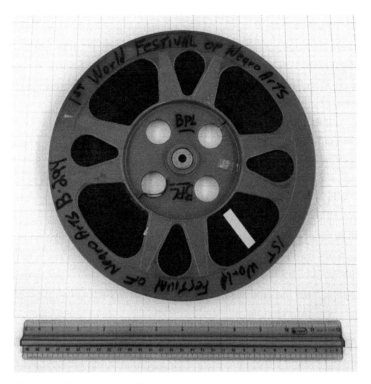

Figure 8-12. An acetate film in an advanced stage of decay, with a strong vinegar odor and some warping of the film.

FILM BASES

The film base originally used (1893 through the early 1950s) for 35 mm film was of cellulose nitrate, which is known for being intensely flammable.[34] For this reason, only a projectionist could project it. It was not used in the home or school markets, and it was never used in any smaller gauge film formats. A notable problem with nitrate films is that they were prone to decompose and catch fire, which resulted in the destruction of several archival film storage facilities. A common practice in the film community is to transfer nitrate films to safety film, which is any kind of film that is not nitrate-based.[35] Most nitrate films are stored in vaults at cold temperatures and kept by staff experienced with these aging films (e.g., at the Library of Congress's Packard Campus of the National Audio-Visual Conservation Center). Nitrate films are often labeled as "nitrate" on the film reel, are most often 35 mm gauge, and would date through the mid-1950s. If you believe your archives has a nitrate film in its possession, and you do not have the proper facilities for storing it, it may be best to deaccession it to an archives that has the proper facilities.

Nitrate film was replaced by film on a cellulose acetate base, often called safety film. Acetate film was used in 35 mm and all smaller gauge films, such as 16 mm, 8 mm, and Super 8 mm, from 1909 onward. The problem with acetate is that it is prone to vinegar syndrome, or acetate decay, which is accelerated by heat and high humidity.[36] The beginnings of vinegar syndrome can be detected when the film starts to smell like vinegar. Later stages of vinegar syndrome include the curling or warping of the film. The Image Permanence Institute sells a product called A-D Strips, which are small strips of chemically sensitive paper that can be placed in a film container and that will change color if the film is undergoing vinegar syndrome.[37] In figure 8-12, an acetate film is shown with a yellow A-D Strip, which indicates an advanced stage of decay. The film has a strong vinegar odor, and some slight warping is visible. Films that are decaying can be shrink-wrapped and kept at freezing temperatures. Also worth noting is that vinegar syndrome can spread from one film to another because the vapors released can start the chemical reaction in other films.[38] For this reason, films affected by vinegar syndrome are best stored separate from other acetate films.

Polyester film (plastic) has many advantages over both nitrate and acetate in that it is nonflammable, does not decompose, and is very durable—thus, it has become a suitable replacement for acetate film. Polyester began to be used in the mid-1950s and continues to be used to this day.[39] Polyester film is used by Hollywood film studio archives to store films, and if stored in a cool and dry environment, they are expected to last for at least a hundred years.[40]

How does one tell the difference between an acetate film and a polyester film, as both films may be labeled as safety film? First, if the film smells at all like vinegar, then it is an acetate film. However, if no odor is present, then one way to test it is to hold up the film reel to the light and wave your hand behind it. If you are able to see your hand through the film, then it is most likely a polyester film (figure 8-13). If no light comes through the film and you cannot see your hand, then it is an acetate film (figure 8-14).

COLOR FADING AND SHIFTING

Despite the apparent advantages of polyester film, a notable preservation issue is color fading and shifting.[41] Color fading, which also affects films on bases other than polyester, occurs when the dyes used in the motion picture film fade over time through a process of chemical decomposition. Color shifting—a related problem also caused by chemical decomposition—occurs when a set of colors changes into another set of colors. Colors fade and shift differently depending on the film stock. For example, in some films the cyan and yellow fade or shift first, leaving the film a magenta color. Other films fade or shift differently, leaving a greenish hue. A significant challenge in identifying what films will fade is that the companies that produce (or produced) film—such as Kodak, Fuji, Konica, and Agfa—produced many different varieties of motion picture film over many decades. In general, some of the earliest color film stocks had significant fading troubles, prompting film directors such as Martin Scorsese to advocate that companies such as Kodak and Fuji make longer-lasting color film stocks, both for film negatives and film prints.[42] Through such advocacy, by the mid-1980s, color motion picture film was improved over its earlier predecessors.[43] According to Henry Wilhelm and Carol Brower, "most motion picture color negatives and prints made after the introduction of the Eastman [Kodak] Color process in 1950 until about 1985 have by now suffered significant fading."[44] In this case, it is not because the cyan and yellow components turned red, but rather that the cyan and yellow components faded away, leaving a "ghastly reddish-magenta reminder of what once were brilliant, full-color images."[45] For more discussion about particular varieties of color film and tests of their fading, see the Wilhelm and Brower text referenced above and available online.

Fortunately, color fading and shifting can be addressed by separating the colors of a film into their elementary colors (yellow, cyan, and magenta) and printing them on black-and-white film stocks. By shining those respective colors through the black-and-white film stock, the full-color image can be reconstituted. This process is called creating YCM separation masters on black-and-white film.[46] The advantage of this process is that the YCM masters have the potential to survive for hundreds of years if

Figure 8-13. Polyester film: your hand can be seen through it when the film is held up to a light source.

Figure 8-14. Acetate film: your hand cannot be seen through it when the film is held up to a light source.

kept in the proper storage conditions, with little maintenance needed other than controlling the physical environment. The downside is the cost of creating the costly film prints.

STORAGE ENVIRONMENT

For all types of film, the *Film Preservation Guide* from the National Film Preservation Foundation recommends cold temperatures of 40°F with 30–50 percent relative humidity. They note that freezing films can extend their life. However, films with magnetic elements like magnetic sound tracks should not be frozen because the tracks can be damaged that way. Acetate or nitrate films that are showing signs of decomposition are best kept frozen or as cool as possible, because being kept at room temperature to cool temperatures (54°F to 68°F) is likely to cause further damage.

For most small archives without climate-controlled cold vaults, frost-free freezers can be used to store films showing signs of decomposition or films in need of extended life. The Association of Moving Image Archivists (AMIA) provides a website on how to freeze films.[47] When moving a film from freezing conditions to warmer temperatures, it should be acclimatized so that condensation does not occur. For more information on acclimatizing films, see the *Film Preservation Guide*.

Film should be stored flat or horizontally in rigid containers that protect the reels from dust or physical damage.[48] Containers can be stacked on top of each other. Containers should be made of plastic, acid-free cardboard, and noncorroding metal.

PRESERVATION REFORMATTING

As mentioned earlier, films on black-and-white polyester film stock have the potential to last for centuries if stored in a cold and dry environment. Thus, films that need preservation attention, such as films deteriorating on acetate or nitrate stock, are often rephotographed back onto film.[49] Further, film librarian Elena Rossi Snook of the New York Public Library has suggested that independent filmmakers photograph their born-digital films onto film stock because of its durability and its future-proof decoding requirements.[50] Although many independent filmmakers are unlikely to follow her suggestion because of the high expense of creating film prints, it does highlight strongly held beliefs in the durability of film.

Using digital technology as a preservation medium has only recently become an option.[51] Despite this emerging option, digital technology may well turn out to be a less reliable carrier than film, even in cases where institutions have digital preservation procedures in place, as well as trustworthy repositories. Film can endure more benign neglect than digital technology, which needs regular data migration and maintenance. Film is relatively easily preserved using a "store and ignore" approach that emphasizes controlling the storage environment.[52]

Despite this, it is possible to digitize films and create digital preservation masters. The best way to digitize films is to digitize each frame of the film individually. Equipment to perform this conversion of film to a video format is sometimes called a telecine. Digitizing each frame of film is the process used by filmmakers who continue to use film in the production process, as well as the procedure for restoring films for release or rerelease. Companies with long-standing investment in the film community, such as the German company ARRI, create motion picture film digitization hardware.[53] Despite the availability of quality products for digitizing film, many films, especially those in smaller gauge formats, have been subject to low-quality digitization. In these cases, a film is projected onto a screen and a camcorder, recording at standard-definition or high-definition resolution, records what is projected. Digitization of this sort is often inferior to the original film; however, it is a somewhat easy and cost-effective solution for creating access copies of films. High-quality film digitization hardware can cost well over $100,000. Thus, outsourcing of film digitization is necessary for all but a few archives that specialize in film.

Digitization of film is not unlike scanning still photographs on 35 mm film, whether slides (or film positives) or strip negatives. Scanning images involves sampling elements of the image and mapping those to a grid of dots or pixels.[54] When zooming in on a digitized film frame image using a program like Adobe Photoshop, you can readily see the grid of picture elements (or pixels) that make up the image. Resolution is the number of pixels that make up the image, from left to right and top to bottom. The higher the resolution, the clearer or sharper the image should be. However, as with audio sampling (discussed in the previous chapter), after a certain point the human eye and brain cannot distinguish between a high-resolution image and a very high-resolution image. Although resolutions continue to increase, both in the digital filmmaking community and television, there may come a point where the increased resolution does not matter because of limitations of human anatomy.

In the film and television community, sometimes only the left-to-right pixel resolution is specified, and the top-to-bottom dimension is implied. For example, many films currently shown in theaters have a resolution of 4K, which amounts to 4096 x 2160 pixels. High-definition televisions have a resolution of 1920 x 1080 pixels. A comparison of the various resolutions, including SD (standard-definition television resolution) is shown in figure 8-15. The reason that only one dimension needs to be mentioned is that film and television have aspect ratios that describe the relative proportions of the width of the content to the height. For example, the old, boxy TVs that many people had in their homes until recently have an aspect ratio of 4:3, where the first number is the width and the second is the height. The HDTV more recently adopted has an aspect ratio of 16:9, which indicates that HDTV is much wider than it is high. The aspect ratio used with many post-1950s films is 1.85:1.[55]

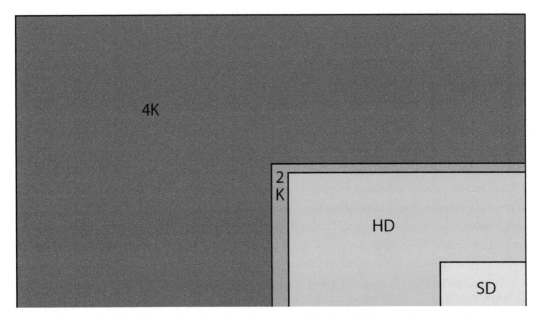

Figure 8-15. Various display resolutions used in television and film. Digital films are often projected in movie theaters at 2K and 4K resolutions.

In addition to resolution, all digitized images have bit depth. Bit depth is the amount of digital data used to capture the color of a single pixel, usually measured in bits.[56] Much like bit depth as discussed in the previous chapter, the greater the bit depth, the greater the range of colors that can be displayed. This range—from the darkest dark to the lightest light—is also known as the dynamic range.[57] Digital technology has tended to struggle with representing images with wide dynamic ranges, but as bit depths have increased and technology has improved, the dynamic range available to image producers has increased dramatically. Frequently used bit depths for digitizing images include 24 bits and 48 bits.

Recent digitization of smaller-gauge films indicates that high-resolution scans offer significant advantages. For example, Ken Burns's *The Civil War*, which was originally shot on 16 mm film in the late 1980s, was digitized at 4K resolution and produced great visual results when the digital version premiered on PBS in 2015.[58] The 4K resolution indicates that approximately four thousand pixels are used to represent one row of pixels from the left to the right of the image. At the time of this writing, most home televisions only support HD resolution, with ultra high-definition 4K televisions beginning to be adopted. Also at the time of this writing, movie theaters project movies at 4K resolution, and some continue to project at 2K, which is not much more resolution than an HD television. Scanning a film at 4K resolution ensures that the film will look as good as possible on ultra high-definition 4K televisions.

There is no set standard for digitizing specific film gauges at particular resolutions. Many films were digitized at SD for release on television. However, this is widely considered an inadequate representation of the original content, even for small-gauge films like 16 mm and even 8 mm. For film digitization, display resolution of at least HDTV resolution (1920 x 1080 pixels) is becoming increasingly common. For 35 mm films and important films on 16 mm, 4K resolution may well be a worthwhile investment in time and resources. Digitized films that have been scanned should be stored in formats that do not lossy compress individual photographic frames, such as formats that are based on uncompressed TIFF or JPEG 2000 images. A format often used for scanning film that does not lossy compress the individual photographic frame is the DPX (Digital Picture Exchange) file format.[59] Once high-quality digital masters of film works are created, access copies can be created depending on the access needs. Examples include compressing the video for streaming over the Internet or burning it onto Blu-ray optical discs.

BORN-DIGITAL FILM

Unlike audio and video discussed in this book, there is no born-digital equivalent of film. Rather, many things that we call "films," such as feature-length Hollywood "films," are technically computer files distributed to theaters on hard drives called DCPs, or Digital Cinema Packages.[60] "Film" has become a term of respect for certain kinds of moving image works and denotes the artistic and intellectual ambitions of the creators. It may insult some filmmakers if they were to be called video makers, and it may delight others! In any case, the terms "film" and "filmmaker" persist as signifiers. Although there are still some directors and cinematographers who shoot films on film, the film is always digitized for editing and post-production, and it is almost always now projected digitally.[61]

A personal example illustrates some of the interesting uses of language around motion pictures. In 2013, I worked on some digital projects for the PBS television program *POV*, which broadcasts independent documentaries during the summer months. One of their initiatives is distributing copies of independent documentaries to public libraries, schools, and community centers for screening, and hosting discussions afterwards.[62] Therefore, they need to duplicate a large number of DVDs for distribution. I remember hearing a staff member say to a visitor, "this is where we make the films," referring to the machine that duplicates DVDs. I found this use of language very interesting because no piece of physical film was ever used in the production or distribution process, and clearly the DVD duplicator was not doing anything with film. However, referring to works such as independent documentaries as films—despite the lack of any film use—continues and indicates continuity with earlier traditions and respect for the creators.

Archivists will not have to worry about DCPs showing up in their archival collections. DCPs are encrypted and can only be decrypted using a Key Delivery Message (KDM), which authorizes the film to play on a specific projector for a set period of time.[63] These encryption measures were designed to prohibit piracy of movies. Even if a DCP were not returned to a studio and arrived in someone's donated collection, it would be nearly impossible to access the content on it. Further, attempting to break the encryption would be a violation of the US Digital Millennium Copyright Act, which makes it illegal to break encryption mechanisms designed to protect copyrighted works.[64] If a filmmaker wants to donate a born-digital film to an archives, the master files should be submitted unencrypted as computer files on hard drives or other high-capacity digital carriers. Files should be migrated off hard drives and ingested into trustworthy digital repositories.

FILM WITHOUT THE CAMERA

Up until this point, it has been assumed that films—be they born-digital or those on motion picture film—are created via a camera. In this scenario, the camera captures light waves through the lens from the physical world onto some recordable medium. With film cameras, this medium is the film negative, which is developed to form the film positive. With digital cameras, this medium is the sensor, which comprises an array of millions of light-detecting pixels or photosites.[65] In filmmaking and video production, capturing action through the camera is also referred to as capturing live action.[66] In animation—not live action—capturing images through a camera was also common practice. Before the widespread use of computer-generated imagery (CGI) animation, photographing a succession of drawings or models was often used to create animation, although this was not the only way to produce animations.[67] Pixar's *Toy Story* (1995) radically broke from this model, creating all visible elements with computerized 3-D models and dispensing with the camera almost entirely.[68] Even in the case of *Jurassic Park* (1993), which was a landmark use of CGI, the animated dinosaurs were captured with a film camera from the CRT screens of computers.[69] It is a marvel that the film looks as good as it does, considering this seemingly rudimentary solution.

Works of Hollywood animation are not the only types of moving image and sound record being created that do not rely on cameras. One popular application is the rendering of architectural interiors and exteriors, which can be viewed both as interactive models (with the ability to pan, zoom in and out, etc.) and as video renderings that take viewers through a designed space. Although the preservation of 3-D architectural models is beyond the scope of this book, renderings of architectural spaces as motion graphics are increasingly common and may well find themselves in archival collections.[70]

Moving image and sound records that are based not on raster images but rather on vector images present some interesting preservation challenges. Raster images are like those discussed earlier in this chapter: an image composed of a matrix of pixels. Vector images dispense with pixel matrices and instead use intricate layers of shapes with properties attached to them, like X-Y coordinates, width, and height. Computer algorithms and software can be applied to such assemblages to give them motion and have them interact with other elements as needed. These works prompt a myriad of preservation challenges: for example, should they be preserved more like digital video, or more like computer software? To preserve CGI-based works, the recommendation made here is to treat the work both as digital video *and* as computer software. First, the master digital video versions should be preserved. (Recommendations for preserving such records are discussed in chapter 10, "Digital Video Collections.") As all CGI-based works eventually get rendered as raster images for exhibition, whether for theatrical exhibition or for broadcast, physical media, or Internet distribution, retaining this raster version of the work is an important first step.

In addition to the digital video version, there is reason to also preserve the version of the work as computer software, or the vector graphics computer files, if resources permit. This allows the vector graphics to be remixed, reused, studied, and analyzed, among many other possible uses. In treating the work more as computer software, it is necessary to maintain the files created for the work, as well as a copy of the software used to render the vector graphics. This can be a challenge, as eventually the software may not operate on present-day computers and may need emulation to function properly. For a thorough discussion of preserving records such as these based on software, see chapter 11, "Complex Media."

CONCLUSION

Archivists may encounter motion picture film in their collections; these materials can include 8 mm, Super 8 mm, 16 mm, 35 mm, and—in rare cases—70 mm films. This chapter has discussed preservation concerns for film and ways to address these concerns through proper storage conditions, as well as options for digital reformatting for preservation and access. The chapter has also discussed issues in filmmaking in the digital era, including some notable trends such as the filmmaking community, ironically, dispensing with both film and cameras.

NOTES

1. This assumes that we are not considering the sound track, which is not so trivial to decode.

2. David Bordwell, *Pandora's Digital Box: Films, Files, and the Future of Movies* (Madison, WI: Irvington Way Institute Press, 2012).

3. Leo Enticknap, *Moving Image Technology: From Zoetrope to Digital* (London: Wallflower, 2005).

4. Illustration from John Barnes Linnet, *Zeitgenössische Illustration* (1886), https://commons.wikimedia.org/wiki/File:Linnet_kineograph_1886.jpg, permalinked on April 22, 2016, at https://perma.cc/K4V6-VPDS.

5. Illustration from Amédée Guillemin, *El mundo físico: gravedad, gravitación, luz, calor, electricidad, magnetismo, etc.* (Barcelona: Montaner y Simón, 1882), https://flic.kr/p/7b7CcN, permalinked on April 22, 2016, at https://perma.cc/UA3A-363X.

6. Photograph of Mutoscope made by American Mutoscope and Biograph Company circa 1899, on display at Museum of the Moving Image, Queens, New York.

7. Kristin Thompson and David Bordwell, *Film History: An Introduction,* 2nd ed. (Boston: McGraw Hill, 2003).

8. Jean Clottes, *Chauvet Cave: The Art of Earliest Time*s (Salt Lake City: University of Utah Press, 2003); Marc Azéma and Florent Rivère, "Animation in Palaeolithic Art: A Pre-echo of Cinema," *Antiquity 86* (2012): 316–24; *Cave of Forgotten Dreams,* directed by Werner Herzog (Los Angeles: Creative Differences, 2010).

9. Thompson and Bordwell, *Film History.*

10. Ibid.

11. Image from website of Ministère de la Culture et de la Communication, France, http://archeologie.culture.fr/chauvet/, permalinked on April 22, 2016, at https://perma.cc/E8BE-AAMF.

12. Academy of Motion Picture Arts and Sciences, "305 Feature Films in Contention for 2015 Best Picture Oscar," https://www.oscars.org/news/305-feature-films-contention-2015-best-picture-oscarr, permalinked on April 22, 2016, at https://perma.cc/4UKJ-QMLQ.

13. Thompson and Bordwell, *Film History.*

14. Robert Sklar, *A World History of Film* (New York: Harry N. Abrams, 2002).

15. Joshua M. Greenberg, *From Betamax to Blockbuster: Video Stores and the Invention of Movies on Video* (Cambridge, MA: MIT Press, 2010).

16. Sklar, *A World History of Film.*

17. Bordwell, *Pandora's Digital Box.*

18. Ibid.

19. Ibid.

20. Avid, http://www.avid.com/, permalinked on April 22, 2016, at https://perma.cc/ML9D-EZCX.

21. Bordwell, *Pandora's Digital Box.*

22. Ibid.

23. Richard Verrier, "End of Film: Paramount First Studio to Stop Distributing Film," *Los Angeles Times,* January 17, 2014, http://articles.latimes.com/2014/jan/17/entertainment/la-et-ct-paramount-digital-20140117, permalinked on April 22, 2016, at https://perma.cc/87HE-45J4.

24. This issue is discussed in depth in the film *Side By Side,* directed by Christopher Kenneally (Los Angeles, CA: Company Films, 2002).

25. Enticknap, *Moving Image Technology.*

26. Thompson and Bordwell, *Film History.*

27. Vadim Rizov, "39 Movies Released in 2014 Shot on 35 mm," *Filmmaker Magazine,* January 15, 2015, http://filmmakermagazine.com/88971-39-movies-released-in-2014-shot-on-35mm/, permalinked on April 22, 2016, at https://perma.cc/C9CY-RFT3.

28. Image courtesy of Wikimedia Commons, https://en.wikipedia.org/wiki/35_mm_film#/media/File:35mm_film_audio_macro.jpg, permalinked on April 22, 2016, at https://perma.cc/4KSN-LUFD.

29. "Reversal film," *Wikipedia,* https://en.wikipedia.org/wiki/Reversal_film, permalinked on February 15, 2017, at https://perma.cc/8P2A-YFD9.

30. Brian R. Pritchard, *Identification of 16mm Film* (2013), http://www.brianpritchard.com/16mm%20Identification%20Version%201.02.pdf, permalinked on February 15, 2017, at https://perma.cc/FF3Y-BYK2.

31. "Quentin Tarantino on 'Hateful Eight' and Why 70 mm 'Might Be Film's Saving Grace,'" *Hollywood Reporter,* December 24, 2015, http://www.hollywoodreporter.com/news/quentin-tarantino-hateful-eight-why-851136, permalinked on April 22, 2016, at https://perma.cc/DD6P-GQTH; Lucas Kavner, "Paul Thomas Anderson's 'The Master' on 70 mm Harkens Back to Hollywood Epics," *Huffington Post,* September 7, 2012, http://www.huffingtonpost.com/2012/09/07/paul-thomas-anderson-the-master_n_1862890.html, permalinked on April 22, 2016, at https://perma.cc/ZRW9-5Z8Z.

32. "List of 70 mm Films," *Wikipedia,* https://en.wikipedia.org/wiki/List_of_70_mm_films, permalinked on April 22, 2016, at https://perma.cc/A7B5-CB4H.

33. Alan D. Kattelle, "The Evolution of Amateur Motion Picture Equipment 1895–1965," *Journal of Film and Video* 38, no. 3/4, (1986): 47–57.

34 National Film Preservation Foundation, *The Film Preservation Guide: The Basics for Archives, Libraries, and Museums* (San Francisco: National Film Preservation Foundation, 2004), http://www.filmpreservation.org/preservation-basics/the-film -preservation-guide-download, permalinked on April 22, 2016, at https://perma.cc/2Z5A-LYXW.

35 Anthony Slide, *Nitrate Won't Wait: A History of Film Preservation in the United States* (Jefferson, NC: McFarland, 2000).

36 National Film Preservation Foundation, *Film Preservation Guide.*

37 A-D Strips, Image Permanence Institute, https://www.imagepermanenceinstitute.org/imaging/ad-strips, permalinked on April 24, 2016, at https://perma.cc/9SSX-M7ZF.

38 National Film Preservation Foundation, *Film Preservation Guide.*

39 Ibid.

40 Enticknap, *Moving Image Technology;* Science and Technology Council of the Academy of Motion Picture Arts and Sciences, *The Digital Dilemma: Strategic Issues in Archiving and Accessing Digital Motion Picture Materials* (Beverly Hills, CA: Academy of Motion Picture Arts and Sciences, 2007), https://www.oscars.org/science-technology/sci-tech-projects/digital-dilemma, permalinked on September 15, 2016, at https://perma.cc/Y5M2-KESS.

41 National Film Preservation Foundation, *Film Preservation Guide.*

42 Henry Wilhelm and Carol Brower, *The Permanence and Care of Color Photographs: Traditional and Digital Color Prints, Color Negatives, Slides, and Motion Pictures* (Grinnell, IA: Preservation Publishing Company, 1993), http://wilhelm-imaging.com /pdf/HW_Book_01_of_20_HiRes_v1c.pdf, permalinked on September 14, 2016, at https://perma.cc/YDF5-TAD4.

43 Ibid.

44 Ibid., 26.

45 Ibid., 26.

46 Science and Technology Council, *Digital Dilemma.*

47 Association of Moving Image Archivists (AMIA), *Film Forever: The Home Film Preservation Guide,* http://www.filmforever .org/, permalinked on April 22, 2016, at https://perma.cc/QKF6-DUZL.

48 National Film Preservation Foundation, *Film Preservation Guide.*

49 Ibid.

50 Elena Rossi Snook, "How does your film become preserved and discoverable?" (presentation at the Documentary Preservation Summit, New York, NY, March 31–April 1, 2015).

51 Giovanna Fossati, *From Grain to Pixel: The Archival Life of Film in Transition* (Amsterdam: Amsterdam University Press, 2009).

52 Science and Technology Council, *Digital Dilemma.*

53 ARRISCAN, https://www.arri.com/archive_technologies/arriscan/, permalinked on April 22, 2016, at https://perma.cc /H85E-9HY8.

54 Cornell University Library, *Moving Theory into Practice: Digital Imaging Tutorial* (2003), http://www.library.cornell.edu /preservation/tutorial/contents.html, permalinked on April 22, 2016, at https://perma.cc/V5AS-HNJ8.

55 David Bordwell and Kristin Thompson, *Film Art: An Introduction* (New York: McGraw-Hill, 1997).

56 Cornell University Library, *Moving Theory into Practice.*

57 Ibid.

58 Paul Barnes, *The Civil War: Restoring the Film* (PBS, 2015), http://www.pbs.org/kenburns/civil-war/restoring-film/, permalinked on April 22, 2016, at https://perma.cc/FC6W-9A8F.

59 Digital Picture Exchange, https://en.wikipedia.org/wiki/Digital_Picture_Exchange, permalinked on December 6, 2016, at https://perma.cc/YP3P-7W7L.

60 Bordwell, *Pandora's Digital Box.*

61 Carolyn Giardina, "Christopher Nolan Urges Hollywood to Step Up Efforts to Preserve Film," *Hollywood Reporter,* March 8, 2015, http://www.hollywoodreporter.com/behind-screen/christopher-nolan-urges-hollywood-step-779986, permalinked on April 22, 2016, at https://perma.cc/KRR2-UNRF.

62 Anthony Cocciolo, "Public Libraries and PBS Partnering to Enhance Civic Engagement: A Study of a Nationwide Initiative," *Public Library Quarterly* 32, no. 1 (2013): 1–20.

63 Bordwell, *Pandora's Digital Box.*

64 Heather Briston, "Understanding Copyright Law," in *Rights in the Digital Era,* ed. Menzi L. Behrnd-Klodt and Christopher J. Prom (Chicago: Society of American Archivists, 2015).

65 Michael Freeman, *The Complete Guide to Light and Lighting in Digital Photography* (New York: Lark Books, 2007).

66 Tom Sito, *Moving Innovation: A History of Computer Animation* (Cambridge, MA: MIT Press, 2013).

67 Ibid.

68 Ibid.

69 Ibid.

70 For some background on preserving architectural 3-D models, see Anthony Cocciolo, "Digitally Archiving Architectural Models and Exhibition Designs: The Case of an Art Museum," *Practical Technology for Archives,* no. 4 (2015), http:// practicaltechnologyforarchives.org/issue4_cocciolo/, permalinked on April 22, 2016, at https://perma.cc/BF3S-99FK.

CHAPTER 9

Analog Video Collections

OVERVIEW

As with audio collections, the best practice in maintaining video collections for long-term preservation is to migrate the content to digital files that are then stored in trustworthy digital repositories. Acknowledging that this is an expensive, time-consuming, and labor-intensive prospect, this chapter will discuss ways that this work can be delayed, as well as steps for beginning to do the work. However, before format migration is discussed, some basic background on analog video is presented.

BRIEF HISTORICAL BACKGROUND

Analog video encompasses a wide range of uses, with most occurring from the 1950s through the early 2000s. Its earliest use was recording of broadcast television for rebroadcast in the various time zones of the United States.[1] In an interesting intersection of popular culture and media history, the actor and singer Bing Crosby invested in early efforts by the Ampex Corporation to record television to magnetic tape after his successful investment in Ampex's audio recording technology.[2] Through the efforts of Ampex, video recording of television began with the introduction in 1956 of Quadruplex format, which recorded monochrome video onto two-inch-wide open-reel tape.[3] Although television had been available in the United States since 1946, recording television—if it was recorded at all—required photographing it onto film using a device called the kinescope (a process called telerecording in the United

Kingdom).[4] Videotape had the advantage of being reusable, allowing tapes to be overwritten for the next broadcast.[5] This unfortunately led to the loss of much important early television.[6]

Color television was authorized for broadcast in the United States in 1953; however, it was not until the early 1960s that color television sets were purchased in large numbers by viewers.[7] Further, not all television content was broadcast in color until the early 1960s.[8] To be broadcast in color, the program had to be either live or played back from color film. This began to change, however, with Ampex's introduction of a color videotape recorder in 1958.[9]

Innovations in professional video recording proceeded through the 1950s, 1960s, and 1970s, especially spawned by competition among US companies such as Ampex and RCA and Japanese companies such as Sony, Panasonic, and JVC.[10] Innovations include the introduction of cartridge-based videotapes and portable video recorders that could be used by television news agencies.[11]

Video sprang from the broadcast centers and into individuals' homes with the advent of Betamax and VHS in the late 1970s, which made rerecordable video technology available to consumers.[12] This brought with it a burgeoning market for films on video, first on VHS and eventually on DVD and Blu-ray. Films on video became available for rental through video stores, including stores owned by individuals as well as large chain stores such as Blockbuster Video and Hollywood Video.[13] Video stores are now nearly extinct—although some persist—as rental of video was surpassed first by Netflix circulating DVDs through the postal service, and more recently by Internet streaming services offered by Amazon and Netflix.[14]

As video developed for commercial distribution of film works, it brought with it the rise of video for recording family activities (unseating small-gauge film formats like Super 8) and for documenting meetings and events.[15] Throughout this time, video as a concept has shifted away from being very much about broadcast television; now, as described by media studies professor Michael Z. Newman, "video has come to include practically any kind of object combining motion pictures and sound."[16]

SIGNAL ENCODING

The earliest form of video is analog video, where a representation of the image and sound is encoded in a wide range of electromagnetic signals onto some physical medium like magnetic tape. While the sound track uses similar technology to that discussed in chapter 7, "Audio Collections," the moving image in analog video does not use any technology similar to film. With film, the images are encoded as individual photographic frames that are shown in quick succession with a brief blackout frame in between. Relatedly, analog video differs from digital photography, where images have pixels with bit depths. Although there are frames in analog video, there are no pixels, as the moving image is made up of lines that are drawn on the screen. The earliest form of video provided for 480 lines drawn from left to right—a format called NTSC (National Television System Committee). NTSC was adopted in the United States in 1953 and used in other countries such as Canada, Japan, and parts of Latin America.[17] Television was broadcast in this format in the United States until 2009. This format showed the viewer about 30 frames every second (29.97 frames, to be exact).[18]

Interestingly, different regions of the world encode the video signal using other schemes. For example, in the United Kingdom, they use a format called PAL (Phase Alternating Line), and in France a format called SECAM (*Séquentiel couleur avec mémoire*), both of which provide for 576 lines.[19] For an

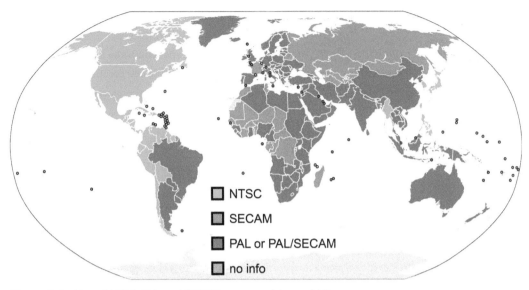

Figure 9-1. Map of NTSC, PAL, and SECAM use around the world.[20]

archivist, knowing the encoding format of a work is important; one can try to play a videotape and conclude wrongly that there is something wrong with it because it plays back garbled video. However, it is possible that the tape is simply encoded differently. Some video players support the three different encodings (NTSC, SECAM, and PAL); however, this is rare, and most players only support the predominant format in the country the player was sold in. Also, a video player generally does not indicate that it is attempting to play a video encoded in a different format. For a map of which countries used which standard, see figure 9-1.

Video that is encoded with 480 lines of NTSC or 576 lines for SECAM or PAL represent standard-definition (SD) video. This was the type of video or television that most people grew up with, which was watched on the boxy televisions. SD video has been superseded by high-definition video displayed on flat-panel televisions.

An analog video camera breaks an image into a series of scan lines. Typically, consumer formats can represent fewer scan lines than professional videotape formats of the same era. Magnetic videotape encodes a range of electromagnetic signals corresponding to the colors represented within the line. For example, the color orange is represented with a specific electromagnetic signal (or voltage), and that signal is used each time that color needs to be represented in the line.[21]

ANALOG VIDEO COLOR SPACE

Also worth noting about analog video is that it uses a color space that is different from the color space used to display video on computers. Computers use the RGB color space, where numbers are used to specify the red, green, and blue parts of an image. If you have ever created a web page and had to specify colors using hexadecimal values such as "#FF0000" for red or "#FFFF00" for yellow, then you have some experience with the RGB color space. The aforementioned examples represent 24-bit color, where the first 8 bits are for red, the second 8 bits are for green, and the last 8 bits are for blue. The numbers are represented as hexadecimal digits that are more compact than ordinary numbers, also known as base-10 numbers. For example, "FF" in hexadecimal is "255" in base-10 numbers. Instead of RGB, color analog video uses a color space called YCrBr, where the black-and-white component of the image (or the luminance) is separated from the color components (or the chrominance).[22] In the computer applications, this color space is often referred to as YUV. Separation of the color from the black-and-white signal was needed to accommodate the introduction of color television and the need to maintain backward compatibility (e.g., the ability to watch color broadcast on a black-and-white television). When displaying analog video on modern-day computers, it is necessary for the computer to convert from that color space to the RGB color space upon playback.

DISPLAY TECHNOLOGY

When analog video was broadcast over television or recorded onto video, the image was interlaced. Since the entire image could not be sent at once because of limitations of broadcast technology, all of the even lines would be sent first, and then the odd lines.[23] Because this process of interlacing happens very quickly, viewers generally did not notice how the image was being woven together in this way, much as they did not notice the blackout frames in film. This is something to keep in mind when digitizing video, as most computer users have stopped using CRT (cathode-ray tube) displays that interlace the image in favor of progressive scan displays, such as flat-panel displays like LCD or LED.[24] For access copies, it may be necessary to deinterlace the video so it renders the image smoothly on progressive scan displays.

ANALOG VIDEO PRESERVATION CHALLENGES

According to the Association of Moving Image Archivists (AMIA) *Videotape Preservation Fact Sheets*, all analog video formats except VHS are threatened, endangered, critically endangered, or extinct.[25] VHS is not endangered because of the wide variety of players available and the fact that replacement models can still sometimes be purchased new. However, in 2016 the final manufacturer of VHS players ceased production, which will likely result in VHS players having to be purchased used like many other video players.[26] All other formats are endangered because manufacture of the machines has ceased, or even more endangered because there is a dwindling supply of spare parts for fixing them. For example, a *Washington Post* reporter interviewed Paul Klamer, the video lab supervisor at the Library of Congress's Packard Campus of the National Audio-Visual Conservation Center: "Today there are barely one hundred working Ampex [Quadruplex] units in the world, Klamer says, making them rarer than Edsels. Packard owns twenty-seven of the machines (original price $100,000), only two of which are operational."[27] Thus, when making digital reformatting decisions, it may make sense to deprioritize VHS in favor of any other analog tape formats.

Figure 9-2. The ubiquitous VHS tape, found in most archival collections.

FREQUENTLY OCCURRING FORMATS: VHS AND ITS DERIVATIVES

Analog video always appears on specialized magnetic tape carriers. The format most archivists are likely to encounter, in extensive quantities no doubt, is VHS, short for "Video Home System." (See figure 9-2.) VHS is a low-image-quality consumer format that was introduced in 1976 and rose to popularity in the early 1980s; it is still used in some niche markets today. Because of its low cost and ubiquity, it was used to create home videos and also was used in low- to mid-resourced professional contexts, such as recordings of oral histories, meetings, and events. For example, sessions of Congress were recorded on professional videotape formats, not VHS, but many educational projects and low-resourced film projects were recorded onto VHS.[28] Further, commercial works like Hollywood films were widely released onto VHS, which allowed for consumers to purchase films on VHS as well as rent them from video stores.[29]

Although broadcast technology was able to render 480 lines of image resolution, VHS is only able to render 240 lines of resolution from left to right.[30] Thus, images recorded from broadcast television to VHS should look less sharp and include less detail. Since analog video, like VHS, is comprised not of pixels but of lines, the only way to determine a pixel dimension or resolution is to perform an estimation. In *DVD Demystified*, Jim Taylor estimates that VHS tapes have image resolutions of 333 x 360 pixels.[31]

Most VHS players, like other videotape players, allow for the recording of tapes at SP (standard play), LP (long play), and SLP (super long play) or EP (extended play) modes.[32] If recorded at SP mode, a sixty-minute tape will allow for sixty minutes of content recorded. LP mode allows for one and a half to two times that amount of content to be recorded; however, LP mode degrades the image quality.[33] EP or SLP mode allows for three or more times the recording time of SP mode, further degrading the image quality.[34] Usually the VHS player selects the correct playback mode. However, if it does not, there is usually a button on the front of the player or on the remote that allows you to select other modes. The mode that renders the image and sound with the least errors is typically the correct mode.

S-VHS

Although much less common than VHS, this format will be discussed here because of its close relationship to VHS. S-VHS looks just like a VHS tape; however, it should include an S-VHS logo rather than a VHS logo. Despite the similarities in appearance, S-VHS tapes will not play on VHS players. However, VHS tapes will play on S-VHS players. S-VHS tapes use 400 scan lines, thus making for much sharper and more detailed images than VHS tapes afford.[35] S-VHS never became very popular, despite the increase in resolution. Introduced in 1987, the players and tapes were more expensive than VHS and did not incorporate HDTV—which was emerging in the late 1980s—thus inhibiting adoption.[36]

VHS-C AND S-VHS-C

VHS-C and S-VHS-C use VHS and S-VHS technology, respectively; however, the tape cartridge is smaller and is designed to fit inside a camcorder. These tapes can be played on VHS and S-VHS players, respectively, but require an adapter. (See figure 9-3.)

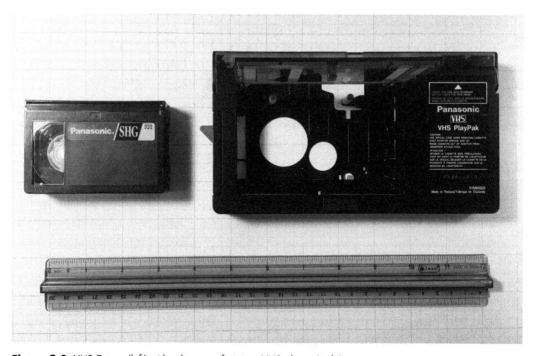

Figure 9-3. VHS-C tape (left) with adapter to fit it to a VHS player (right).

Figure 9-4. Two sizes of U-matic and U-matic SP tapes.

PROFESSIONAL FORMATS

An archives can find a variety of professional analog videotape formats depending on the communities that it collects from. These tapes look similar to VHS tapes, which most archivists are familiar with; however, they require playback equipment specific to each format. Professional formats that occur with some frequency include U-matic, Betacam, and Betacam SP, all of which should be labeled as such. (See figure 9-4.)

U-matic tapes were introduced by Sony in 1971 and provided for 250 lines of resolution.[37] These tapes were used for recording television programs and other programming requiring professional videography. U-matic SP ("superior performance") tapes were introduced in 1986 and provided for 300 lines of resolution. U-Matic SP VTRs can play U-matic tapes, but not vice versa. Because of the age of these

Figure 9-5. Two sizes of Betacam and Betacam SP tapes.

tapes and the dwindling number of players available for the format, they should be prioritized for digital reformatting.[38] U-matic tapes come in two sizes, as shown in figure 9-4.[39]

Betacam tapes were introduced in 1982 and offered 360 lines of resolution. Betacam SP ("superior performance") was introduced in 1986 and provided for 450 lines of resolution. Betacam and Betacam SP tapes come in two sizes, as shown in figure 9-5. Betacam SP players can play Betacam tapes, but not vice versa. Like U-matic tapes, these tapes were used for recording television programs and other activities needing professional videography.

Many professional videotape formats such as Betacam include time code information that is not shown to the viewer. Time code records the hours, minutes, and seconds in the recording; it is used for editing and synchronizing videos. (Consumer formats like VHS do not have time code.) When digitizing professional videotape formats, the time code should also be digitized because it is part of the original video artifact and can provide insight into the making of the video.

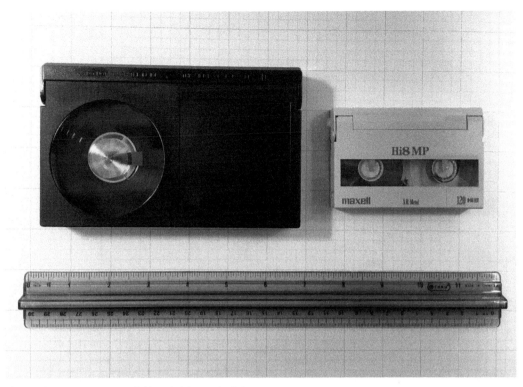

Figure 9-6. Betamax tape (left) and Hi8 tape (right).

ADDITIONAL CONSUMER FORMATS

In addition to the professional formats mentioned above, archivists could encounter analog formats designed more for the consumer market. These include Betamax, Video8, and Hi8. Betamax and Hi8 tapes are shown in figure 9-6. Video8 and Hi8 tapes look the same but are labeled differently.

Betamax was introduced to the consumer market in 1975 and provided consumers with 250 lines of resolution, thus providing a somewhat better image than VHS.[40] Because of the age of this format, players are becoming more difficult to find. For this reason, migration of Betamax tapes to digital files is recommended.

Video8 and Hi8 tapes were used in camcorders in the consumer market. Video8, also known as 8 mm video or Standard 8, was introduced in 1984 and provided for 260 lines of resolution.[41] Hi8 replaced Video8 in 1989 and provided for 400 lines of resolution. Tapes in these formats can often be read by Digital8 camcorders, which ultimately replaced both Video8 and Hi8. A Digital8 camcorder in shown in figure 9-7.

Lesser-known consumer formats include tapes labeled VCR (1971), VCR Long Play (1975), and SVR / Super Video (1978).[42] These VCR acronyms should not be confused with the more common meaning of VCR, videocassette recorder. These videotapes appear in identical cassettes but require separate players. Lastly, Video 2000 (1979) was another consumer tape format that can be found.[43]

Figure 9-7. A Digital8 camcorder, which can play Digital8, Hi8, and Video8 tapes.

ADDITIONAL PROFESSIONAL FORMATS

A variety of professional videotape formats may crop up in archives. These include the oldest video-tapes, which are open-reel formats that come in sizes of a half inch, one-inch, and two-inch tape. These tape formats were used from the 1950s into the 1970s, when they were superseded by cartridge-based videotapes such as U-matic.[44] The earliest makers of videotape players include the Ampex Corporation. A two-inch tape (the size used in Ampex's earliest machines, often called a two-inch Quad, short for Quadruplex) and one-inch tape are shown in figure 9-8.[45] Because there are few players left for playing these formats, it is imperative to digitize such tapes.

Other professional videotape formats that may be encountered are tapes labeled MII; they were introduced in 1986 and come in two sizes.[46]

ANALOG VIDEO REFORMATTING: PLAYBACK

When digitizing analog video, the necessary components are the playback equipment, a capture device, and a computer for receiving the captured digital file. Each videotape format requires specific playback equipment. Purchasing well-maintained equipment that has been cleaned or restored by a reputable seller is recommended.

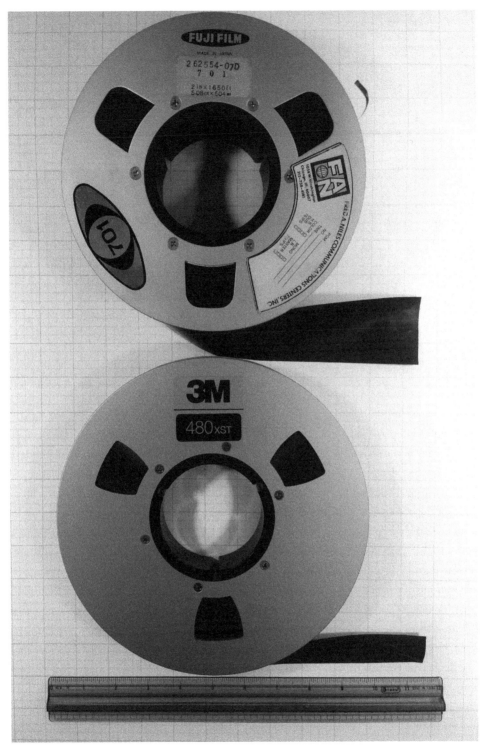

Figure 9-8. Open-reel videotapes: two-inch tape (top) and one-inch tape (bottom).

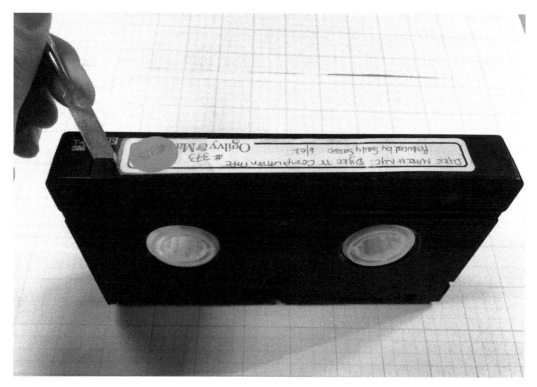

Figure 9-9. Removing the tab from a VHS tape keeps it from being recorded over.

Although VHS players can still sometimes be bought new, I find that some of the high-end devices from the heyday of the technology provide image quality that is superior to that of the newer devices.

Some devices allow for cleaning through the use of cleaning cartridges, which remove interior debris from the playback equipment. Also, always test a video player with a test tape before putting in an archival tape, especially after cleaning. Further, be sure to engage the write protection on the tape before digitizing so that if the record button on the player is accidentally hit, it will not record over the tape. For example, on VHS tape, you can use a minispatula to pop out the write-protection tab. (See figure 9-9.)

Before putting a tape in the player, inspect it for any physical damage or deterioration. This can include warping of the plastic tape housing. Also, open the plastic door protecting the tape and make sure that the tape does not have any damage, such as wrinkling or warping. On VHS tapes, there is a small button that, when depressed, allows you to open the plastic door. (See figure 9-10.) If a tape is damaged, it is more likely to get jammed in the player, which may damage the tape further and possibly damage the player. For this reason, if a tape shows signs of physical deterioration, contact a video conservator. The Specs Bros LLC, who are audio and video preservation specialists, provide a useful white paper on inspecting the physical condition of videotape, which includes looking for bent or ripped tape, fungus, smells that indicate deterioration, and other kinds of decomposition.[47]

As the tape is playing, if you hear any unusual sounds, stop the tape immediately and eject it. If a tape gets stuck in a player and will not eject, it is necessary to not yank the tape out but rather to unscrew the cover from the player and manually remove the tape. Avoid touching the tape; if it must be touched, use cotton gloves so as not to leave fingerprints and hand oils on the tape. Alternatively, use tweezers or other clean tools.

Figure 9-10. Inspecting the tape inside a VHS cartridge for deterioration or damage.

During playback, it may be necessary to adjust the tracking controls. These controls allow for slight modifications in the speed at which the tape is played, thus permitting some variation in how tapes are manufactured and recorded.[48] Unlike audiotapes—which, when played faster or slower, sound fast or slow—if a video is played too fast or slow, the image will degrade with static and lines. Many newer VCRs will adjust the tracking automatically. However, if the tracking is not adjusted automatically, it can be adjusted manually with the control on the front of the device or on the remote control. The best approach is to start in the middle and try it different ways until the image stabilizes.

ANALOG VIDEO REFORMATTING: SIDE-BY-SIDE TESTING

The objective of analog video digitization is to render the video as a computer file with no loss of the original content. This is possible; however, it requires some care in selecting the capture hardware and ensuring the quality of the digitization. When selecting a capture device, my recommendation is to test the capture device first for image and sound quality. To do this, use the capture device to digitize a few minutes of video. Then, connect the player to a CRT television, and compare the digitized playback with the version shown on the CRT monitor. Alternatively, if your configuration allows, watch the digitized output on the computer side by side with the version on the CRT television concurrently. CRT monitors are the boxy televisions that many people had in their homes until recently, when they were replaced by flat-panel HDTVs. It is possible to find high-quality CRT televisions for nearly no money at all. It may be somewhat embarrassing to admit, but on trash day one can find some very nice CRT televisions on the curbs of New York City streets!

The CRT version should represent the original look of the image, as long as the tape itself has not degraded and the tape player is functioning properly. When comparing the two versions, look for any reduction of detail in the digitized version, reduction in the range of colors displayed, or introduction of any digitization artifacts. Digitization artifacts are elements that are not in the original video signal but are introduced during the digitization process. These artifacts can include elements such as lines running side to side or up and down across the images. Also, use headphones to listen for the introduction of any noises that are not present in the CRT version.

The human eye and brain can be very forgiving and can make sense of images even with a wide range of distortions. It is very easy for someone to look at the playback of a VHS tape using a low-quality capture device and assume that the image quality is low because "that's how things were back then." When comparing the digitized video side by side with the original CRT version, you may well find that a great deal of image quality is being lost and that many digitization artifacts are being introduced. If this is the case during your test, it is necessary to use another capture device.

I have tested a variety of capture devices and can attest that some are very low quality. Using capture devices that go straight to formats such as MPEG4/H.264 and do not include higher-quality output options should be avoided, even in the most resource-constrained contexts. The image quality produced by such devices is usually inferior, resulting in image stability issues, erosion of color, and introduction of digitization artifacts. High-quality makers of capture devices include Blackmagic Design and AJA Video Systems; however, their devices should still be tested for quality assurance.[49]

DIGITIZATION ARTIFACTS

A wide range of artifacts can be introduced during the process of digitization. These include artifacts of digitization but can also include problems with the analog video signal that become apparent during the digitization process. The goal with digitization of analog video is to eliminate those artifacts or to make them as negligible as possible. Since analog video uses lines, not pixels, the introduction of any pixilation or boxiness in images is likely an artifact of digitization or compression of the digital imagery. These artifacts have names like mosquito noise, which introduces pixels around a part of the image, or quilting, which makes images blocky, like a quilt. There are so many possible artifacts that the Bay Area Video Coalition (BAVC) created the *A/V Artifact Atlas*, which catalogs and describes many possible artifacts that can occur during playback and digitization.[50] The excellent *Compendium of Image Errors in Analogue Video* also includes a catalog of errors that may appear, with possible causes.[51]

FORMATS FOR DIGITIZATION OF ANALOG VIDEO: CODECS

Before discussing formats for digitizing video, some background information is necessary. All born-digital or digitized video files are wrapped in a container or wrapper. Within the wrapper, there can be multiple streams, typically an audio stream and a video stream. Each of the audio and video tracks—collectively often called the essence—is encoded using a codec.[52] The codec is necessary for encoding the video and audio, as well as decoding them. A simple video encoder may arrange 30 TIFF files per second in succession, which is a simple encoding scheme similar to how an uncompressed video codec works.[53] Lossy compression codecs—to save disk space and transmission requirements—may encode video differently. For example, for a blue screen that lasts 10 seconds, it is much more economical to encode something like "blue screen-10 seconds," rather than have to store 300 identical TIF files.

Whereas file extensions like .MOV and .AVI indicate the wrapper of a file and the best program to open the video (QuickTime and Windows Media Player, in these cases), they do not indicate the codec used to encode the video or audio. For example, a single AVI file could have content that is encoded with dozens—if not hundreds—of different types of codecs. When considering the ability to digitally preserve a particular video format, it is necessary to think about the preservation of the wrapper as well as the essence. In sum, a file extension alone does not tell you a great deal about the codecs needed to play back a video. Rather, the software that plays the video needs to read the contents of the file and determine the appropriate codec needed to play back the video.

RECOMMENDED CODECS AND WRAPPERS

The best practice in digitizing analog video is to create 10-bit uncompressed YUV video.[54] This standard allows for 10 bits for red, 10 for green, and 10 for blue, which allows for a wide range of colors (1,024 variations of each color). These files can be wrapped using wrappers like MOV, AVI, and MXF. The image dimensions should be 720 x 486 pixels.[55] This configuration is as faithful to the original analog video as possible, maintaining both the color space and the interlacing of frames.

Figure 9-11 illustrates a configuration that enables the creation of these files. In this figure, a Sony U-matic VTR (right) is connected via a composite video cable and two audio cables to a Blackmagic Design UltraStudio 4K analog-to-digital converter (center, middle). The VTR is also connected to an analog monitor (center), which shows the output of the VTR playback. The analog-to-digital converter is connected to an iMac computer via a Thunderbolt cable. The software program Blackmagic Media Express is used to capture 10-bit uncompressed YUV files wrapped in QuickTime (MOV) wrappers. An advantage of this configuration is that the analog playback and the digital capture can be readily compared for accuracy.

The audio should be encoded using 24-bit bit depth and 48 kHz sampling rate with pulse-code modulation (PCM).[56] For more background on this audio encoding, see chapter 7, "Audio Collections."

The downside of 10-bit uncompressed YUV video is that one hour of standard-definition video can result in a file about 100 GB in size.[57] Thus, compressing video makes a lot of sense. However, avoid using lossy video encoders, such as the popular MPEG4/H.264, which discard visual information from the video. These lossy formats work well for access but should not be used to create preservation masters. These encoders remove visual information from the image that the algorithm developers think the viewer will not notice. If lossy formats such as MPEG4/H.264 are used for reasons of economics, their use should be reserved for videos that will not be exhibited in any way and in which the visual information is of low importance. See chapter 1, "Appraisal and Reappraisal," for considerations on using lossy video compression.

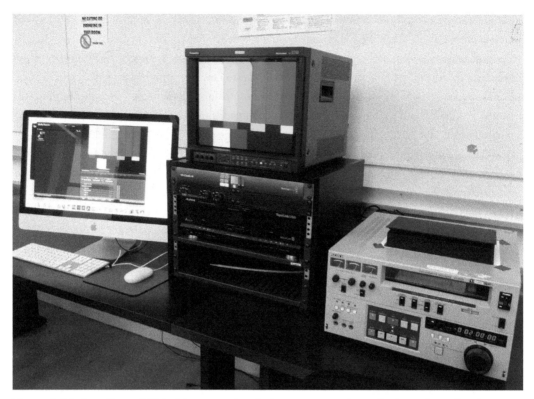

Figure 9-11. Sony U-matic VTR (right) connected to Blackmagic Design UltraStudio 4K analog-to-digital converter (center, middle) connected to an iMac via a Thunderbolt cable.

Lossless compression shrinks the file size but does not remove any visual information. ZIP files are the perfect example of lossless compression: nothing is lost between when files are zipped up and then unzipped for use. Strategies for shrinking file sizes in a lossless way may include reconfiguring how the bits are used. For example, 10-bit video reserves 10 bits for red, enabling 1,024 variations of red. However, what if only 180 shades of red are used in a given video? In this case, it would be possible to remap those shades of red onto an 8-bit universe. Although saving two bits does not sound like much, if you consider that every analog video frame has almost thirty frames a second, and a video can run more than an hour, the savings start to add up. A lossy compression algorithm can work in this way: Although 180 shades of red are detected, some are similar enough that they could be considered the same, and thus only 120 variations get encoded into the file. However, once those 60 shades have been discarded from the file, there is no way to get them back—thus we call this form of compression "lossy."

There are lossless video encoders that compress the file size but do not discard any of the original information. One format is Motion JPEG 2000, which is used by the Library of Congress.[58] This encoder shrinks videos by more than half, leading to the file size of an hour of standard-definition video being about 50 GB.[59] Another lossless encoder is the FFV1 format, which is used by the archives of CUNY TV, among others.[60] The popular MPEG4/H.264 codec is almost always used for creating lossy videos; however, there are some options that can be passed to the encoder for creating lossless videos. Despite these options, this codec is rarely used for encoding lossless videos, and using it for this purpose is not highly recommended.

The advantage of all these codecs is that there is open documentation for them; thus they align well with digital preservation standards.

ALTERNATIVES

Although creating 10-bit uncompressed YUV master video, or using lossless compression on such videos using Motion JPEG 2000 or FFV1, is the best option, there are some suboptimal solutions. For low-quality consumer formats like VHS, one option is to play back the VHS to a DV deck or DV camcorder (like a MiniDV camcorder) and import DV versions of the video over FireWire using software like Adobe Premiere or Apple Final Cut Pro.[61] Related options include importing DV files using a dedicated analog-to-DV converter device. DV is a digital video format that was introduced in 1996 and stores video as digital information (1s and 0s) rather than as a range of electromagnetic signals.[62] The file size for standard-definition video imported as DV is about 12 GB for an hour, making this a very economical option.[63] The downside of this option is that although the images are stable and have good detail, the color conversion is of lower quality. Specifically, when doing a side-by-side comparison of a digitized DV version of a video with the analog counterpart displayed on a CRT monitor, I notice that the DV color can be slightly washed out. This is likely because this variety of DV only supports 8-bit color, which allows for 8 bits for red, 8 bits for green, and 8 bits for blue, amounting to only 256 shades of each color. This is considerably less than 10-bit color, which allows for 1,024 shades of each color. Thus, this option should be reserved for the most low-resourced institutions.

Figure 9-12. VHS player and DVCAM deck connected via RCA cables.

Figure 9-12 illustrates a Samsung VHS player (capable of playing NTSC, PAL, and SECAM encoded tapes), with a Sony DVCAM DSR-11 deck on top connected via RCA cables (the yellow cable for video and the red and white cable for stereo audio). The DVCAM deck is connected to a computer via FireWire. The VHS tape is played back to the DVCAM deck, which then converts the signal to digital information and sends it to Adobe Premiere over FireWire. (See figure 9-13.)

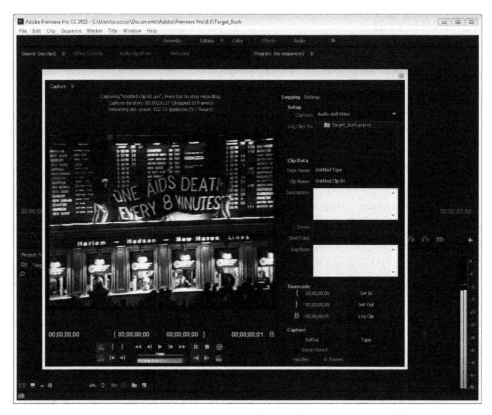

Figure 9-13. The DVCAM deck converts an analog signal to digital information and sends it via FireWire to the computer, where it is captured in Adobe Premiere.[64]

CAPTURE SOFTWARE

When capturing video using a capture device, software such as Adobe Premiere or Apple's Final Cut Pro can be used. Alternatively, the software that is available from makers of the capture device (like Blackmagic Media Express) can be used.[65]

TRIAL AND ERROR

Unfortunately, with analog video, there is no one perfect player or capture device for some formats. Often, when reformatting, you may need to try more than one player and more than one capture device. Try to find a player that preserves the image detail and color and introduces the fewest errors, such as lines running across the screen. Once this has been achieved, try more than one capture device (if you have more than one) and use the one that produces the best digital version. Then it will not be necessary to settle for a problematic digitization; trial and error can achieve a better result. The drawback of trial and error is that it can be labor intensive; it may need to be reserved for the most important records. If you do not have the time or inclination to engage in this sort of trial and error, consider working with a reputable video reformatting firm.

HOUSING AND STORAGE

The life of analog video carriers can be extended through storage in a stable environment that controls for temperature and humidity. The storage environment for analog video is the same as for analog audio collections, and thus they can be stored together in the same room. The recommended room temperature is between 46°F and 53°F, with 25–35 percent relative humidity; videotapes should never be subjected to freezing temperatures.[66] Videotapes should be stored upright in their original containers, in acid-free boxes or directly on shelves.[67]

AFTER DIGITIZATION

As with audio collections, the original video carrier should be retained unless storage pressures are present. See chapter 7, "Audio Collections," for recommendations on what to do with the original carriers; the recommendations are largely the same for video collections.

After preservation masters have been created, derivatives based on those masters should also be created. Derivatives can include a mezzanine file, which is a high-quality version of the master that should satisfy most users. This file may differ from the master in that it has been deinterlaced and subjected to some compression. Additionally, an access file or files can be created from the mezzanine file, based on the needs of users. For example, streaming files over the Internet usually requires additional compression, which may include shrinking the dimensions of the video to make the file more compact. See chapter 5, "Access and Outreach," for more discussion on making digitized video available to users.

OUTSOURCING OF VIDEO DIGITIZATION

The advice provided in chapter 7, "Audio Collections," applies well to video and can be used for thinking about outsourcing a video digitization project. Further, New York University provides a helpful RFP (request for proposals) template for digitizing video for long-term preservation.[68] This resource should be consulted when assembling an RFP.

CONCLUSION

The recommended practice in preserving analog video is to reformat it as digital files and store the files in trusted digital repositories. As analog video is obsolete, and tape players for nearly all formats are dwindling in number, it is necessary to think about format migration. VHS tapes—found in large quantities in archives—have an abundance of players that can be found for playback, and thus formats other than VHS should be prioritized for preservation reformatting. However, historically significant or frequently accessed content on VHS could be prioritized. Digitization can be delayed to some extent through storing tapes in a stable, cold, and dry environment. However, even in such an environment, the media will eventually deteriorate, and players will become increasingly scarce.

NOTES

1. Jim Wheeler, Peter Brothers, and Hannah Frost, *Videotape Preservation Factsheets* (Hollywood, CA: Association of Moving Image Archivists, 2007), http://www.amianet.org/sites/all/files/fact_sheets_0.pdf, permalinked on April 4, 2016, at https://perma.cc/XZ9Q-QQGE.

2. Finn Jorgensen, "Early Fixed-Head Video Recorders," in *Magnetic Recording: The First 100 Years*, ed. Eric D. Daniel, C. Denis Mee, and Mark H. Clark (Piscataway, NJ: IEEE Press, 1999), 137–52.

3. Frederick M. Remley, "The Challenge of Recording Video," in *Magnetic Recording: The First 100 Years*, 124–36.

4. Roy Armes, *On Video* (London: Routledge, 1988); Leo Enticknap, *Moving Image Technology: From Zoetrope to Digital* (London: Wallflower Press, 2005).

5. Enticknap, *Moving Image Technology*.

6. William T. Murphy, *Television and Video Preservation 1997: A Report on the Current State of American Television and Video Preservation* (Washington, DC: Library of Congress, 1997), https://www.loc.gov/programs/static/national-film-preservation-board/documents/tvstudy.pdf, permalinked on April 4, 2016, at https://perma.cc/8UZ4-868Y.

7. Giraud Chester, Garnet R. Garrison, and Edgar E. Willis, *Television and Radio,* 3rd ed. (New York: Appleton-Century-Crofts, 1963).

8. Ibid.

9. Albert Abramson, *The History of Television: 1942 to 2000* (Jefferson, NC: McFarland, 2003).

10. Hiroshi Sugaya, "Helical-Scan Recorders for Broadcasting," in *Magnetic Recording: The First 100 Years*, 170–81.

11. Ibid.

12. Enticknap, *Moving Image Technology*.

13. Daniel Herbert, *Videoland: Movie Culture at the American Video Store* (Berkeley, CA: University of California Press, 2014).

14. Ibid.

15. Eugene Marlow and Eugene Secunda, *Shifting Time and Space: The Story of Videotape* (New York: Praeger, 1991).

16. Michael Z. Newman, *Video Revolutions: On the History of a Medium* (New York: Columbia University Press, 2014), 73.

17. Johannes Gfeller, Agathe Jarczyk, and Joanna Phillips, *Compendium of Image Errors in Analogue Video* (Zurich: Schweizerisches Institut für Kunstwissenschaft, 2012).

18. George Blood, *Refining Conversion Contract Specifications: Determining Suitable Digital Video Formats for Medium-term Storage* (Washington, DC: Library of Congress, 2011), http://www.digitizationguidelines.gov/audio-visual/documents/IntrmMastVidFormatRecs_20111001.pdf, permalinked on April 5, 2016, at https://perma.cc/L58A-38NV.

19. Ibid.

20. Public domain image courtesy of https://en.wikipedia.org/wiki/NTSC#/media/File:PAL-NTSC-SECAM.svg, permalinked on April 5, 2016, at https://perma.cc/SXK6-LABL.

21. James Snyder, "Moving Image Archiving: Digitizing Present and Future," Issues and Answers in Digitization Workshop Series, Library of Congress, Washington, DC, January 24, 2011, http://www.cendi.gov/activities/01_24_11_video_digitizing.html, permalinked on April 5, 2016, at https://perma.cc/K78R-5ZLM.

22. Keith Jack, *Video Demystified: A Handbook for the Digital Engineer*, 5th ed. (Amsterdam: Newnes, 2007).

23. Marcus Weise and Diana Weynand, *How Video Works: From Analog to High Definition,* 2nd ed. (Amsterdam: Elsevier, 2007).

24. Ibid.

25. Wheeler, Brothers, and Frost, *Videotape Preservation Factsheets*.

26. Jonah Engel Bromwich, "The Long, Final Goodbye of the VCR," *New York Times*, July 21, 2016, http://www.nytimes.com/2016/07/22/technology/the-long-final-goodbye-of-the-vcr.html, permalinked on September 1, 2016, at https://perma.cc/CK55-DELV.

27. W. Barksdale Maynard, "Rescuers Rush to Preserve TV Shows Shot on Fragile Videotape," *Washington Post*, July 15, 2013, https://www.washingtonpost.com/national/health-science/rescuers-rush-to-preserve-tv-shows-shot-on-fragile-videotape/2013/07/15/ef6e2ee4-cd3c-11e2-8845-d970ccb04497_story.html, permalinked on April 5, 2016, at https://perma.cc/5N7A-WMSE.

28. Robert X. Browning, "The C-SPAN Video Archives: A Case Study," *American Archivist* 77, no. 2 (2014): 425–43.

29. Joshua M. Greenberg, *From Betamax to Blockbuster: Video Stores and the Invention of Movies on Video* (Cambridge, MA: MIT Press, 2010).

30. Gfeller, Jarczyk, and Phillips, *Compendium of Image Errors*.

31. Jim Taylor, *DVD Demystified* (New York: McGraw-Hill, 1998).

32. Gfeller, Jarczyk, and Phillips, *Compendium of Image Errors*.

33. Ibid.

34. Ibid.

35. Ibid.

36 Taylor, *DVD Demystified.*

37 Gfeller, Jarczyk, and Phillips, *Compendium of Image Errors*; "U-matic," *Wikipedia*, https://en.wikipedia.org/wiki/U-matic, permalinked on September 18, 2016, at https://perma.cc/3YHY-A873.

38 Wheeler, Brothers, and Frost, *Videotape Preservation Factsheets.*

39 Jeff Martin, *Curriculum Module: 3/4" U-matic Videotape* (2007), http://www.nyu.edu/tisch/preservation/program/modules/Martin_UmaticTape.pdf, permalinked on September 16, 2016, at https://perma.cc/4GY7-RUVK.

40 Gfeller, Jarczyk, and Phillips, *Compendium of Image Errors.*

41 Ibid.

42 Ibid.

43 Ibid.

44 Enticknap, *Moving Image Technology.*

45 Mona Jimenez and Lisa Platt, *Videotape Identification and Assessment Guide* (Austin: Texas Commission on the Arts, 2004), http://www.arts.texas.gov/wp-content/uploads/2012/04/video.pdf, permalinked on September 15, 2016, at https://perma.cc/PCL8-ZXQQ.

46 Gfeller, Jarczyk, and Phillips, *Compendium of Image Errors.*

47 Specs Bros LLC, *Whitepaper: Basic Inspection Techniques to Sample the Condition of Magnetic Tape* (n.d.), http://www.specsbros.com/white-paper-basic-inspection-techniques-to-sample-the-condition-of-magnetic-tape.html, permalinked on September 16, 2016, at https://perma.cc/KW4J-PZHM.

48 Ibid.

49 Blackmagic Design, https://www.blackmagicdesign.com/, permalinked on April 5, 2016, at https://perma.cc/SEH5-27NQ; AJA Video Systems, https://www.aja.com/, permalinked on April 5, 2016, at https://perma.cc/A7Q4-A58J.

50 Bay Area Video Coalition, *A/V Artifact Atlas*, http://avaa.bavc.org/, permalinked on April 5, 2016, at https://perma.cc/Z27V-3QH7.

51 Gfeller, Jarczyk, and Phillips, *Compendium of Image Errors.*

52 Chris Lacinak, *A Primer on Codecs for Moving Image and Sound Archives & 10 Recommendations for Codec Selection and Management* (Brooklyn, NY: AVPreserve, 2012), http://www.avpreserve.com/wp-content/uploads/2010/04/AVPS_Codec_Primer.pdf, permalinked on April 5, 2016, at https://perma.cc/42EW-378C.

53 Ian Bogus et al., *Minimum Digitization Capture Recommendations* (Chicago: Association for Library Collections and Technical Services Preservation and Reformatting Section, 2013), http://www.ala.org/alcts/resources/preserv/minimum-digitization-capture-recommendations#video, permalinked on April 5, 2016, at https://perma.cc/9E7H-6E54.

54 Blood, *Refining Conversion.*

55 Ibid.

56 Ibid.

57 Snyder, "Moving Image Archiving."

58 Blood, *Refining Conversion.* Also recommended in Jim Linder et al., *Digital Video Preservation Reformatting Project* (Washington, DC: Dance Heritage Coalition and New York: Media Matters, 2004), http://www.danceheritage.org/digitalvideopreservation.pdf, permalinked on September 15, 2016, at https://perma.cc/EPF3-683N.

59 Snyder, "Moving Image Archiving."

60 "FFV1," *Wikipedia*, https://en.wikipedia.org/wiki/FFV1, permalinked on September 16, 2016, at https://perma.cc/X7TW-NG3D.

61 "PrestoSpace Migration Paths for Video Media," http://www.preservationguide.co.uk/RDWiki/pmwiki.php?n=Main.Roadmap, permalinked on April 5, 2016, at https://perma.cc/2UEC-C3MY.

62 Wheeler, Brothers, and Frost, *Videotape Preservation Factsheets.*

63 Assumes 25 Mbit/sec DV.

64 Video being captured is from *Target Bush*, AIDS Community Television, 1993, from the collection of the Lesbian Herstory Archives.

65 Blackmagic Design Media Express, https://www.blackmagicdesign.com/products/intensity/mediaexpress, permalinked on April 5, 2016, at https://perma.cc/Q4H5-FCW3.

66 Dietrich Schüller and Albrecht Häfner, eds., *Handling and Storage of Audio and Video Carriers: Technical Committee Standards, Recommended Practices, and Strategies* (London: International Association of Sound and Audiovisual Archives, 2014).

67 Ibid.

68 Paula De Stefano et al., *Digitizing Video for Long-Term Preservation: An RFP Guide and Template* (New York: New York University Libraries, 2013), http://library.nyu.edu/preservation/VARRFP.pdf, permalinked on April 5, 2016, at https://perma.cc/69B5-FD78.

CHAPTER 10

Digital Video Collections

Perhaps it is a somewhat obvious point, but born-digital video does not need to be digitized for preservation because it is already digital. However, this does not mean that there are no preservation challenges. Like analog video carriers, digital video carriers face deterioration and obsolescence challenges, and thus the recommended practice is to migrate the video to computer files and store them in trusted digital repositories. Before these practices are outlined, a brief historical background on digital video is provided.

BRIEF HISTORICAL BACKGROUND

The possibility of using digital technology as a video capture and storage medium intensified with the maturation of the semiconductor industry.[1] The earliest interest in recording video as digital information grew out of military needs of the 1960s, such as the need to encrypt video transmissions of the color television network connecting major US military sites.[2] Since it is nearly impossible to encrypt analog television signal, digital technology was thought to have the most potential to make encryption possible. There was also a desire to improve video quality for broadcast and home viewing, thus resulting in intense competition in the 1970s among Bosch, Sony, Ampex, and RCA.[3] By 1986, the first digital video recorders were made by Sony and Bosch, with Ampex introducing models soon after.[4]

Important in the early development of digital video was the introduction and standardization of video compression, which was needed to make high-quality video available over limited transmission channels.[5] This led to the formation in 1988 of the Moving Picture Experts Group (MPEG), which set standards for video and audio compression.[6] Video compression was originally intended to be used in video transmission, not capture; however, when used in video capture it has the advantage of reducing the amount of media needed, which is a significant cost saving for professional broadcasters.[7] In 1992, Ampex introduced the first professional digital video recorder that used data compression.[8] It was followed in 1993 by the introduction of Sony's Digital Betacam. Digital video became widespread with the introduction in 1995 of Sony's DV and MiniDV, which were used for semiprofessional and amateur videography.[9] Both Sony's Digital Betacam and DV formats made use of data compression.

The demise of analog technology in favor of digital technology was underlined with the end of analog television broadcast, which occurred in the United States on June 12, 2009.[10] This switch was made in part to free up the radio frequency spectrum for other devices, such as mobile phones.[11] A DTV (digital television) signal replaced the analog signal but required a digital-to-analog converter device to be viewed on analog televisions.

The development of digital video recording and data compression made possible the development of HDTV (high-definition television), which provides more image resolution than standard-definition video. (See the resolution comparisons in figure 8-15 in chapter 8, "Film Collections"). HDTV may soon be surpassed by ultra HDTV, which provides even more image resolution than HDTV (equivalent to 4K resolution). In sum, the movement of video and television from analog to digital technology was driven by the need to increase image and sound quality in ways that consumers have come to expect. It is also part of a larger trend of media convergence around digital technology and digital networks.

DIGITAL VIDEO BASICS

Early digital video relied extensively on magnetic tape, but instead of encoding a wide range of electromagnetic signals onto the tape like analog video, it encoded binary data. Whereas each analog VCR can interpret a VHS tape's signals slightly differently, digital video has the advantage of being decodable in one way only, helping ensure consistent video across platforms.

Many formats of digital video preform lossy compression during the time of creation. For example, the popular DV format encodes individual frames, with each frame subjected to lossy compression, similar to the compression engine used to create JPGs.[12] When preserving digital video that is already lossy compressed, it is important to not subject the video to additional lossy compression. However, it is impossible to "go back in time" and undo the lossy compression that happened at the time of creation.

In addition to video in specialized tape cartridges or optical disc formats, digital video also includes video in unspecialized carriers like computer files on hard drives. Today, much digital video is created on solid-state media, such as computer files, that can be readily ingested into computers without special playback equipment.

EARLY PROFESSIONAL TAPE-BASED DIGITAL VIDEO FORMATS

A wide variety of digital video formats exist on tape. The earliest ones produce standard-definition video, and newer ones are able to capture high-definition video. Early professional tape formats that archivists could encounter include D-1 (1986), D-2 (1988), D-3 (1991), Digital Betacam (1993), D-5 (1994), D-6 (1995), Betacam SX (1996), Digital-S or D-9 (1996), and MPEG-IMX (2000), which may come in multiple tape sizes, with some able to capture HD video.[13] Fortunately, manufacturers such as Sony created video players that had backward compatibility. For example, the Sony J-30 series of videotape players are able to read Betacam, Betacam SP, Betacam SX, MPEG-IMX, and Digital Betacam tapes.[14]

DV AND ITS DERIVATIVES

The digital video format on tape that archivists are most likely to encounter is the MiniDV, which was introduced in 1995 and used in semiprofessional and amateur contexts for producing standard-definition video (figure 10-1).[15] The format was often used to record meetings, events, and interviews, as well as to produce creative works. It is important to note that DV is much more than just MiniDV. Introduced at the same time as MiniDV, DV was a larger tape and was used in semiprofessional contexts. DV was enhanced for professional contexts with the introduction of Sony's DVCAM (1996), available in two tape sizes, and Panasonic's DVCPRO (1995) and DVCPRO 50 (1999), both available in three tape sizes.[16] All of these formats produced standard-definition video. DVCAM players can also read DV and MiniDV tapes.[17]

DIGITAL8

For consumers, the Digital8 format was created in 1999, with tapes coming in the same size as analog Hi8 and Video8 tapes.[18] Many Digital8 camcorders could play Hi8 and Video8 tapes. Along with MiniDV, this is a standard-definition video format that archivists may well encounter. Other consumer digital video formats include D-VHS (1998); these tapes have the same tape dimensions as VHS.[19]

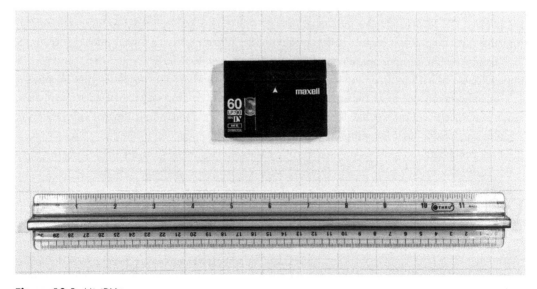

Figure 10-1. MiniDV tape.

HD VIDEO ON TAPE

The advent of high-definition television spawned formats for capturing and playing back HD resolution video, including HDCAM (1997), HDCAM SR (2003), and HDV (2004), all available in two tape sizes.[20] Panasonic's DVCPRO format was upgraded for HD with DVCPROHD (2005), available in three tape sizes.[21]

DIGITAL VIDEO ON OPTICAL DISC: DVD

Making video available on optical disc grew in popularity with the advent in 1996 of the DVD, which unseated VHS as the format for distributing commercial films to home viewers.[22] Unlike the tapes discussed in the previous section, video cameras never recorded to DVD. Rather, video was often recorded onto tape and then imported into a computer for editing and creating master video files; finally, versions of the video were created for DVD. Like compact discs discussed in chapter 7, "Audio Collections," DVDs were first available as pressed discs, where the digital information is encoded as depressions in the disc's plastic, which is then coated with a glossy metal.[23] To fit an entire film on a DVD as standard-definition video, it is necessary to compress the video using lossy compression. Despite the compression, the images look far better than VHS, so most users at the time were satisfied with what they saw. DVDs with films or videos on them—rather than file systems—are referred to as DVD Video.[24] DVDs with computer files on them are referred to as DVD-ROMs.

Similar to the CD-R format, DVD-R (1999) and DVD+R (2002) became available; they are one-time writeable DVD discs.[25] This family of discs is referred to as DVD±R because of their similarity. Like CD-Rs, the information is burned into chemical dyes; the difference between the formats is how the laser beam reads the data from the disc.[26] Also like CD-Rs, because of the unstable nature of the chemical dyes and fading of dyes, DVD±Rs are a less stable storable medium than professionally pressed DVDs.[27]

Following the introduction of DVD±R was DVD±RW, which, like CD-RW, allowed the discs to be rewritten. Instead of information being burned into chemical dyes, information is encoded into metal alloys that can be reprogrammed.[28] In studying the persistence of information on DVD±RW, Joe Iraci notes that DVD±RW indicates "substantially less stability when compared to the most stable DVD+R and DVD-R" and that these "discs are not recommended for the long-term storage of digital information."[29]

BLU-RAY DISC AND ITS DERIVATIVES

The Blu-ray disc is designed to hold high-definition video and is the successor to DVD. Released in 2006, "Blu-ray" refers to the blue laser that is used to read the disc, which allows for a greater density of impressions than the red laser used in DVDs and CDs.[30]

Like CDs and DVDs before them, Blu-ray discs can be professionally pressed. BD-ROMs can include file systems and computer files, whereas BD Video contains video streams. Writeable discs are also available, including BD-R, writable a single time, and BD-RW and BD-RE, recordable multiple

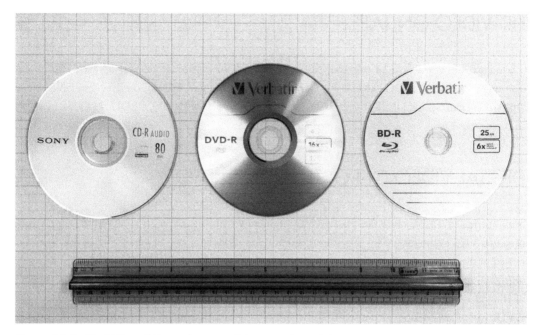

Figure 10-2. CD, DVD, and Blu-ray discs are all the same physical dimension.

times.[31] Both use technology similar to the DVD technology previously discussed, but they pack much more information into the same size discs. Figure 10-2 illustrates the identical dimensions of CDs, DVDs, and Blu-rays.

The Blu-ray disc will eventually be replaced by an ultra HD Blu-ray format, which will support the storage of ultra HD video at 4K resolution.[32] Based on past developments in the video industry and considering that 8K resolution televisions are being released, it seems likely that an 8K resolution Blu-ray format will also be developed.[33]

OTHER OPTICAL FORMATS

DVD is not the first optical video format. It was preceded in 1993 by Video CD or VCD, which placed highly compressed versions of video on compact discs that are typically used for listening to sound recordings.[34] Because of the high compression, the image quality was roughly that of VHS, and the format did not gain much traction in the United States.[35]

Before VCD, video could also be put on LaserDisc, which was introduced in 1978 and produced higher quality images than VHS.[36] Like VCD, LaserDisc never gained much traction in North America because it could not record television like VHS. Also, a LaserDisc could only fit one hour of video on each side of the disc, thus requiring that the disc be flipped over when watching a feature-length film.[37] LaserDisc is far larger than CD, DVD, and Blu-ray (figure 10-3).

Blu-ray is not the only HD optical disc format. HD DVD is a format that was discontinued in favor of Blu-ray in 2008 after a protracted format battle.[38] Note that HD DVDs will not play in Blu-ray players; an HD DVD player is needed.

Figure 10-3. Comparison of sizes between a LaserDisc (top) and a DVD-R (bottom).

DIGITAL VIDEO AS COMPUTER FILES

In this decade, the importance of tape—once a primary carrier of video—has faded. For video capture, it has been replaced by computer files stored on removable solid-state memory devices. Two solid-state memory cards are pictured in figure 10-4. Via this mode, video is captured through a camera to a solid-state device and then transferred to a computer for editing and storage. The solid-state memory device—often called a flash drive—can then be cleared for reuse. The solid-state device is often formatted with file systems that are familiar to both the camera and desktop computers, thus allowing files to be easily transferred. Video can be transferred from the camera to the computer by removing the SD card and putting it in the computer, or connecting the camera to the computer via a cable. Examples of cameras that use solid-state memory cards are the Sony XDCAM and many consumer camcorders available on the market.

It is unusual for video to be transferred to an archives via SD card, since the cards are often reused. More likely, video will be delivered via hard disk, either in a solid-state format or a format with spinning platters.

Alternatively, video can be captured to a nonremovable solid-state memory device and copied from the device via cable or wireless network upload. Millions of people do this every day using their smartphones. Smartphone users often create high-definition videos and upload them to web services like YouTube or transfer them to desktop computers for editing, production, and distribution.

For video as computer files, it is important to get accurate technical information on the video codecs used to encode and decode the video. As mentioned in the previous chapter, the file extension indicates the wrapper but not

Figure 10-4. SD card (left) and micro SD card (right).

the codec. Opening the file in a program such as VLC Player and selecting Media Information will show the audio and video codecs used to create the video (figure 10-5).[39]

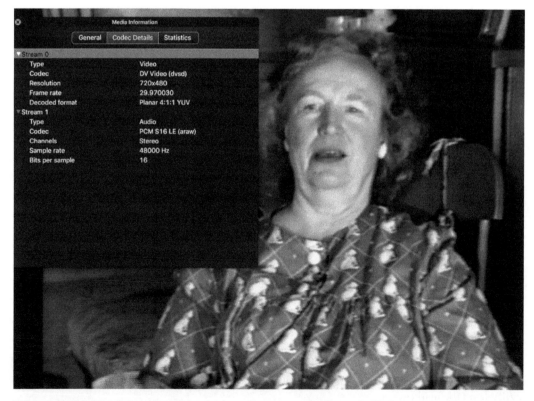

Figure 10-5. VLC Player shows the audio and video codecs contained within an AVI file.[40]

MIGRATION OF DIGITAL VIDEO TO COMPUTER FILES

The recommended practice in preserving digital video is to migrate it to computer files and store the files in trusted digital repositories.

Born-digital video files that are transferred to an archives and stored on devices like hard drives, memory cards, and USB flash drives should be migrated into an archives' trusted digital repository. For these computer files, the highest fidelity version of the computer files should be maintained "as is" as long as the native codec and wrappers are not obsolete or fragile.[41] Obsolete cases include those where the codec and/or wrapper are no longer actively supported, thus making it difficult to find ways to play the video. Fragile video files include those cases where it is difficult to get the media to play properly or reliably. For a discussion of maintaining less than the highest fidelity version of a video, see chapter 1, "Appraisal and Reappraisal."

Since obsolescence is a "moving target"—as described by video expert George Blood—it is necessary to track over time the codecs and wrappers in collections to ensure that they continue to be sustainable.[42] While working on an electronic records project for a US-based museum, I developed a codec and wrapper registry that tracks the video and audio codecs used across accessions (figure 10-6). The notion here is that if a given codec starts to become unsustainable and move toward obsolescence, then the video file can be migrated to a more sustainable format. This is a somewhat low-tech solution, and more elegant solutions may be developed that automatically log the codec and wrapper information on ingestion into a digital archives. Whatever way this information is collected, it should be maintained and reexamined every few years to ensure that the codecs and wrappers are still sustainable.

Codec and Wrapper/Container Registry			
Video codec abbreviations: h264 (MPEG4 AVC Part 10/H.264), DV25 (DV 25 Mbits/sec), DV50 (DV 50 Mbits/sec), Uncompressed 10-bit YUV (10bit), [add others as needed]			
Video wrapper/container abbreviations: avi (Audio Video Interleave), mov (QuickTime movie), dvdiso (DVD disk image), blurayiso (Blu-ray disk image), [add others as needed]			
Audio codec abbreviations: MP3, m4a (MPEG4 AAC), PCM, [add others as needed]			
Accession #	Video codecs used (separate with semicolons)	Video wrappers/containers used (separate with semicolons)	Audio codecs used (separate with semicolons)
0004	h264; 10bit	AVI	M4A; PCM
0009	DV25	MOV	PCM
0011	—	dvdiso; blurayiso	—

Figure 10-6. Codec and wrapper registry.

The Library of Congress maintains a list of file formats and codecs with a description of the sustainability factors.[43] Although the listing does not outright say that a given format is unsustainable, there are a variety of factors one could consider to reach that conclusion. Important factors include if the format is openly documented (e.g., how is data arranged in the file?), what software is available for playing it, and what the future prospects are for the format. For example, the Library of Congress investigates the "RealVideo, Version 10" video format, which was used by the once popular RealPlayer for distribution of video over the web and which has been superseded, first by Flash video and more recently by MPEG4/H.264. The library notes that in terms of documentation, the format is a "proprietary format with little public documentation," which may be good reason to migrate video out of this format to a more sustainable format.[44]

The alternative to maintaining a codec registry is to migrate all videos to a single format. However, this is unappealing for several reasons. First, it takes a great deal of human and computer time to perform video migrations. Second, the original video could better represent the creators' intention and preferences. In either case, if a digital video is migrated to a new format, the original file should be retained as a representation of the original submission. If the original cannot be retained for economic reasons, the original submission should be documented (e.g., with a description of all the original codecs and wrappers). This is consistent with advice from the digital preservation community that submission information packages (SIPs) be created that represent what was submitted by the information producer.[45] Migration efforts should be reserved for videos that have genuine preservation issues, such as difficulties in being played back.[46]

DIGITAL VIDEO AND DIGITAL PRESERVATION INITIATIVES

In the digital preservation community, registries such as the PRONOM database aim to provide a comprehensive listing of known file formats that archivists may encounter.[47] File format extensions alone often do not indicate what software program was used to create a file, and the further back in time one goes, the more obscure the extensions become. The Macintosh platform often does not even use extensions. Accurate identification of file formats is useful both for documentation purposes and for developing strategies for migrating files from obsolete and proprietary formats to more sustainable formats.[48] Included in PRONOM are "signatures" of particular format variations that can be useful in identifying a file created by one version of a software package versus another. A file format signature is a pattern that all files of that type should have, such as a consistent set of bytes at the very beginning or the very end of a file.[49] If a file is determined to have the same pattern of bytes as the signature, then it must be of that format. New tools are being created based on PRONOM to help identify digital file formats in an automated fashion. Two such tools are DROID and Siegfried.[50] Further, the FITS XML format provides a way to standardize formatting of technical information that may be produced by tools such as DROID and Siegfried.[51]

The challenge with tools based on PRONOM is that video files are composed of two elements, the wrapper and the codec. Thus, tools used to map files to particular creating software may not produce useful results in the case of video. For example, running DROID against a batch of MOV files with different codecs did not produce any useful technical information about the files other than the fact that they had the MOV extension. Tools that recognize how video files are composed of a wrapper and essence are more useful. For example, the open-source tool MediaInfo produces much more useful technical metadata on the same set of video files. (See figure 10-7.)[52] This includes information about the wrapper (QuickTime MPEG4), video codec (DV), and audio codec (PCM or pulse-code modulation). Note that such technical data can be readily exported from MediaInfo and used in technical metadata. FITS, an open-source tool that produces FITS XML technical metadata, relies on MediaInfo to extract information from audio and video files.[53]

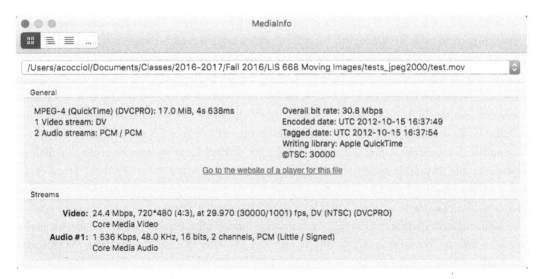

Figure 10-7. MediaInfo provides more detailed information about video formats than tools designed for typical computer files.

MIGRATION OF VIDEO FROM OPTICAL DISC TO COMPUTER FILES

A plethora of optical disc formats support video. Fortunately, most of today's Blu-ray players are backward compatible with DVD and CD. Blu-ray players can be purchased fairly inexpensively and can connect with computers via USB; some computers have a built-in player. When choosing a player to use for migrations, ensure that it offers backward compatibility with formats such as CD, CD-R, DVD, DVD±R, DVD±RW, BD, BD-R, BD-RE, and BD-RW.

For video on CD, DVD, and Blu-ray, the recommended practice is to create a disk image of the optical disc and maintain it in a trusted digital repository.[54] Disk images are a bit-for-bit copy of the contents of the optical disc and thus maintain everything about the disc content such as menus, subtitles, chapters, and more. Disk images usually have file extensions such as .iso and .img. Video players like VLC player can play back ISO files. Many programs exist for creating disk images. For example, the Disk Utility program that is part of Apple's OSX will create disk images of DVDs that can be played back with VLC player.

It is important to note that some legal issues can be introduced by "ripping" DVDs and Blu-rays, which are often encrypted to protect the content from piracy. See chapter 3, "Legal and Ethical Issues," for a discussion of "ripping" such optical media.

MIGRATION OF DIGITAL VIDEO FROM TAPE TO COMPUTER FILES

When migrating digital video from tape to computer files, ideally the digital information on the tape can be read and directly transferred to the computer without any transcoding. Transcoding is the process by which information is migrated from one encoding format to another.[55] This is less than ideal, because transcoding could move the video away from the format that is the most authentic representation of that content. However, it is sometimes necessary due to issues like format obsolescence.

As long as the codec is still supported, and the format supports the movement of information from tape to computer over a cable, the video can be transferred in its native format and wrapped using containers like MOV, AVI, and MXF.[56] Fortunately, this is possible for all varieties of DV format, such as MiniDV. To migrate a MiniDV or DV tape, connect the DV deck or DV camcorder via FireWire to a computer. Software programs such as Adobe Premiere or Final Cut Pro can control the DV deck via FireWire; using its capture options, the program can record the output of the DV deck. The program will store the output of the DV deck in its native DV format wrapped in AVI or MOV containers. Programs like VLC player are able to play back these DV-encoded videos.

Unfortunately, transferring the digital information directly off the tape is not an option with all digital video formats. For formats that do not support direct transfer of digital information, the videotape can be played back to a capture device via the SDI port (for SD content) or HDSDI port (for HD content).[57] Capture devices, such as the Blackmagic UltraStudio 4K device shown in figure 9-11 in the previous chapter, are able to capture this content and transmit it to the computer over a Thunderbolt cable. The computer should capture 10-bit uncompressed video from the SDI or HDSDI port of the capture device.[58] Tape formats that need to be played back in this way include D-1, D-2, D-3, Digital Betacam, D-5, D-6, D-S or D-9, HDCAM/HDCAM SR, Betacam SX (in most cases), and MPEG-IMX.[59]

STORAGE ENVIRONMENT

Migration of digital video to computer files can be delayed to some extent by keeping tapes and optical discs in a cool and dry environment. The same environment described in chapter 9, "Analog Video Collections," can be used; recommended room temperatures are between 46°F and 53°F, with 25–35 percent relative humidity.[60]

Tapes are best stored upright in their original containers, on shelves or in acid-free boxes.[61] Optical media are best stored upright in their original containers, such as jewel cases.

Recent research has indicated that optical discs, especially those burned using consumer CD/DVD/ Blu-ray burners, are not as reliable as pressed discs.[62] These should be prioritized for migration to digital files over pressed discs and possibly even over older videotape formats. The oldest born-digital videotapes should also be prioritized for migration as the equipment becomes increasingly obsolete.

Ideally, video stored as computer files on removable hard drives, solid-state memory devices, or other magnetic disks would be imaged on accession. Imaging creates a bit-for-bit copy of the media; if the media fails while in storage, this should not matter because an exact replica of it has also been retained.[63] Hard disks with spinning platters that are not routinely powered on can suffer from stiction, wherein the disk head lubrication fails and the disk head cannot move across the disk.[64] Other issues include obsolescence of the interfaces. For example, it is now difficult to connect SCSI (Small Computer System Interface) devices to modern computers. This difficulty may occur with FireWire, which is being phased out in favor of other interfaces like Thunderbolt.

For some archives, creating disk images can be too costly, because the images can take up a lot of disk space and are generally not used for researcher access. For these archives, it is recommended to at least copy the files off the disk and ingest them into trusted digital repositories.

For archives that do not have trusted digital repositories, it may be necessary to maintain the physical medium as the primary carrier of the content. If this is the case, a recommended option is to power on spinning hard disks occasionally (at least yearly) to keep them from suffering from stiction. It is also highly recommended to duplicate files to at least one—and preferably two—drives that are occasionally powered on. Research has found that the failure rate for hard drives increases as the drives age.[65] Thus, when taking in a collection, it is a good idea to determine an approximate age for each drive and prioritize migration or duplication of content for hard drives that are more than five years old. See chapter 4, "Digital Preservation," for a more thorough discussion of this issue.

CAPTURING DIGITAL VIDEO FROM THE WEB

Sometimes archivists may encounter video records that document significant institutional activity, but the master videos cannot be found and only copies available on the web persist. In this case, archivists may want to download copies of these videos to preserve them, as they may be removed from the website or the website hosting them may be shut down.

Note that downloading videos in this way may be against the terms of service of some platforms. Many platforms would like users to visit their website to view a video (and any advertising), rather than have it viewed offline. Also, downloading videos may have copyright implications. See chapter 3, "Legal and Ethical Issues," for a discussion of this issue.

CAPTURING YOUTUBE CONTENT

Most video websites do not necessarily make it easy to download videos for offline viewing. On YouTube, for example, if you can log in to the account of the user who uploaded the video, there are options for downloading the compressed version. However, sometimes the account owner cannot be located or is not cooperative. In these cases, it is sometimes possible to download the video using an assortment of tools, such as extensions to Mozilla Firefox or Google Chrome. I have had success downloading videos from YouTube using a Firefox extension called Download YouTube.[66] Despite the feasibility of this, it is against the terms of service for YouTube.[67] A discussion of this practice can be found in chapter 3, "Legal and Ethical Issues."

Many of the platforms that use streaming servers do not make it easy to download videos. In these cases, a Google search for crowd-sourced work-arounds for downloading videos from given platforms can be very instructive.

CAPTURING HTML5 VIDEO

A popular way to make video available today is through HTML5 video players, which allow a video file to reside on a web server and be readily played without the need for sophisticated video streaming servers. When viewing the source of an HTML page in your web browser, you will see that videos available in this way use tags like the following:

```
<video src="willer_tape1.mp4" width="480" height="270" controls>
```

It is almost always possible to directly download videos available in this format. To do so, take the URL of the website that hosts the <video> tag, such as the following:

http://herstories.prattsils.org/bilitis/about.php

Construct the full URL of the video using the host name, directory structure, and filename, producing a URL such as the following:

http://herstories.prattsils.org/bilitis/willer_tape1.mp4

Enter the full URL into a web browser. Most will start downloading the video and playing it. From the File menu of the browser, select "Save Page As" or a similar option to save the video file to your computer.

CONCLUSION

The practice recommended here for preserving digital video is to migrate video to computer files stored in trusted digital repositories. Prioritization of formats for migration can take into account factors such as the importance of the video to the institutional mission, as well as the obsolescence of the format. Like the analog tapes that came before them, digital video on tape eventually needs to be migrated, as new players are not being created for older formats. Optical disc formats such as CD, DVD, and Blu-ray—especially the varieties created with consumer disc burners—have proven less reliable than other storage media. For this reason, media on these formats should be prioritized for migration to computer files.

NOTES

[1] Koichi Sadashige, "Digital Video Recording," in *Magnetic Recording: The First 100 Years*, ed. Eric D. Daniel, C. Denis Mee, and Mark H. Clark (Piscataway, NJ: IEEE Press, 1999), 201–20.

[2] Ibid.

[3] Ibid.

[4] Ibid.

[5] Ibid.

[6] K. F. Ibrahim, *Newness Guide to Television and Video Technology* (Oxford: Elsevier, 2007).

[7] Sadashige, "Digital Video Recording."

[8] Ibid.

[9] Johannes Gfeller, Agathe Jarczyk, and Joanna Phillips, *Compendium of Image Errors in Analogue Video* (Zurich: Schweizerisches Institut für Kunstwissenschaft, 2012).

[10] Michael Starks, *The Digital Television Revolution: Origins to Outcomes* (New York: Palgrave Macmillan, 2013).

[11] Ibid.

[12] Library of Congress, *Sustainability of Digital Formats: Digital Video Encoding (DV, DVCAM, DVCPRO)* (Washington, DC: Library of Congress, 2012), http://www.digitalpreservation.gov/formats/fdd/fdd000183.shtml, permalinked on April 6, 2016, at https://perma.cc/3LC7-E3HT.

[13] Gfeller, Jarczyk, and Phillips, *Compendium of Image Errors*; "D-1 (Sony)," *Wikipedia*, https://en.wikipedia.org/wiki/D-1_(Sony), permalinked on September 16, 2016, at https://perma.cc/ZY3R-9DP3; "D-2 (video)," *Wikipedia*, https://en.wikipedia.org/wiki/D-2_(video), permalinked on September 16, 2016, at https://perma.cc/86FN-R4B9; "D-3 (video)," *Wikipedia*, https://en.wikipedia.org/wiki/D-3_(video), permalinked on September 16, 2016, at https://perma.cc/FX74-VKN6; "D6 HDTV VTR," *Wikipedia*, https://en.wikipedia.org/wiki/D6_HDTV_VTR, permalinked on September 16, 2016, at https://perma.cc/ALC8-YEFJ; "Digital-S," *Wikipedia*, https://en.wikipedia.org/wiki/Digital-S, permalinked on September 16, 2016, at https://perma.cc/C6LA-6HSZ; "Betacam," *Wikipedia*, https://en.wikipedia.org/wiki/Betacam, permalinked on September 16, 2016, at https://perma.cc/UF8B-Z2VP.

[14] Sony J-Series brochure, https://pro.sony.com/bbsc/assetDownloadController/j30-brochure.pdf?path=Asset%20Hierarchy$Professional$SEL-yf-generic-153708$SEL-yf-generic-153751SEL-asset-46298.pdf&id=StepID$SEL-asset-46298$original&dimension=original, permalinked on April 25, 2016, at https://perma.cc/ULG7-SBBK.

[15] Gfeller, Jarczyk, and Phillips, *Compendium of Image Errors*; "DV," *Wikipedia*, https://en.wikipedia.org/wiki/DV, permalinked on September 16, 2016, at https://perma.cc/CJ88-N7RX.

[16] Ibid.

[17] Ibid.

[18] Gfeller, Jarczyk, and Phillips, *Compendium of Image Errors;* "8 mm video format," *Wikipedia,* https://en.wikipedia.org/wiki/8_mm_video_format, permalinked on September 16, 2016, at https://perma.cc/PD35-X6S2.

[19] "D-VHS," *Wikipedia*, https://en.wikipedia.org/wiki/D-VHS, permalinked on September 16, 2016, at https://perma.cc/T5TX-N4LQ.

[20] Gfeller, Jarczyk, and Phillips, *Compendium of Image Errors;* "HDCAM," *Wikipedia,* https://en.wikipedia.org/wiki/HDCAM, permalinked on September 16, 2016, at https://perma.cc/KX9M-7K3R; "HDV," *Wikipedia,* https://en.wikipedia.org/wiki/HDV, permalinked on September 16, 2016, at https://perma.cc/A5QV-GST4.

[21] Gfeller, Jarczyk, and Phillips, *Compendium of Image Errors.*

[22] Jim Taylor, *DVD Demystified* (New York: McGraw Hill, 1998).

[23] Ibid.

[24] *DVD Primer* (2000), from the international organization DVD Forum, http://www.dvdforum.org/tech-dvdprimer.htm#5, permalinked on April 6, 2016, at https://perma.cc/QY6V-XF8Y.

[25] Optical Storage Technology Association (OSTA), *Understanding Recordable and Rewritable DVD* (Cupertino, CA: Optical Storage Technology Association, 2004), http://www.osta.org/technology/dvdqa/pdf/dvdqa.pdf, permalinked on April 6, 2016, at https://perma.cc/4CVP-BN2N.

[26] Kevin Bradley, *Risks Associated with the Use of Recordable CDs and DVDs as Reliable Storage Media in Archival Collections—Strategies and Alternatives* (Paris: UNESCO, 2006).

[27] Ibid.

[28] OSTA, *Understanding Recordable and Rewritable DVD.*

[29] Joe Iraci, "The Stability of DVD Optical Disc Formats," *Restaurator* 32, no. 1 (2011): 39–59.

[30] Jim Taylor et al., *Blu-ray Disc Demystified* (New York: McGraw-Hill Education, 2008).

[31] Ibid.

32   Mike Snider, "New Improved High-res Ultra HD Blu-ray Discs and Players on the Way," *USA Today*, May 12, 2015, http:// www.usatoday.com/story/tech/2015/05/12/ultra-hd-blu-ray-disc-specification/27155765/, permalinked on April 6, 2016, at https://perma.cc/54AF-KZWN.

33   Arjun Kharpal, "Sharp is Selling the World's First 8K TV for $133K," CNBC, September 16, 2015, http://www.cnbc .com/2015/09/16/sharp-is-selling-the-worlds-first-8k-tv-for-133k.html, permalinked on April 6, 2016, at https://perma .cc/4J9P-6GC3.

34   Joshua Paul, *Digital Video Hacks: Tips and Tools for Shooting, Editing and Sharing* (Sebastopol, CA: O'Reilly Media, 2005).

35   Ibid.

36   Taylor et al., *Blu-ray Disc Demystified*.

37   Ibid.

38   Jack Schofield, "Toshiba Drops HD DVD," *The Guardian*, February 19, 2008, https://www.theguardian.com/technology /blog/2008/feb/19/toshibadropshddvd, permalinked on April 6, 2016, at https://perma.cc/RW22-V73D.

39   VLC Media Player is a free and open-source media player available for download at http://www.videolan.org/vlc/, permalinked on April 6, 2016, at https://perma.cc/77RX-JF7D.

40   Edith Eyde is pictured in this video from the Daughters of Bilitis Video Project, Lesbian Herstory Archives, http://herstories .prattsils.org/omeka/items/show/219, permalinked on April 6, 2016, at https://perma.cc/5V5R-3P5A.

41   George Blood, *Refining Conversion Contract Specifications: Determining Suitable Digital Video Formats for Medium-term Storage* (Washington, DC: Library of Congress, 2011), http://www.digitizationguidelines.gov/audio-visual/documents /IntrmMastVidFormatRecs_20111001.pdf, permalinked on April 6, 2016, at https://perma.cc/D2MU-CE2Q.

42   Ibid., 18.

43   Library of Congress, *Sustainability of Digital Formats: Planning for Library of Congress Collections* (Washington, DC: Library of Congress, 2013), http://www.digitalpreservation.gov/formats/, permalinked on April 6, 2016, at https://perma.cc /E33A-G4VM.

44   Library of Congress, *Sustainability of Digital Formats*: Planning for Lirbary of Congress Collections: Real Video 10 (Washington, DC: Library of Congress, 2013), http://www.digitalpreservation.gov/formats/fdd/fdd000050.shtml, permalinked on April 6, 2016, at https://perma.cc/XRD6-CZJA.

45   Brian Lavoie, *The Open Archival Information System (OAIS) Reference Model: Introductory Guide* (York, UK: Digital Preservation Coalition, 2014).

46   For examples of guidelines that suggest not migrating to a single format unless obsolescence is a concern, see Blood, *Refining Conversion*, and Andrea Shahmohammadi, *Born-Digital Video Preservation: A Final Report* (Washington, DC: Smithsonian Institution Archives, 2011), https://siarchives.si.edu/sites/default/files/pdfs/bornDigitalVideoPreservation2011.pdf, permalinked on April 6, 2016, at https://perma.cc/V7UA-KZYH.

47   National Archives of the United Kingdom: The Technical Registry PRONOM, http://www.nationalarchives.gov.uk /aboutapps/PRONOM/default.htm, permalinked on September 14, 2016, at https://perma.cc/57GK-QDDC.

48   Erin O'Meara and Kate Stratton, "Preserving Digital Objects," module 12 in *Digital Preservation Essentials,* ed. Christopher J. Prom (Chicago: Society of American Archivists), 1–73.

49   National Archives of the United Kingdom, *How to Research and Develop Signatures for File Format Identification* (2012), http://www.nationalarchives.gov.uk/documents/information-management/pronom-file-signature-research.pdf, permalinked on September 15, 2016, at https://perma.cc/664M-B9F2.

50   Richard Lehane, Siegfried (on Github), https://github.com/richardlehane/siegfried, permalinked on September 14, 2016, at https://perma.cc/X86L-9BR4; National Archives of the UK: DROID file format identification, http://www.nationalarchives .gov.uk/information-management/manage-information/preserving-digital-records/droid/, permalinked on September 14, 2016, at https://perma.cc/P6P6-8TPF.

51   Harvard University: File Information Tool Set (FITS) XML, http://projects.iq.harvard.edu/fits/fits-xml, permalinked on September 14, 2016, at https://perma.cc/2828-9RTP.

52   MediaInfo, https://mediaarea.net/en/MediaInfo, permalinked on September 14, 2016, at https://perma.cc/MN2U-DSJ3.

53   Harvard University: File Information Tool Set (FITS), http://projects.iq.harvard.edu/fits/, permalinked on September 15, 2016, at https://perma.cc/L9J9-BGYR.

54   Blood, *Refining Conversion*.

55   Huifang Sun, Xuemin Chen, and Tihao Chiang, *Digital Video Transcoding for Transmission and Storage* (New York: CRC Press, 2005).

56   Blood, *Refining Conversion*.

57   Ibid.

58   Ibid.

59   Ibid.

[60] Dietrich Schüller and Albrecht Häfner, eds., *Handling and Storage of Audio and Video Carriers: Technical Committee Standards, Recommended Practices, and Strategies* (London: International Association of Sound and Audiovisual Archives, 2014).

[61] Ibid.

[62] Kevin Bradley, *Risks Associated with the Use of Recordable CDs and DVDs as Reliable Storage Media in Archival Collections— Strategies and Alternatives* (Paris: UNESCO, 2006); Laura Wilsey et al., "Capturing and Processing Born-Digital Files in the STOP AIDS Project Records: A Case Study," *Journal of Western Archives* 4, no. 1 (2013): 1–22.

[63] AIMS Work Group, *AIMS Born-Digital Collections: An Inter-Institutional Model for Stewardship* (2012), http://dcs.library .virginia.edu/files/2013/02/AIMS_final.pdf, permalinked on April 6, 2016, at https://perma.cc/9E3J-8SCH.

[64] Gordon F. Hughes and Joseph F. Murray, "Reliability and Security of RAID Storage Systems and D2D Archives using SATA Disk Drives," *ACM Transactions on Storage* 1, no. 1 (2004), 95–107; Anthony Cocciolo, "FixityBerry: Environmentally Sustainable Digital Preservation for Very Low Resourced Cultural Heritage Institutions" (paper presented at iConference 2015, Newport Beach, CA, March 24–27, 2015), http://www.thinkingprojects.org/fixity_berry_iconf_final.pdf, permalinked on April 6, 2016, at https://perma.cc/9QBC-3VDC.

[65] Eduardo Pinheiro, Wolf-Dietrich Weber, and Luiz Andre Barroso, "Failure Trends in a Large Disk Drive Population," in *Proceedings of the 5th USENIX Conference on File and Storage Technologies (FAST'07)*, February 13–16, 2007, San Jose, CA.

[66] Source of extension is available at https://github.com/gantt/downloadyoutube, permalinked on April 6, 2016, at https:// perma.cc/QZP9-3TDJ; an extension for Firefox based on the same script is available at https://addons.mozilla.org/en-US /firefox/addon/download-youtube/, permalinked on April 6, 2016, at https://perma.cc/A6DQ-8BTM.

[67] "YouTube Terms of Service," https://www.youtube.com/static?template=terms, permalinked on April 6, 2016, at https:// perma.cc/5GTA-F6FK.

CHAPTER 11

Complex Media

Although the media discussed in the previous chapters, such as VHS tapes and compact audiocassettes, are likely to compose the bulk of moving image and sound records stewarded by non-audiovisual-specific archives, archivists may well encounter complex media in need of preservation. Complex media is an umbrella term for a wide variety of media that do not easily fit into the category of digital video or digital audio. Complex media, as it is discussed here, describes digital audio, video, or other moving image items embedded within a larger amalgamation of digital material. The entire record comprises not simply the audio or video but rather the whole assemblage of digital material.

Complex media can contain digital video or audio embedded in software combined with interactive components, such as educational software on CD-ROM, which has become obsolete. It can also refer to digital video or audio contained within a network of web pages. Because of the wide variety of combinations, the preservation challenges for complex media are somewhat different from the other types of media discussed in this book. This chapter offers some strategies for dealing with complex media that archivists may encounter.

BRIEF HISTORICAL BACKGROUND

Complex media, as it is discussed here, is intimately related to the rise of the computing industry. Unlike digital video, which traces its roots to competition among established analog video companies such as

Sony and Ampex, complex media can be traced back to a particular strand of the computing industry: the emergence of personal computers. Whereas computers had been used for business, military,
and space applications in the 1960s, it was not until the 1970s that notable technologies were developed to create significant human-computer interactions (HCI). This includes the introduction of the
WYSIWYG ("what you see is what you get") interface at Xerox PARC in 1973, followed soon after by
the cut-and-paste word processor and the GUI (graphic user interface) with icons, menus, and overlap-
ping windows.[1] These interfaces were popularized by Apple Computer in 1984 with the Macintosh and
later adopted by Microsoft for its Windows operating system.[2]

Through user-friendly interfaces, computers increasingly became tools with which to make things,
including cultural and artistic works. For still images, Photoshop was developed in 1987 and released
by Adobe in 1990, facilitating the endless manipulation of bitmap images.[3] Although not the first tool
to allow such manipulation, its long-standing and continued impact on the creation of graphic images
makes it noteworthy. For moving images, Apple's Final Cut Pro was released in 1999, allowing the editing of everything from simple videos to feature-length motion pictures and making personal computers key tools in composing digital video and digital films.[4] Also not the first video editing program, it
is noteworthy in that it was a tool used by both amateurs and professional filmmakers. For example,
Hollywood films such as *The Social Network* (2010) and *The Curious Case of Benjamin Button* (2008)
were edited using Final Cut Pro.[5]

In addition to being used as tools for cultural production, computers were increasingly used for
educational and learning applications from the 1980s onward, including games and hypermedia applications that combined nonlinear text with still images.[6] Beginning with the release of high-storage-
capacity media such as the CD-ROM, educational and learning applications could include audio, video,
high-resolution images, and complex animations. Particularly memorable educational CD-ROMs
include Microsoft's Encarta, available from 1993 to 2009; it was a hypermedia encyclopedia with extensive audiovisual media content.[7]

Today, much of cultural production occurs in the realm of digital media. This trend is highlighted
by the notion of media convergence, as old and new media merge through their use of digital technology
and their interactions with users through the Internet.[8]

For our purposes, "complex media" is an important concept because it draws our attention to
the possibilities of increased interaction between the user and the media item. Whereas some of the
technologies discussed in this book, such as analog video and audio, can only be played, paused, fast-
forwarded, and rewound, complex media items can be designed such that there is an unlimited number
of ways users can interact with them. For this reason, complex media can present novel preservation and
access challenges.

ARCHIVISTS AND COMPLEX MEDIA

Before proceeding further, it is worth noting the issue of the archivist's role. Is it the archivist's responsibility to preserve and provide access to complex media? Part of the difficulty in determining this is
that digital technology has somewhat blurred the lines of who takes care of what. Traditionally, museums steward three-dimensional objects, archives groups of paper records, and libraries books and other
published materials. However, complex media challenge this arrangement. Are complex media more

like three-dimensional objects or more like records? The answer is inevitably case by case. Interestingly, archives, libraries, and museums are beginning to preserve computerized items, and in some cases, they are making use of common infrastructure. However, who preserves what depends on the reason the media item was acquired in the first place.

Take an example from an art museum context. Art museums acquire born-digital artwork in need of digital preservation. At the same time, museum archives collect media that document institutional activity, such as web archives of museum websites and smartphone apps. As this case illustrates, both museum archives and museum curatorial units need to engage in digital preservation of complex media, such as preserving bits, migrating them to new hardware when needed, making geographically dispersed copies, and documenting how to make "it" function as intended. However, the difference in who acquires, preserves, and makes accessible the item has more to do with why it was acquired. Archives take in complex media that document the functions of the museum, while curators, with the help of conservators, acquire complex media that complement the museum's collection and address some need in the collection. In this respect, archivists and digital conservators may well find themselves engaging in similar kinds of digital preservation activities for complex media, although the media are acquired and preserved for different reasons.

DESKTOP COMPUTER SOFTWARE

Archives may find themselves interested in preserving computer software. For collecting institutions, this can include software developed by a donor and included in a donation; for institutional archives, this can include software developed by the parent institution. Computer software can vary from computer games to software-based artworks to educational multimedia on CD-ROM. For software contained on removable media such as CD-ROMs and floppy disks, the recommended first step is to create a disk image of the media item—a bit-for-bit copy—and maintain it in a trusted digital repository, so that if the original should fail, the data can continue to be maintained. This is a similar process to that described in chapter 10, "Digital Video Collections."

CREATING DISK IMAGES

Many programs exist for creating disk images. For example, FTK Imager is a free tool that works well for creating disk images; it is also used in the criminal forensics community for making bit-for-bit copies of a disk's contents.[9] The forensics community is particularly interested in documenting pieces of evidence while eliminating the chance of tampering, like disk contents being inadvertently or deliberately changed. Accessing information from a disk using a bit-for-bit copy of it helps preserve the integrity of what was on the disk as it was first encountered by authorities and helps the forensic examiner ensure that he or she need not worry about the disk failing. This method of getting an authentic and complete copy of a disk, as well as other practices from the forensics community, has been incorporated into the practices of some archives.[10] The use of digital forensics is best captured in the BitCurator project, an effort to assemble a collection of open-source digital forensic tools for use by the library, archives, and museum community.[11]

When creating a disk image, it is important to note the number of read errors. A read error could indicate that part of a disk is corrupted, which could result in the entire file system being rendered unreadable. Relatedly, read errors can render files unable to be opened and software unable to be executed. Fixing or repairing corrupted disks is beyond the scope of this book, and seeking assistance from a data recovery specialist may be necessary.

After a disk image is made, the original disk can be put into storage. It is recommended that imaged disks be put in envelopes that clearly label the disk as having been imaged. This way, should someone encounter the disk in the future, they can mount the disk image to access its contents rather than the original disk. Disk images can be mounted into operating systems using tools such as OSFMount, as well as options built into operating systems.[12] Reports produced by the imaging program, such as a listing of files and directories contained on the image, are useful to maintain.

One challenge with mounting disk images is figuring out the file system used to encode the contents of the disk. File systems make meaning of the bits encoded on the disk, such as translating a seemingly random assemblage of bits into directories, files, and properties of files such as "date modified" and "date created." Common file systems used today include FAT12 (File Allocation Table), FAT16, FAT32, exFAT (Extended File Allocation Table), NTFS (New Technology File System), Mac OS Extended, and others. Often, the tool used for mounting the file system can decipher what file system was used. However, sometimes it may be necessary to install software for reading file systems that are not native to your operating system. In other cases, it may be necessary to mount the disk image in an operating system that is able to read that disk format. As mentioned earlier, disk images that result in read errors may not be able to be opened with any file system. Some educated trial and error may be the best strategy for decoding what file system a disk has used. Try mounting the disk image using file systems that were in use during the time frame in which the disk was created (and based on information on the disk's label). Figure 11-1 shows some file systems, when they were introduced, and how they were/are used.

File System	Year Introduced	How Used
FAT12[13]	1987	Used for formatting floppy disks on DOS/Windows computers.
FAT16	1988	Used for formatting hard drives in MS DOS 4.0 and greater.
FAT32	1996	Began to be used in Windows 95, with continued use today, especially for formatting USB hard drives and flash drives.
exFAT	2006	Often used today to format USB hard disks and flash drives.
NTFS[14]	1993	Often used to format internal hard drives for Windows NT and greater computers (e.g., Windows 2000, XP, Vista, etc.).
Mac OS Extended[15]	1998	Also known as HFS Plus, used to format hard drives on Macintosh computers.

Figure 11-1. Frequently encountered file systems.

WRITE PROTECTION

When inserting a disk—such as floppy disks that are writeable—into a computer, it is recommended that you engage the write-protection tab. Modern operating systems often write content such as invisible files or other information to a disk. Further, simply opening a file can modify the file system metadata, such as a file's "date last accessed" property, which is indeed an interesting and important property to

Figure 11-2. A 5.25-inch floppy disk (left) and 3.5-inch diskette (right) with their write-protection tabs open, meaning the disks cannot be written to.

preserve. Figure 11-2 shows a 5.25-inch floppy disk and a 3.5-inch diskette with their write-protection features engaged.

For media items that do not have built-in write protection, a hardware write blocker can help prevent data being written to the disk. For example, the CRU WiebeTech Forensic UltraDock device can be used to prevent data from being written to hard disks, and the CRU WiebeTech USB WriteBlocker device (figure 11-3) can be used to prevent data from being written to removable USB flash drives.[16] Using a software write blocker is another way to prevent disks from being written to. However, this can get quite technical to set up, so a hardware write blocker may be easier to use. For optical devices that

Figure 11-3. CRU WiebeTech USB WriteBlocker connected to a SanDisk USB flash drive.

cannot be readily written to, such as pressed CDs, DVDs, or Blu-rays, write protection is not needed because the disc is inherently read-only.

DEDICATED WORKSTATION

When reading obsolete media, assembling a dedicated workstation for imaging that is disconnected from the rest of the network is a recommended practice. The reason to have a dedicated workstation is that if there is a virus on the media that is being read, it will not infect the entire network. After obsolete media is imaged, the mounted image can then be scanned for viruses using any preferred virus scanner.

When purchasing devices for reading media, it is best to get the newest incarnation of the reader that also has backward compatibility. For example, when purchasing an optical disc reader, it is best to get a Blu-ray reader that has backward compatibility with DVDs and CDs.

Disk drives that read 3.5-inch diskettes can still be purchased new and connected to modern computers through USB. However, other devices need to be purchased used, as they are no longer being manufactured. For example, Iomega Jaz drives and Zip drives can be purchased used through resellers like eBay. In some cases, it may be necessary to purchase interfaces to connect these devices to modern USB interfaces. For example, Jaz drives may require converters from a SCSI interface to a USB interface. Three kinds of drives are illustrated in figure 11-4.

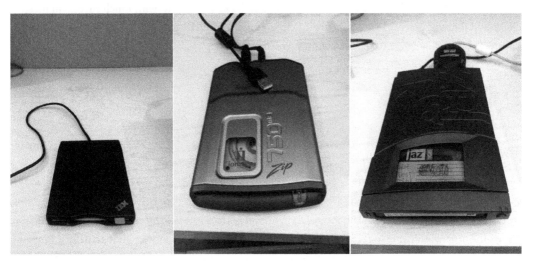

Figure 11-4. Obsolete removable disk drives: 3.5-inch diskette drive (left), Iomega Zip drive (center), and Iomega Jaz drive (right).

When purchasing used devices, it is best to buy ones that are advertised as "tested" from well-reviewed sellers. Also, when using a device for the first time, it is necessary to test it with a nonarchival disk. This way, if the used device damages the disk, the test disk will be damaged, rather than an archival item.

Drives that read 5.25-inch floppy disks also need to be purchased used through resellers like eBay. Devices for connecting 5.25-inch disk drives to modern computers include a product by Device Side Data that makes these drives accessible via USB and includes software for doing the disk imaging.[17] I

Figure 11-5. Device Side Data USB device (left) connected to a 5.25-inch floppy disk drive (right).

have used this device, with 5.25-inch floppy drives purchased from eBay, with much success in imaging DOS and Commodore disks. (See figure 11-5.) Another product called the KryoFlux can be used to connect obsolete hardware to modern computers.[18]

EMULATION

For archives, it is insufficient to simply maintain the software bits. It is necessary to be able to provide researchers access to the intellectual content of the software itself. Software that is designed for operating systems that are obsolete may not run on current operating systems and may need to be run in their native operating systems. Archivists do not have to find old computers to run old software. It is possible to run old operating systems in contemporary computer environments through emulation. Emulation allows the original software to think that it is running on the original hardware, but actually it is operating on a piece of software called a virtual machine that mimics the behavior of the original hardware. For example, it is possible to run DOS 6.2, Windows 3.1, and Windows XP through the virtual machine software Virtual Box on a Mac laptop running OSX.[19] Imaged disks can then be mounted into these obsolete operating systems, and the software can be run as if on a twenty-year-old computer.

When setting up a virtual machine, it is necessary to install the original operating system that you need, which requires that you purchase a vintage copy of it. Software on original media can be obtained through reseller sites such as eBay. Although copies of obsolete operating systems can be found online, and using such copies can get you up and running that operating system more quickly, this option is illegal and also opens up your institution to risk. For example, such software copies can include viruses and other spyware. Further, since copyright for corporate works extends for ninety-five years from publication, the copyright holder (e.g., Microsoft, IBM, or Apple) can still enforce its copyright. Although most software companies are unlikely to dedicate much effort to enforcing their copyright on very old software, it is still illegal to copy such software. The long copyright term on software and the paucity of options for working around this problem endangers the ability of libraries, archives, and museums to preserve software—an issue that is beyond the scope of this book.

Virtual machines that mimic an entire hardware environment are not the only way to do emulation. Enthusiasts of vintage computing have developed stand-alone emulation software for running software on a wide variety of obsolete platforms. For example, there is Stella for Atari, Mini vMac for emulating the Macintosh Plus, DosBox for running DOS applications, CCS64 and Vice for emulating Commodore 64, and SheepShaver for emulating older Macintosh computers, among many others.[20] Figure 11-6 illustrates a modern iMac (right) running software designed for the Mac SE (left) through the emulator Mini vMac.

As Jon Ippolito points out in *Re-collection: Art, New Media, and Social Memory,* preserving born-digital media requires experimenting with tools developed not only by professional conservators and archivists but also by computing enthusiasts. He notes that " . . . emulators are not the product of software engineers working for a commercial enterprise . . . but are hacked together by acned kids on laptops in bedrooms . . . ." and that the "quantity and quality of . . . [these] emulators is astounding."[21] As the technology industry strives to deliver the latest, newest technology, it is quick to render its past creations obsolete. Therefore, it is necessary to embrace nontraditional solutions, like crowd-sourced emulators, in order to render obsolete computer-based media.

Figure 11-6. A 1984 Mac SE (left) with modern iMac running the Mini vMac emulator (right).

DOCUMENTING COMPLEX MEDIA

Once the disk image has been created, and the program has been run using a modern computer or emulator, it is important to document the activities needed to make the software function again. This documentation can be consulted when a researcher needs to gain access to the software. The information can be entered into a simple text file kept in the same directory as the disk image. Alternatively, the information can be included in the finding aid, within the technical access element, under the conditions of access and use section.[22] Further, the software needed to run the program, such as virtual machines or emulators, should be available on a public-access researcher computer or laptop.

The following example provides a sample text file for running a piece of obsolete CD-ROM software that can be maintained with the disk image:

> Paul Hindemith: Leben und Werk / Life and Work
>
> by Art Transfer Multimedia
>
> Published 1998
>
> Hardware Requirements: Windows 3.1, Windows 95, PowerPC Mac
>
> To run CD-ROM, copy Paul_Hindemith_Leben_und_Werk_1998.iso to computer with Windows 3.1 or Windows 95 virtual machine installed on it. Start Virtual Box (or other virtual machine software), and start Windows 3.1 or 95 VM. Does not work in Windows XP. Mount the CD image using the mount options available in the VM. Run the setup.exe program. After setup, run the application from the icon it creates.
>
> Technical notes by Anthony Cocciolo (2015).

Note that this documentation will likely need to be updated at least once a decade to ensure that the method still works on present-day computers and is intelligible to current archivists and researchers. Since preserving software-based media can be labor intensive, such items should be accessioned judiciously.

In looking at a library catalog's "System Details" field (or MARC field 538), which describes system requirements for running software available in the collection, it becomes clear that such instruction can become anachronistic. For example, the following "System Details" entry for a CD-ROM available for checkout at the Pratt Institute Libraries includes the following:[23]

> System requirements: MAC Quadra 700 or better; 4 MB of RAM; 4 MB of hard disk space; QuickTime 2.0; double speed CD-ROM drive; 13 in. or larger color monitor with at least 8-bit color.

This information can be useful for setting up an emulator or virtual machine, but it is unlikely that a present-day researcher will seek out a Quadra 700 to run this software—and the "or better" Macintosh of today will certainly not run that software without emulation. For this reason, the information needed to run a computer program should be updated at least once a decade and should include instructions on using emulators to run the software.

WEB-BASED RECORDS

Archivists may well need to preserve moving image and sound records that appear on the web. Such records may be embedded in a complex network of web pages that form the overall record, thus requiring the related web pages to be preserved as well. Archiving records such as these requires web archiving, which entails copying and preserving web pages before they are rendered inaccessible.

Web archiving is necessary because the web provides a sense of permanence that is only now beginning to be widely recognized as illusory.[24] Because some websites persist for long periods of time, the web can appear to have everything ever created for it still available. For example, Warner Brothers' *Space Jam* website—made for the film of the same name—appears seemingly exactly as it did in 1996.[25] The *New York Times* website provides access to the newspaper's archives going back to 1851. However, this sense of permanence and completeness that seems to surround websites still in the custody of their creators is rather tenuous. Redesigning a website often mean "retiring" web pages that are no longer viewed as applicable, or are outright embarrassing, to present-day tastes. In addition to redesigns that do away with parts of websites, mass deletions by media companies further endanger web pages. Some of the best-known examples of mass inaccessibility include Yahoo's deletion of GeoCities—one of the earliest web self-publishing platforms—and the removal of user-created blogs from MySpace.[26] The web can be best described as an active publishing platform that reflects the present, rather than a comprehensive "archive" of the past.

Some of the methods used to archive web content are client-side archiving, server-side archiving, and nonweb archiving.[27] Client-side archiving is the most popular form of web archiving and is used by the Internet Archive's Wayback Machine.[28] In this approach, web crawlers act like normal web users and "start from seed pages, parse them, extract links, and fetch the linked document," then reiterate.[29] This method works well for simpler web pages but could work less well when encountering web pages that exchange content between web page loads, which is popularly known as the Asynchronous JavaScript and XML (AJAX) approach to creating web interfaces. Many social media sites make extensive use of this approach. Without special provisions for web archiving, this could make retrieving such content challenging. The challenges can be overcome but may require manual intervention by a skilled web archivist. Client-side archiving is also challenged when attempting to download large collections of web pages, which could take a long time. For example, Julien Masanès notes that a website with one hundred thousand pages would take approximately three days to download.[30]

Some of the limitations of client-side web archiving are overcome by server-side web archiving, in which files are copied directly from the server with the site owner's cooperation. This method is currently being used by the Library of Congress to create a Twitter archive.[31] The limitations of this approach are reanimating the web pages so that they are authentic to what the user would have experienced and the extensive effort required to negotiate the transfer of data.

Perhaps the simplest form of web archiving is to create nonweb archives, where web content is printed out or converted to a format such as PDF or PNG and stored using something other than the web (e.g., physical file folders or directories on a computer).[32] Although this method has some appeal because of its simplicity, it loses both the context in which users experienced the content and the hyperlinked navigation. It also could lose some of the graphical look and feel of the web page, as is readily evident when web pages are saved as PDFs or printouts.

CREATING CLIENT-SIDE WEB ARCHIVES

Producing WARC (Web ARChive) files, an ISO standard format for web archives, is one of several methods for creating client-side web archives.[33] One limitation of this approach is that you need a program to read the WARC files. A less complex solution is to use the Wget program to download the web pages as files into a directory.[34] The Wget program is able to crawl an entire website and download all related HTML, image files, and other media that might be linked to the page.[35]

Issuing the command below via the command line prompt (e.g., using the Mac OSX terminal application) will download my entire website:

```
wget -mpk http://www.thinkingprojects.org
```

The "-mpk" parameter is a series of options to Wget. The "m" specifies that all contents stemming from the home page should be downloaded. The "p" command causes Wget to download all the files that are necessary to properly display a given HTML page. The "k" option converts links within the document to make them amenable to local viewing. A listing of all Wget options is available on the Wget website.[36]

New web archiving tools are being created regularly to make web archiving more feasible and easier to complete. For example, a tool released by Ilya Kreymer and Rhizome called the Webrecorder creates WARC files; Kreymer also provides the tool WebArchivePlayer that allows the WARC file to be played back and explored by the user.[37] Testing of this tool shows that it works well for web archiving content. The only downside is that it requires users to visit every page that they want to web archive, which is only feasible for small web-based projects.

As mentioned in chapter 5, "Access and Outreach," video embedded in web pages can be difficult to download. Programs such as Wget should be able to download video embedded in web pages using HTML5 media elements; however, Wget is unlikely to download video that uses streaming servers. Therefore, one option is to first use Wget to download web pages and then try other means to extract the video. For example, using server-side archiving, or contacting the webmaster to get a copy of digital video, are methods that can be used to fill in holes left by client-side archiving.

Another option for creating client-side archives is to use the open-source Heritrix web crawler, which is the web crawler that powers the Internet Archive's Wayback Machine.[38] One advantage of Heritrix is that it creates WARC files, which are an international standard format for preserving web archives. The web archives are viewable in WayBackMachine, another piece of open-source software created by the Internet Archive.[39] Heritrix can be quite difficult to set up; however, Mat Kelly has created a software package called WAIL (Web Archive Integration Layer) that makes setting up Heritrix and WayBack relatively easy on a Mac and PC.[40]

Another option for creating web archives is to become a client of the Internet Archive's Archive-It service, a hosted service that archives websites for clients.[41] Other web archiving services are available; however, Archive-It is the most popular, no doubt a result of the Internet Archive's long-standing commitment to archiving the web. The downside of the Archive-It service is that it can be costly for small institutions. One approach is to share an Archive-It subscription among a consortium of archives working within a particular collecting area.

Once web-archived files have been created—either as a directory of files or as WARC files—they can be maintained like any other files in need of digital preservation. See chapter 4, "Digital Preservation," for more about this topic.

SMARTPHONE APPLICATIONS

Moving image and sound records can be embedded in smartphone applications, such as apps created for museum visitors. Unfortunately, because of the way that smartphone applications are controlled and circulated (e.g., through the Apple iTunes store), it is difficult to get a copy of the executable code as well as an environment in which to run it, as you can do with desktop computer software. Archivists can maintain the app's source code if they have access to it; in these cases, the app can be emulated on desktop computers (e.g., using Xcode in Mac OSX). However, smartphone environments are complex for most archives to maintain and serve up to users. One method to preserve iPhone and other smartphone applications is to create screencasts—video captures of the device's screen—of the app. Since screencasts are video, they can be preserved as digital video and do not require complex emulation. Although a screencast of an app is not the same thing as the app itself, such screencasts can be augmented with videos of patrons using the app, thus providing a representation of the app experience that future researchers can understand.

Fortunately, the moving image and sound records included in apps are usually access copies of the media; the masters can be found elsewhere. Because of this, it is not necessary to preserve the entire app in order to preserve the video and audio included in it. In sum, screencasts provide a work-around for documenting apps in a manner that is easy to preserve and provide access to.

CONSOLE-BASED GAMES

The likelihood that an archivist will need to preserve console video games is fairly remote, especially compared to other types of complex media like computer software or web-based records. The reason for this is that console-based games, like those developed for Nintendo, Sega, PlayStation, and Xbox, among others, are likely to be preserved by others, such as conservators at museums like the Strong National Museum of Play and the Museum of Modern Art, as well as in a more open fashion by the Internet Archive.[42] Therefore, console-based games are not dealt with in any depth in this book. However, recommended resources for preserving console-based games, as well as other gamelike environments such as virtual worlds, are included in this chapter's notes.[43]

CONCLUSION

Moving image and sound records can be embedded in complex media, such as in now-obsolete educational CD-ROMs. Preservation of software-based complex media can be accomplished through creating disk images, with software reanimated through emulators and virtual machines for access. Complex media that originate on the web can be preserved through web archiving, which is a method of copying websites and subjecting these copies to digital preservation activities.

NOTES

[1] Douglas K. Smith and Robert C. Alexander, *Fumbling the Future: How Xerox Invented, Then Ignored, the First Personal Computer* (New York: William Morrow, 1988).

[2] Lev Manovich, *The Language of New Media* (Cambridge, MA: MIT Press, 2001).

[3] Computer History Museum, "Timeline of Computer History: 1990," http://www.computerhistory.org/timeline/1990/, permalinked on April 25, 2016, at https://perma.cc/NFR6-XTK4.

[4] "Final Cut Pro," *Wikipedia*, https://en.wikipedia.org/wiki/Final_Cut_Pro, permalinked on April 25, 2016, at https://perma.cc/2LQJ-LS3E.

[5] Ibid.

[6] History of Computing in Learning and Education Project Wiki, http://hcle.wikispaces.com/, permalinked on April 25, 2016, at https://perma.cc/Z3CA-GD2U.

[7] "Encarta," *Wikipedia*, https://en.wikipedia.org/wiki/Encarta, permalinked on April 25, 2016, at https://perma.cc/WX2T-856H.

[8] Henry Jenkins, *Convergence Culture: Where Old and New Media Collide* (New York: New York University Press, 2008).

[9] AccessData's FTK Imager, http://accessdata.com/, permalinked on April 25, 2016, at https://perma.cc/GWA5-G845.

[10] AIMS Working Group, *AIMS Born-Digital Collections: An Inter-Institutional Model for Stewardship* (2012), http://dcs.library.virginia.edu/files/2013/02/AIMS_final.pdf, permalinked on April 25, 2016, at https://perma.cc/9E3J-8SCH; Julianna Barrera-Gomez and Ricky Erway, *Walk This Way: Detailed Steps for Transferring Born-Digital Content from Media You Can Read In-house* (Dublin, OH: OCLC Research, 2013), http://oclc.org/content/dam/research/publications/library/2013/2013-02.pdf, permalinked on April 25, 2016, at https://perma.cc/GBN6-WLXL; Martin J. Gengenbach, "'The Way We Do It Here': Mapping Digital Forensics Workflows in Collecting Institutions (master's thesis, University of North Carolina, Chapel Hill, 2012), http://digitalcurationexchange.org/system/files/gengenbach-forensic-workflows-2012.pdf, permalinked on April 25, 2016, at https://perma.cc/ANX6-MT9K.

[11] Christopher A. Lee et al., "BitCurator: Tools and Techniques for Digital Forensics in Collecting Institutions," *D-Lib Magazine* 18, no. 5/6 (2012), http://mirror.dlib.org/dlib/may12/lee/05lee.html, permalinked on April 25, 2016, at https://perma.cc/F5VF-UGKH.

[12] OSFMount, http://www.osforensics.com/tools/mount-disk-images.html, permalinked on April 25, 2016, at https://perma.cc/QFB6-X4TA.

[13] File Allocation Table, https://en.wikipedia.org/wiki/File_Allocation_Table, permalinked on April 25, 2016, at https://perma.cc/68AD-VSQK.

[14] NTFS, https://en.wikipedia.org/wiki/NTFS, permalinked on April 25, 2016, at https://perma.cc/GHA4-LRGS.

[15] HFS Plus, https://en.wikipedia.org/wiki/HFS_Plus, permalinked on April 25, 2016, at https://perma.cc/3TTY-TXQH.

[16] Cru WiebeTech UltraDoc FUD, https://www.cru-inc.com/products/wiebetech/forensic-ultradock-v5-5/, permalinked on April 25, 2016, at https://perma.cc/J6LA-C4C7; Cru WiebeTech USB Write Blocker, https://www.cru-inc.com/products/wiebetech/usb_writeblocker/, permalinked on April 25, 2016, at https://perma.cc/PH6W-5NT6.

[17] Device Side Data's 5.25 to USB device, http://www.deviceside.com/, permalinked on April 25, 2016, at https://perma.cc/H7F2-7Z47.

[18] KryoFlux, http://www.kryoflux.com/?page=kf_features, permalinked on April 25, 2016, at https://perma.cc/5642-MW2B.

[19] Oracle VirtualBox, https://www.virtualbox.org/, permalinked on April 25, 2016, at https://perma.cc/R7GL-6LF9.

[20] Stella Atari emulator, http://stella.sourceforge.net/, permalinked on April 25, 2016, at https://perma.cc/8YLB-2U7J; Mini vMac emulator, http://www.gryphel.com/c/minivmac/, permalinked on April 25, 2016, at https://perma.cc/M6H7-RKG2; DosBox emulator, http://www.dosbox.com/, permalinked on April 25, 2016, at https://perma.cc/S69Y-3A9J; CCS64 Commodore 64 emulator, http://www.ccs64.com/, permalinked on April 25, 2016, at https://perma.cc/UMS7-36P7; VICE Commodore 64 emulator, http://vice-emu.sourceforge.net/, permalinked on April 25, 2016, at https://perma.cc/UMS7-36P7; SheepShaver emulator, http://sheepshaver.cebix.net/, permalinked on April 25, 2016, at https://perma.cc/YWW7-GVXG.

[21] Jon Ippolito, "Generation Emulation," *Re-collection: Art, New Media, and Social Memory*, eds. Richard Rinehart and Jon Ippolito (Cambridge, MA: MIT Press), 119.

[22] Technical access element is included in section 4.3 of *Describing Archives: A Content Standard*, 2nd ed. (Chicago: Society of American Archivists, 2013).

[23] Catalog record for CD-ROM available at http://cat.pratt.edu/record=b1096081~S0, permalinked on April 25, 2016, at https://perma.cc/RTC7-GTRT.

[24] Several articles about the need to archive the web have appeared in major publications. See, for instance, Adrienne LaFrance, "Raiders of the Lost Web," *Atlantic,* October 14, 2015, http://www.theatlantic.com/technology/archive/2015/10/raiders-of-the-lost-web/409210/, permalinked on April 25, 2016, at https://perma.cc/5J25-J6QL.

25 *Space Jam* website, Warner Brothers, http://www.warnerbros.com/archive/spacejam/movie/jam.htm, permalinked on April 25, 2016, at https://perma.cc/TH63-UQJ3.

26 Anthony Cocciolo, "Youth Deleted: Saving Young People's Histories after Social Media Collapse," paper presented at International Internet Preservation Consortium General Assembly, Paris, France, May 19–23, 2014, http://www .thinkingprojects.org/youth_deleted_iipc.pdf, permalinked on April 25, 2016, at https://perma.cc/RU5N-CH3P.

27 Julien Masanès, *Web Archiving* (Berlin: Springer, 2006).

28 Internet Archive Wayback Machine, http://archive.org, permalinked on April 25, 2016, at https://perma.cc/7B4U-4E89.

29 Masanès, *Web Archiving*, 23.

30 Ibid., 24.

31 Gayle Osterberg, "Update on the Twitter Archive at the Library of Congress," *Library of Congress Blog*, January 4, 2013, http://blogs.loc.gov/loc/2013/01/update-on-the-twitter-archive-at-the-library-of-congress/, permalinked on April 25, 2016, at https://perma.cc/XS2P-T4KS.

32 Masanès, *Web Archiving*, 36.

33 ISO 28500:2009: WARC file format, http://www.iso.org/iso/catalogue_detail.htm?csnumber=44717, permalinked on April 25, 2016, at https://perma.cc/GX5K-Z38J.

34 Ben Fino-Radin, "Wget Cheat-Sheet," May 25, 2012, http://notepad.benfinoradin.info/tag/wget/, permalinked on April 25, 2016, at https://perma.cc/2YKV-H8B2.

35 Anthony Cocciolo, "Unix Commands and Batch Processing for the Reluctant Librarian or Archivist," *Code4Lib Journal* 23 (2014), http://journal.code4lib.org/articles/9158, permalinked on April 25, 2016, at https://perma.cc/7DEE-TPZB.

36 *Wget Manual*, http://www.gnu.org/software/wget/manual/wget.html, permalinked on April 25, 2016, at https://perma .cc/3KS8-SE7V.

37 Web Recorder, https://webrecorder.io/, permalinked on September 6, 2016, at https://webrecorder.io/; WebArchivePlayer, https://github.com/ikreymer/webarchiveplayer, permalinked on September 6, 2016, at https://perma.cc/LLX4-UNBJ.

38 Heritrix, https://webarchive.jira.com/wiki/display/Heritrix/Heritrix, permalinked on April 25, 2016, at https://perma .cc/5KG7-XJPR.

39 Wayback software download, http://archive-access.sourceforge.net/projects/wayback/downloads.html, permalinked on April 25, 2016, at https://perma.cc/MB9Q-Z2CA.

40 Mat Kelly's Web Archive Integration Layer (WAIL), http://matkelly.com/wail/, permalinked on April 25, 2016, at https:// perma.cc/ZW9F-97XQ.

41 Internet Archive's Archive-It service, https://archive-it.org/, permalinked on April 25, 2016, at https://perma.cc /ER75-VRKC.

42 The Strong National Museum of Play, http://www.museumofplay.org/, permalinked on April 25, 2016, at https://perma .cc/2BD6-63VN; Museum of Modern Art, http://www.moma.org/, permalinked on April 25, 2016, at https://perma.cc /SKP4-GLSC; Internet Archive, http://www.archive.org/, permalinked on April 25, 2016, at https://perma.cc/7B4U-4E89.

43 Useful resources on preserving console-based computer games and other types of complex game and gamelike environments include Mark Guttenbrunner, Christopher Becker, and Andreas Rauber, "Keeping the Game Alive: Evaluating Strategies for the Preservation of Console Video Games," *International Journal of Digital Curation* 5, no. 1 (2011): 64–90, http://www.ijdc .net/index.php/ijdc/article/view/147, permalinked on April 25, 2016, at https://perma.cc/JEP2-4SNE; Megan A. Winget, "Videogame Preservation and Massively Multiplayer Online Role-Playing Games: A Review of the Literature," *Journal of the American Society for Information Science & Technology* 62, no. 10 (2011): 1869–83; Alasdair Bachell and Matthew Barr, "Video Game Preservation in the UK: Independent Games Developers' Records Management Practices," *International Journal of Digital Curation* 9, no. 2 (2014): 137–70, http://www.ijdc.net/index.php/ijdc/article/view/9.2.170/375, perma-linked on April 25, 2016, at https://perma.cc/NF2H-7T6W; Jerome McDonough et al., *Preserving Virtual Worlds Final Report* (2010), https://www.ideals.illinois.edu/handle/2142/17097, permalinked on April 25, 2016, at https://perma.cc /WAM9-ZRMQ.

Epilogue

The goal of this book has been to provide practical guidance on managing moving image and sound collections for the archivist who may be more well versed in managing paper collections. This is a challenging moment for archives, which are facing increasing quantities of moving image and sound records in need of stewardship, often accompanied with few additional resources to ensure long-term preservation and accessibility. This book aimed to offer some solutions for ensuring the long-term persistence of moving image and sound records, such as do-it-yourself digitization, low-cost digital preservation, and open-source access tools. I will conclude with some thoughts on the future of moving image and sound archives by taking into account the culture in which they are embedded. But first, I offer three factors to keep in mind when managing moving image and sound collections.

The first factor relates to media age. By this, I mean that media age should not be the sole determinant in reformatting decisions. As has been explored in this book, some born-digital media, such as burned optical discs, may be more susceptible to failure than far older media, such as black-and-white film on a polyester base. Other issues unique to digital technology, such as digital rights management (DRM), can further endanger the accessibility of records. Thus, the particularities of the media and the condition of the item itself should be considered when making decisions about reformatting. If some media are newer or digital, that does not make them better or less likely to fail.

The second factor to keep in mind is that archives need to move away from the "media in the box" perspective as the main way to preserve electronic and audiovisual records. For most media, such as video, audio, and complex media, the eventual goal for most archives should be to reformat content to digital files and store those files in trustworthy repositories. Although this can be delayed to some extent through preservation-standard storage environments, it is unlikely that this solution will be sufficient indefinitely. At the very minimum, digital repositories that store archival files should hold at least two independent copies of the data, with some separation (e.g., not kept in the same room). Beyond this, there are many worthwhile goals, such as having the technology, resources, and organization of the archives focused explicitly on preserving digital assets. Results of such activities could include creating three independent copies of the data using enterprise storage technology, dispersing the copies geographically, and engaging in file fixity checks, among other elements. As I like to tell my students, Tupperware is not a trustworthy repository!

The last factor to keep in mind is the capacity of the human brain and the senses to ignore distortions in moving images and sound reproductions. For example, when digitizing analog video, it is easy to ignore reduction in color quality or the introduction of digital artifacts. Anyone who has ever taken a driver training class and learned about blind spots—the way that the brain fills in information that it does not see but thinks should be there—may be familiar with the ability of the human perceptual system to gloss over details. For this reason, when engaging in digitization or format migration, it is necessary to do side-by-side comparisons between the master and the digitized or migrated copy. In doing so, one should look closely at and listen attentively for the introduction of artifacts or the degradation of original elements. You may well be surprised to find that what you have digitized is inferior to the original. Luckily, using better equipment can often rectify this.

THOUGHTS ON THE FUTURE

Although recorded moving image and sound were inventions of the nineteenth century, they became more than curiosities and made a substantial impact on culture in the twentieth century. Musical recordings on discs and cylinders, followed by silent films and eventually "talkie" films, ushered in an era of popular culture and mass entertainment. The midcentury invention of the television built on the path forged by radio by bringing news and entertainment into the homes of millions, further solidifying the bonds between producers of moving image and sound records and their consumers. As the century progressed, continual innovation in moving image and sound technology brought color, richer sound recordings, and more detailed video images. As technology evolved, the means of producing and dispersing moving image and sound records multiplied. The tools for capturing live action, whether through small-gauge film, VHS tape, or iPhone, have made the creation of such records increasingly possible with each successive decade, resulting in widespread recordings of meetings and events as well as amateur films. The ability to transmit such creations over the Internet, coming within reach of millions with the introduction of YouTube and other platforms, has irrevocably impacted how humans share information, knowledge, and culture.[1] What might these developments mean for human culture more generally? Further, what might they mean for archives and archivists? Although it is impossible to predict the future, some of these issues are explored in this epilogue.

The first position I will take is that moving image and sound records will only increase in prominence and importance as the twenty-first century progresses. The basis of this assertion is that audio and video recordings enable orality, or more specifically, the use of the spoken word as a primary vehicle for communication. The work of communication theorist Walter Ong is particularly useful here. In *Orality and Literacy*, he argues that modern humans have existed for tens of thousands of years; however, written language is a fairly recent invention, beginning around 3500 BC with the Sumerians in present-day Iraq.[2] Written language is rare, too, as most languages ever spoken never developed a written equivalent.

Through evolution, humans developed the ability to speak, and, unlike with writing, all individuals who have the physical and cognitive ability to hear and speak easily learn spoken language. For tens of thousands of years, humans transmitted information primarily through oral communication and storytelling; stories were often repeated, memorized, and set to a rhythm so that they could be passed from one generation to the next. The ability of twenty-first-century humans to transmit information, knowledge, and culture through oral communication using video and audio recordings allows for a return to the oldest form of communication, albeit in a new, mediated way. Technologies such as radio, television, and the telephone have all furthered a culture of orality.

Some have argued that reading and writing are in trouble. Sociologists Wendy Griswold, Terry McDonnell, and Nathan Wright find that "the era of mass reading, which lasted from the mid-nineteenth through the mid-twentieth century in northwestern Europe and North America, was the anomaly" and that "we are now seeing such reading return to its former social base: a self-perpetuating minority that we shall call the reading class."[3] Reading and writing will persist but will likely be used in addition to—and perhaps in service of—other forms of electronically mediated oral communication. Concepts that highlight this transformed literacy landscape include multiple literacies, new literacies, multimodal literacy, digital literacies, media literacy, and visual literacy. Although each of these concepts is different, they emphasize a need for understanding and being able to operate in a communicative landscape that includes more than print literacy. For example, educational researchers Gunter Kress and Carey Jewitt note that "now the screen is the dominant medium; and the screen is the site of the image and its logic"; they find that even in books "now writing is often subordinated to image."[4]

Institutional archivists may well recognize this change in their own archives, with some archivists noting that narrative reports on activities have given way to short bursts of email.[5] Research has indicated that the web, originally the great carrier of text, has seen a decline in text on web pages since 2005 as means to transmit information in other ways has increased (e.g., audio and video).[6] Given these currents in culture, it is likely that moving image and sound records will continue to take on an increasingly large role in facilitating human orality.

Beyond the increased importance of moving image and sound records, the second position I take is that new web-based distribution channels are likely to complicate the relationship between archives and their users. Before I articulate this position more thoroughly, it is useful to reflect on the evolution of media distribution. One of the most remarkable changes in the last decade has been the ability to make video available to audiences at little or no cost via Internet distribution channels. It was not so long ago that getting moving image and sound records to sizeable audiences was expensive and time-consuming, requiring producers to either have the funds themselves or appeal to groups that had such funds. An example from my own experience highlights this change. In 2007 I worked on a project that sent thirty thousand DVD copies of Spike Lee's documentary film *When the Levees Broke: A Requiem in Four Acts* via US mail to community centers, schools, and libraries throughout the country. A large portion of the nearly $1 million grant went toward copying, distributing, and shipping these DVDs.[7] During the project, the Internet was only then becoming reliable enough to transmit high-quality video to all the destinations that could benefit from the film. This example illustrates the great effort and expense necessary to distribute video until fairly recently.

Beyond copying DVDs or VHS tapes, other means of getting moving image and sound works to be seen by sizeable audiences required appealing to broadcasters, such as the Public Broadcasting Service (PBS). In working on a research project about public broadcasting, I learned about some PBS programs that erupted in controversy and failed to be aired. One prominent example was the airing of *Tongues Untied*, a story by Marlon Riggs about the experience of being a black gay man living with AIDS. Although PBS scheduled it to be broadcast in 1991, local affiliates refused to air it in cities such as Houston, Milwaukee, Denver, Portland, Memphis, Nashville, Dayton, Kansas City, Oklahoma City, and others, believing that it was pornographic and inappropriate for mainstream audiences.[8] In 1997, B. J. Bullert noted that "it was the first—and so far the only—program about the experience of being black and gay on public television."[9] Other works, such as the halt of the airing on PBS of *Stop the Church* in 1991, further illustrate the obstacles to broadcasting. This film depicted a demonstration by ACT UP (the AIDS Coalition to Unleash Power) at Saint Patrick's Cathedral in New York to draw attention to the Catholic Church's anti–safe sex policies amid the height of the AIDS pandemic. The film was pulled from its airdate two weeks before its expected broadcast.[10] In this case, as well as others, the "culture wars" of the 1990s prevented important works from reaching sizeable audiences.

A distinct advantage of web distribution is that videos do not have to meet the same "moral" or quality standards of broadcasters. This has not been without its troubles. For example, in 2012 a video on YouTube that was offensive to Muslims was suspected to have been the cause of violence in the Middle East, specifically in Libya and Egypt; the US government asked for the video to be taken down.[11] YouTube did not comply but did post a warning message before playing the video. This example is interesting in that it highlights the ability of small groups to produce and circulate videos that reach wide audiences without the consent of the kinds of gatekeepers present during the *Tongues Untied* incident. More pedestrian examples like the Internet celebrity, who may gain millions of followers (and millions of dollars!) through video blogs, illustrate a transformed capacity to share and communicate via video.[12]

With the newfound ease of circulating video online, the challenge for archives is highlighted by Rick Prelinger, who notes that "YouTube quickly fashioned itself into what most members of the public regard as the world's default media archive," making traditional archives "appear to be less useful, less accommodating, less relevant, and ultimately less important than YouTube."[13] Although YouTube makes no claim to preserve video and acknowledges that it can remove any content for any reason, the existence of such large quantities of video from all eras makes it appear to the public as the de facto archive. Archives' prioritization of preservation over access, as well as respect for the rights of creators, make archives appear less user-centered than YouTube and similar sites. Given users' ability to create, consume, and share video productions with such ease, the need to have an organization tasked with preserving and providing access to such work can appear somewhat superfluous.

Because archives are put in competition with YouTube—not by their own doing but by the perceptions of users and the public—it is necessary to begin to be able to operate on this assumption and even try to chip away at this perception. One way to do this is for archives to more assertively make works available to the public. The legal and technical work to achieve this is no small feat, but it is indeed necessary for researchers who are coming to expect everything to be available at the click of a mouse. Comparisons between archives and YouTube (or similar sites) are likely to persist. For example, Australian television researcher Alan McKee authored a research study published in the journal *Television & Media* titled "YouTube Versus the National Film and Sound Archive: Which Is the More Useful Resource for Historians of Australian Television?"[14] The study found that there were advantages and disadvantages to each, but it does highlight the perception of a competition between YouTube and archives.

One way that archives can more effectively "compete" with YouTube and related sites is to learn from what makes these sites successful and even engage in some imitation. Indeed, imitation is the sincerest form of flattery! The first way archives can do this is to invest in making their access points more participatory. Karen F. Gracy has argued that "not all cultural institutions will see user-defined value as of primary importance, yet many should consider how to incorporate it within their own systems."[15] This can be as simple as allowing users to make comments on a video. Further, research has indicated that designing repositories so that users can contribute to them positively impacts use.[16]

Additionally, incorporating tools into access points that help make the researcher experience more time efficient, such as streamlined ability to request items for viewing, can help endear archives to their end users. For example, Princeton University Library finding aids include a "request this box," "ask a question," and "suggest a correction" button on each webpage that draws from a finding aid.[17] Such access points invite users to use items and contribute their own knowledge, making it clear from web interface alone that interaction and use are encouraged.

Lastly, in addition to simply putting copies of work online, engaging in outreach and educational activities that help make moving image and sound records meaningful to users is increasingly important in a world where large quantities of "content" are available immediately. Nonprofit archives, whether based at colleges and universities, museums, historical societies, or other organizations, have the distinct advantage of being more interested in education, learning, and scholarship than in producing monetary value. For this reason, archives have more to offer than "content," especially when they imbue their services with an educational and scholarly mission to provide insight, understanding, and even joy to their patrons.

FURTHER READING

Appraisal and Reappraisal

Although the only published books that have sections explicitly about appraising moving image and sound records are the ones by Kula and Gracy, some implications for moving image and sound records can be drawn from the other works. For example, in an institutional archives context, the Robyns book can help develop an understanding of functional analysis, which can be applied to moving image and sound records created by an institution. The Huth piece provides useful advice on appraising digital records, especially through his drawing attention to the need for technical appraisal. The Boles book discusses issues essential to any type of appraisal, such as the need to craft mission statements and collecting policies that drive appraisal decisions.

Boles, Frank. *Selecting and Appraising Archives and Manuscripts*. Chicago: Society of American Archivists, 2005.

Gracy, Karen F. *Film Preservation: Competing Definitions of Value, Use, and Practice*. Chicago: Society of American Archivists, 2007.

Huth, Geof. "Appraising Digital Records." Module 14 in *Appraisal and Acquisition Strategies,* edited by Michael Shallcross and Christopher J. Prom, 7–68. Chicago: Society of American Archivists, 2016.

Kula, Sam. *Appraising Moving Images: Assessing the Archival and Monetary Value of Film and Video Records*. Lanham, MD: Scarecrow Press, 2003.

Robyns, Marcus C. *Using Functional Analysis in Archival Appraisal: A Practical and Effective Alternative to Traditional Appraisal Methodologies*. Lanham, MD: Rowman & Littlefield, 2014.

Accessioning, Arrangement, and Description

The readings below offer more on descriptive practices using an aggregate or finding aid approach as well as an item-level approach. For the finding aid approach, the Hackbart-Dean and Slomba, Roe, and Santamaria books are recommended; they include examples of audiovisual groupings in finding aids. Item-level practices, such as MARC records, are discussed in the *AMIA Compendium of Moving Image Cataloging Practice*, and PBCore is discussed in the Rubin article.

Hackbart-Dean, Pam, and Elizabeth Slomba. *How to Manage Processing in Archives and Special Collections*. Chicago: Society of American Archivists, 2013.

Martin, Abigail Leab. *AMIA Compendium of Moving Image Cataloging Practice*. Beverly Hills, CA: Association of Moving Image Archivists, 2001.

Roe, Kathleen D. *Arranging and Describing Archives and Manuscripts*. Chicago: Society of American Archivists, 2005.

Rubin, Nan. "The PBCore Metadata Standard: A Decade of Evolution." *Journal of Digital Media Management* 1, no. 1 (2012): 55–68.

Santamaria, Daniel A. *Extensible Processing for Archives and Special Collections: Reducing Processing Backlogs*. Chicago: Neal-Schuman, 2015.

Legal and Ethical Issues

Rights in the Digital Era provides a thorough overview of the major legal and rights issues that an archivist may encounter, and the reader can readily draw implications for moving image and sound records. The Besek article is essential for addressing pre-1972 recordings. The Hirtle piece provides useful information on determining the copyright status of a particular recording; he updates it yearly.

Behrnd-Klodt, Menzi L. *Navigating Legal Issues in Archives*. Chicago: Society of American Archivists, 2008.

Behrnd-Klodt, Menzi L., and Christopher J. Prom. *Rights in the Digital Era*. Chicago: Society of American Archivists, 2015.

Besek, June M. *Copyright and Related Issues Relevant to Digital Preservation and Dissemination of Unpublished Pre-1972 Sound Recordings by Libraries and Archives*. Washington, DC: Council on Library and Information Resources, 2009. http://www.clir.org/pubs/reports/pub144/pub144.pdf, permalinked on April 21, 2016, at https://perma.cc/U4F8-2CEY.

Hirtle, Peter B. *Copyright Term and the Public Domain in the United States, January 1, 2017*. http://copyright.cornell.edu/resources/publicdomain.cfm, permalinked on January 30, 2017, at https://perma.cc/WAY6-MAYV.

Digital Preservation

General digital preservation practices and advice, such as offered in the modules by O'Meara and Stratton in *Digital Preservation Essentials*, are indeed useful for digitized and born-digital moving image and sound collections. However, the reader should keep in mind some of the issues discussed in this book that are unique to moving image and sound records (e.g., very large file sizes and differences between video files and other computer files). Additional resources on digital preservation are provided.

Bantin, Philip C., ed. *Building Trustworthy Digital Repositories: Theory and Implementation.* Lanham, MD: Rowman & Littlefield, 2016.

Lavoie, Brian F. *The Open Archival Information System Reference Model: Introductory Guide.* 2nd ed. Dublin, OH: OCLC Office of Research, 2012. http://dx.doi.org/10.7207/twr14-02, permalinked on April 21, 2016, at https://perma.cc/7KVK-D5JM.

Marks, Steve. *Module 8: Becoming a Trusted Digital Repository.* Trends in Archives Practice. Chicago: Society of American Archivists, 2015.

O'Meara, Erin, and Kate Stratton. *Digital Preservation Essentials.* Trends in Archives Practice. Chicago: Society of American Archivists, 2016.

Access and Outreach

Unfortunately, the literature on accessing moving image and sound records is not as vigorous as it could be. The Gracy articles provide some background on challenges that archives face when engaging in digitization for preservation and access. Literature on educational outreach is growing, as seen in the other readings. Although books such as *Past or Portal* do not directly mention moving image and sound records, some of the educational activities can be redeveloped to use such records.

Gracy, Karen F. "Distribution and Consumption Patterns of Archival Moving Images in Online Environments." *American Archivist* 75, no. 2 (2012): 422–55.

Gracy, Karen F. "Ambition and Ambivalence: A Study of Professional Attitudes toward Digital Distribution of Archival Moving Images." *American Archivist* 76, no. 2 (2013): 346–73.

Mitchell, Eleanor, Peggy Seiden, and Suzy Taraba, eds. *Past or Portal? Enhancing Undergraduate Learning through Special Collections and Archives.* Chicago: Association of College and Research Libraries, 2012.

Prom, Christopher J., and Lisa Janicke Hinchliffe. *Teaching with Primary Sources.* Chicago: Society of American Archivists, 2016.

Interactions with Moving Image and Sound Producers

General advice and practices for working with donors are useful regardless of whether moving image and sound records are implicated; such advice is available in the Purcell book. *The Digital Dilemma 2* is a well-researched investigation of the relationship between independent filmmakers and nonprofit archives.

Purcell, Aaron. *Donors and Archives: A Guidebook for Successful Programs.* Lanham, MD: Rowman & Littlefield, 2015.

Science and Technology Council of the Academy of Motion Picture Arts and Sciences. *The Digital Dilemma 2: Perspectives from Independent Filmmakers, Documentarians and Nonprofit Audiovisual Archives.* 2012. https://www.oscars.org/science-technology/sci-tech-projects/digital-dilemma-2, permalinked on September 15, 2016, at https://perma.cc/3NET-TGZC.

Audio Collections

The *ARSC Guide to Audio Preservation* is thorough, well illustrated, and highly recommended. Other resources include all of the publications from the International Association of Sound and Audiovisual Archives (IASA), which are available online.

Brylawski, Sam, Maya Lerman, Robin Pike, and Kathlin Smith, eds. *ARSC Guide to Audio Preservation*. Washington, DC: Council on Library and Information Resources, 2015. https://www.clir.org /pubs/reports/pub164/pub164.pdf.

Bradley, Kevin, ed. *Guidelines on the Production and Preservation of Digital Audio Objects*. 2nd ed. Aarhus, Denmark: IASA, 2009. http://www.iasa-web.org/tc04/audio-preservation, permalinked on September 15, 2016, at https://perma.cc/4DFY-E47Q.

Schüller, Dietrich, and Albrecht Häfner, eds. *Handling and Storage of Audio and Video Carriers*. Aarhus, Denmark: IASA, 2014. http://www.iasa-web.org/handling-storage-tc05, permalinked on September 15, 2016, at https://perma.cc/JSV2-8VDC.

Film Collections

The Film Preservation Guide is highly recommended as a film care and preservation manual. The Enticknap book provides a thorough historical treatment of moving image technology, including film and video. The Bordwell and Academy of Motion Picture Arts and Sciences publications discuss the emergence of digital technology in the Hollywood film community.

Bordwell, David. *Pandora's Digital Box: Films, Files, and the Future of Movies*. Madison, WI: Irvington Way Institute Press, 2012.

Enticknap, Leo. *Moving Image Technology: From Zoetrope to Digital*. London: Wallflower, 2005.

National Film Preservation Foundation. *The Film Preservation Guide: The Basics for Archives, Libraries, and Museums*. San Francisco: National Film Preservation Foundation, 2004. http://www.filmpreservation .org/preservation-basics/the-film-preservation-guide-download, permalinked on April 22, 2016, at https://perma.cc/2Z5A-LYXW.

Science and Technology Council of the Academy of Motion Picture Arts and Sciences. *The Digital Dilemma: Strategic Issues in Archiving and Accessing Digital Motion Picture Materials*. Beverly Hills, CA: Academy of Motion Picture Arts and Sciences, 2007. https://www.oscars.org/science-technology /sci-tech-projects/digital-dilemma, permalinked on September 15, 2016, at https://perma.cc /Y5M2-KESS.

Analog and Digital Video Collections

The publications by Jimenez and Platt and Gfeller, Jarczyk, and Phillips are useful to help identify videotape formats; the latter can also be used to help recognize video playback problems. The Bogus and Blood articles are useful for their discussions of video reformatting and technical specifications. The *Videotape Preservation Factsheets* provide information in an easily digestible format.

Blood, George. *Refining Conversion Contract Specifications: Determining Suitable Digital Video Formats for Medium-term Storage*. Washington, DC: Library of Congress, 2011. http://www.digitizationguidelines.gov/audio-visual/documents/IntrmMastVidFormatRecs_20111001.pdf, permalinked on April 5, 2016, at https://perma.cc/L58A-38NV.

Bogus, Ian, George Blood, Robin L. Dale, Robin Leech, and David Matthews. *Minimum Digitization Capture Recommendations*. Chicago: Association for Library Collections and Technical Services Preservation and Reformatting Section, 2013. http://www.ala.org/alcts/resources/preserv/minimum-digitization-capture-recommendations#video, permalinked on April 5, 2016, at https://perma.cc/9E7H-6E54.

Gfeller, Johannes, Agathe Jarczyk, and Joanna Phillips. *Compendium of Image Errors in Analogue Video*. Zurich: Schweizerisches Institut für Kunstwissenschaft, 2012.

Jimenez, Mona, and Lisa Platt. *Videotape Identification and Assessment Guide*. Austin: Texas Commission on the Arts, 2004. http://www.arts.texas.gov/wp-content/uploads/2012/04/video.pdf, permalinked on September 15, 2016, at https://perma.cc/PCL8-ZXQQ.

Wheeler, Jim, Peter Brothers, and Hannah Frost. *Videotape Preservation Factsheets*. Hollywood, CA: Association of Moving Image Archivists, 2007. http://www.amianet.org/sites/all/files/fact_sheets_0.pdf, permalinked on April 4, 2016, at https://perma.cc/XZ9Q-QQGE.

Complex Media

The following texts offer discussions of a variety of complex media items, including artworks, video games, simulations, and 3-D content.

Delve, Janet, and David Anderson. *Preserving Complex Digital Objects*. London: Facet, 2014.

Rinehart, Richard, and Jon Ippolito. *Re-collection: Art, New Media, and Social Memory*. Cambridge, MA: MIT Press, 2014.

NOTES

[1] A thorough and engrossing discussion of how networks more generally transform information and knowledge sharing is provided by Yochai Benkler in *The Wealth of Networks* (New Haven: Yale University Press, 2006).

[2] Walter J. Ong, *Orality and Literacy: The Technologizing of the Word* (London: Routledge, 2002).

[3] Wendy Griswold, Terry McDonnell, and Nathan Wright, "Reading and the Reading Class in the Twenty-First Century," *Annual Review of Sociology* 31 (2005): 127–41.

[4] Gunter Kress and Carey Jewitt, *Multimodal Literacy* (New York: Peter Lang), 16.

[5] For example, Linda Levy of the Archives of the American Jewish Joint Distribution Committee (JDC) noted such changes in the JDC Archives during a 2012 class visit (personal communication).

[6] Anthony Cocciolo, "The Rise and Fall of Text on the Web: A Quantitative Study of Web Archives," *Information Research* 20, no. 3 (2005), http://www.informationr.net/ir/20-3/paper682.html, permalinked on April 21, 2016, at https://perma.cc /D4ZQ-K4E4.

[7] Teaching the Levees, http://www.teachingthelevees.org, permalinked on April 20, 2016, at https://perma.cc/25G7-3K7U.

[8] B. J. Bullert, *Public Television: Politics and the Battle over Documentary Film* (New Brunswick, NJ: Rutgers University Press, 1997).

[9] Ibid., 119.

[10] Robert Hilferty, "Why 'Stop the Church' Was Televised" (letter to the editor), *New York Times*, October 4, 1981, http://www .nytimes.com/1991/10/04/opinion/l-why-stop-the-church-was-televised-112091.html, permalinked on April 20, 2016, at https://perma.cc/YT4S-5EBG.

[11] Claire Cain Miller, "As Violence Spreads in Arab World, Google Blocks Access to Inflammatory Video," *New York Times*, September 13, 2012, http://www.nytimes.com/2012/09/14/technology/google-blocks-inflammatory-video-in-egypt-and -libya.html, permalinked on April 20, 2016, at https://perma.cc/YT4S-5EBG.

[12] Madeline Berg, "The World's Highest-Paid YouTube Stars 2015," *Forbes,* October 14, 2015, http://www.forbes.com/sites /maddieberg/2015/10/14/the-worlds-highest-paid-youtube-stars-2015/, permalinked on April 20, 2016, at https://perma .cc/KZ8Q-6FPW.

[13] Rick Prelinger, "The Appearance of Archives," *The YouTube Reader,* eds. Pelle Snickars and Patrick Vonderau (Stockholm: National Library of Sweden), 268–74, http://www.kb.se/dokument/aktuellt/audiovisuellt/youtubereader/youtube_reader _052009_endversion.pdf, permalinked on September 15, 2016, at https://perma.cc/E5UB-6U9R.

[14] Alan McKee, "YouTube Versus the National Film and Sound Archive: Which Is the More Useful Resource for Historians of Australian Television?," *Television & Media* 12, no. 2 (2011): 154–73.

[15] Karen F. Gracy, "Moving Image Preservation and Cultural Capital," *Library Trends* 56, no. 1 (2007), 183–97.

[16] Anthony Cocciolo, "Can Web 2.0 Enhance Community Participation in an Institutional Repository? The Case of PocketKnowledge at Teachers College, Columbia University," *Journal of Academic Librarianship* 36, no. 4 (2012): 304–12.

[17] Princeton University Library finding aids, http://findingaids.princeton.edu/, permalinked on January 30, 2017, at https:// perma.cc/36CM-SERZ.

Glossary

Note: Terms that are more commonly known by their acronym are listed under that acronym.

10-bit uncompressed video: A format for converting analog video to digital video that does not compress any of the video frames and provides 10 bits for red, 10 bits for green, and 10 bits for blue.

16 mm film: A color or black-and-white film format that is 16 mm wide; often used for educational films, television, and low-budget films (in contrast to Hollywood feature films). Can include sound via magnetic strip or optical sound track.

2K resolution: A resolution used in digital cinema that provides for about 2,000 pixels (from left to right) of image resolution.

35 mm film: A film format that is 35 mm wide, used for commercial film productions or those that have substantial budgets. Can include a sound track or be silent.

4K resolution: A resolution used in digital cinema that provides for about 4,000 pixels (from left to right) of image resolution. Ultra high-definition television also uses this resolution.

8 mm film: A film format that is 8 mm wide, used for personal and family use and for low-budget film productions.

A/D (analog-to-digital) converter: In audio, a device used to convert analog sound to digital sound. Can also refer to a video device that converts an analog video signal to a digital signal.

A-D Strips: A chemical-sensitive paper from the Image Permanence Institute that indicates the extent to which acetate film is undergoing vinegar syndrome.

AAC (Advanced Audio Coding): An audio standard for lossy compression of audio, designed to be the successor to MP3.

AACR2 (Anglo-American Cataloguing Rules, second edition): Formerly the official cataloguing rules for library materials, used in the United States (among other countries); superseded by RDA (Resource Description and Access).

Access copy: A copy of a record (e.g., a video or audio record) that is convenient for researcher use, such as compressed files that easily fit onto a DVD.

Accession: Taking physical and legal custody (i.e., ownership) of records, and recording some basic information about those being transferred (e.g., assigning an accession number to the collection and providing a brief inventory of the boxes and their contents).

Acclimatization: The process of slowly moving a film or other media from cold storage to room temperature to prevent condensation.

Acetate decay: See **vinegar syndrome**.

Acetate film, also **cellulose acetate film:** Also known as safety film, this form of film preceded polyester film and can be found in a variety of gauges. This type of film is susceptible to vinegar syndrome.

Acid-free: A type of paper or material that is pH neutral or slightly basic, but not acidic.

Administrative metadata: Metadata for managing administrative aspects of a record, such as location, preservation issues, and intellectual property.

AJAX (Asynchronous JavaScript and XML): A method of developing interactive web pages where information is exchanged between page loads by a web client and web server.

Analog: A system for representing audio and video on a physical medium that uses a wide range of electromagnetic signals, as opposed to the discrete signals used in digital technology (ones and zeros).

Appraisal: The process of determining that records have permanent or archival value. Does not imply determining the market value of a work. Contrast with **monetary appraisal**.

Archival description: The process of creating a finding aid, elucidating the arrangement, and providing information about the person, family, or organization that created the records.

Archival master or **archival copy:** The original of a media asset, or a copy of it that is as faithful to the original as technically possible.

ArchivesSpace: A web-based archival management system and access tool that merges the functions of Archivists Toolkit and Archon.

Archivists Toolkit: A desktop tool for managing an archives and creating EAD-compatible finding aids; can run on multiple platforms; is currently unsupported software and was replaced by ArchivesSpace.

Archon: A web-based archival management system and access tool that is currently unsupported and was replaced by ArchivesSpace.

Arrangement: The task of organizing materials with respect to provenance and original order, which typically means organizing information in a way that respects the ways in which the creator kept the records.

Artifact or **digitization artifact:** In reference to digitization—often of video—an element introduced into the image or sound that was not present in the original signal and was produced during the digitization process. *Artifacts* can also refer to playback errors present in the analog signal (elements in the signal that were not present when the tape was mastered). Artifacts should be eliminated, if possible.

Aspect ratio: The proportion of the width to the height of a video or cinematic work. Most standard-definition television uses an aspect ratio of 4:3; high-definition television uses an aspect ratio of 16:9.

AtoM (Access to Memory): An archival management and access tool created by the company Artefactual Systems.

Audacity: An open-source software that can record and edit audio; runs on multiple platforms.

Audio track: The audio portion of a video work, embedded in a video file or written to a magnetic tape.

AVI (Audio Video Interleave): A wrapper file created by Microsoft that can include audio and video.

Azimuth: The angle of the tape head relative to the magnetic tape. Adjusting the angle of the tape head can improve the playback of an audiotape.

Backlog: A term used by archivists to denote collections that have not been processed yet and are typically unavailable to researchers.

Bequest: A gift made through a will.

Betacam, Betacam SP, Betacam SX: Formats of professional videotape. Betacam and Betacam SP are analog formats, and Betacam SX is a digital format. These formats should not be confused with **Betamax**.

Betamax: A consumer videotape format introduced in 1975; not to be confused with **Betacam**.

Binder: In magnetic tape, the substance between the tape back coat and the magnetic layer, which holds the magnetic layer to the back coat.

Bit depth: The number of bits used to represent a sample (e.g., the number of bits to represent a pixel, the number of bits to represent a tiny slice of digitized sound, etc.).

Bit rot: The corruption of data on media because of hardware failure.

Blu-ray: A digital optical disc format introduced in 2006 and often used for storing compressed versions of high-definition video.

Born digital: Information that is created on computers and that may not have an analog equivalent (e.g., a printout or videotape).

BWF (Broadcast Wave Format): An uncompressed audio format similar to Microsoft Wave files (WAV) except that it includes extra space for embedded metadata.

Carrier: The medium used to hold information (e.g., VHS tape, vinyl disc, etc.).

Cartridge tape media: Videotapes or audiotapes that are enclosed in plastic containers. Contrast with open-reel media, which have no cartridge.

CD (compact disc): A digital optical disc often used for storing digital audio. Also appears in versions that can be written or rewritten to by consumers.

CGI (computer-generated imagery): Two-dimensional and three-dimensional imagery—such as animated characters and architectural scenes—created on a computer.

Checksum: A value that is generated by an algorithm, such as MD5 or SHA-256, which represents a file uniquely, such that if a file is changed even in a minor way, its checksum will change. Checksums are often used for monitoring file fixity. See **hash**.

Chrominance: In analog video signals, the color part of the signal that was added to broadcast transmissions with the invention of color television. See **luminance**.

Coarse groove: A groove on phonograph records that is larger than microgroove, usually appearing on early records such as 78 rpm records.

Codec: The system for encoding a video or audio file, as well as the system for decoding it (e.g., MPEG4/H.264, a popular codec for streaming video over the web).

Color fading: The chemical decomposition of color dyes (often cyan, yellow, and magenta) used in color film, causing the dyes to fade, which is a major preservation concern.

Color shifting: The chemical decomposition of color dyes used in color film, causing the dyes to change color, which is a major preservation concern.

Compact audiocassette: An analog audiotape format in a cartridge that was widely popular and is still used in some niche markets today.

Component signal: A video signal that carries the luminance and chrominance signals separately.

Composite signal: A video signal that carries the luminance and chrominance signals together.

Copyright: The exclusive rights of a work's creator to make copies of his/her work and to publicly perform his/her work, as defined by US copyright law.

Creative Commons: A system that allows copyright owners to assign downstream rights to use their work.

CRT (cathode-ray tube): A video display technology in wide use before replacement by flat-panel LCD and LED displays. This is the technology behind the older "boxy" televisions.

Cubic feet: See **linear feet**.

D-9: An early professional video format.

DACS (Describing Archives: A Content Standard): A standard from the Society of American Archivists that tells archivists how to compose each element of a finding aid.

Dailies: Raw footage, often the footage filmed the previous day, watched by the cast and crew working on a film set.

DAT (Digital Audio Tape): A cartridge-based and obsolete digital audio recording technology.

DCP (Digital Cinema Package): A device, usually a hard drive, that is used to convey digital cinema files, such as audio and moving image files.

Deaccession: Offering records to another institution, returning them to the donor, or destroying them because they do not have permanent value.

Deinterlace: The process of making an analog video image—which draws all the even lines and then all the odd lines, resulting in an interlaced image—display correctly on noninterlaced screens, such as progressive-scan displays (e.g., LED and LCD flat-panel screens).

Descriptive metadata: Information about a record, such as the title, the date it was created, its creator, and a description of the contents.

Digital Betacam: See **Betacam**.

Digital Millennium Copyright Act (DMCA): A US law passed in 1998 that governs the use of digital material and provides for intellectual property protections for the copyright owner.

Digital preservation: A field of research and practice related to the long-term persistence of digital information.

Digital-S: The same format as **D-9**.

Digital8: A digital videotape format used by consumers. The tape is the same size as Video8 and Hi8 tapes.

Digitization: With moving image and sound records, the process of taking an analog signal and making a reproduction of it using digital technology.

DRM (Digital Rights Management): Access control strategies used to protect proprietary content, such as strategies that prevent the duplication of DVDs.

DROID: An open-source tool developed by the National Archives of the United Kingdom that uses file format signatures, specifically those that are part of the PRONOM technical registry, to determine what format a file is.

Dropout: During playback of video, part of the image or audio that is not read properly, resulting in the omission of that information from playback.

DTV (digital television): The broadcast of a television signal as digital information. Most countries of the world have transitioned from analog television to DTV.

Dublin Core: A descriptive metadata scheme with fifteen fields (e.g., title, creator, date, etc.) that can be used to describe most recorded works.

DV: A digital video format introduced in 1995 for semiprofessional and amateur video creators, with MiniDV as the most well-known instance of DV.

DVCAM: A professional version of the DV digital video format created by Sony in 1996.

DVCPro: A professional version of DV created by Panasonic in 1995.

DVD: A digital optical disc format introduced in 1996 and often used for storing standard-definition video.

Dynamic range: For images, refers to the range of colors (or shades of gray in grayscale works) between the darkest dark and the lightest light. For audio, refers to the range of sound from the highest amplitude to the lowest. Typically, for both images and sound, systems that can represent a wider dynamic range can produce higher quality reproductions.

EAD (Encoded Archival Description): A machine-readable version of a finding aid that is encoded in XML.

Embedded metadata: Metadata that is kept directly in a file.

Emulation: Running software, often obsolete, in modern operating systems by having it run on top of software that mimics the environment the software was intended to operate in.

Emulsion: The layer of film that contains the photographic image.

EP (extended play): Same as **SLP** (super long play).

Essence: The part of an audio or video file representing the recorded signals (as opposed to other aspects of a file like embedded metadata or the wrapper).

exFAT (Extended File Allocation Table): A file system developed by Microsoft for use in flash drives; released in 2006.

Exhibition copy or **exhibition print:** Typically the same as **access copy**.

Fair use: Use allowed by section 107 of the US Copyright Act of 1976, which allows for educational and scholarly use of recorded information without the permission of the copyright holder if the use satisfies four conditions: 1) the purpose of the use, 2) the nature of the copyrighted work; 3) the amount of the work used, and 4) the effect on the market for the work.

FAT (File Allocation Table) and **FAT32:** File systems used in floppy disks and hard disks, especially in DOS and Windows systems from the 1990s. FAT32 allowed for larger disks and files than standard FAT and was used in Windows 2000 and later.

Feature film: A film that is at least forty minutes long; also referred to as a feature-length film.

FFV1 (FF video codec 1): A lossless video codec beginning to be used for encoding master video.

File format signature: A pattern that all files of that format should have, such as a consistent set of bytes in the very beginning or the very end of a file. Used in the PRONOM registry.

File system: The structures and methods for organizing disk space into files, folders, and other file properties.

Film base: The clear plastic-like material used to support the photographic elements. Typical film bases include cellulose nitrate, cellulose acetate, and polyester.

Film gauge: The width of the film (e.g., 35 mm, 16 mm, 8 mm, etc.).

FireWire: A hardware interface for connecting external devices to computers, now increasingly considered obsolete.

FITS XML: An XML format for representing technical information on file formats.

Fixity information: See **checksum**.

Flash: A format created by Macromedia, now owned by Adobe, for displaying video and vector graphics and creating interactive experiences. This format was popular for exhibiting video online, especially during the 2000s, but has since fallen out of favor.

FLV: Flash Video, often used as a file extension. See **Flash**.

Format migration: The process of transforming a record from one format to another, usually because of issues related to format obsolescence.

Frame: A single rectangular image from motion picture film or video.

Frame rate: The number of frames shown to a viewer per second.

Hash: See **checksum**.

HD (high definition): A video capture and display format and television broadcast standard that typically allows for 1920 x 1080 pixels of image resolution. Can also indicate video resolutions that are higher than the resolution of standard-definition video.

HDCAM: A professional video format introduced in 1997 that is capable of capturing high-definition video.

HDSDI (high-definition Serial Digital Interface) ports: Ports that output uncompressed HD video that can be used for migrating video from HD videotapes to computer files.

Hexadecimal: A way to represent numbers in a more compact fashion than typical numbers, also known as base-10 numbers. For example, counting from one to twenty in hexadecimal looks like the following: 1, 2, 3, 4, 5, 6, 7, 8, 9, A, B, C, D, E, F, 10, 11, 12, 13, 14.

Hi8: An analog video format introduced in 1989 for consumer camcorders that improved upon Video8 and was superseded by Digital8.

HTML5: An HTML (HyperText Markup Language) standard adopted in 2014 that includes new features such as media elements for playing audio and video.

HVAC: Heating, ventilating, and air-conditioning. Often used by archives to control the temperature and humidity of a facility.

Hydrolysis: The process in which water is absorbed into a substance. In audiovisual archives, hydrolysis often refers to water absorbed into the binder of magnetic tape, often through moisture in the air, which can result in sticky shed syndrome.

Hygrometer: A device for measuring relative humidity.

Hz (Hertz): A unit for measuring wave cycles that can be readily converted to "times per second"; often used in audio capture to describe the samples taken per second. For example, once per second is equivalent to 1 Hz. Often expressed as kHz (kilohertz), where 1 Hz equals .001 kHz.

Inactive records: Records that are no longer used by individuals during the normal course of their work and thus may be eligible for archival retention or destruction.

Intellectual control: The information that describes what is contained in a collection, which should help researchers identify information pertinent to their interests and should remind the archivist what is in the collection.

Interlacing: See **deinterlace**.

ISO image: A bit-for-bit copy of the contents of an optical disc, including the file system and all files or streams contained within it.

JPEG 2000 and **Motion JPEG 2000:** JPEG 2000 is an image compression standard that is capable of lossless image compression. Motion JPEG 2000 uses JPEG 2000 image compression on moving images, thus making it capable of lossless video compression and making it appropriate for archiving master video.

kHz (Kilohertz): See **Hz**.

Kineograph: A flip-book.

Kinescope: A device for recording television to film.

Lacquer disc: A type of phonograph record with a surface coated in lacquer.

LaserDisc: A digital optical disc format introduced in 1978 and often used for storing standard definition video; predecessor to the CD and DVD.

LCD (liquid-crystal display): A flat-panel, progressive-scan display that (along with LED) has superseded CRT television and computer displays. Makes use of liquid crystals to reflect light.

LED (light-emitting diode) display: A flat-panel, progressive-scan display that (along with LCD) has superseded CRT television and computer displays. Makes use of light-emitting diodes.

Linear feet: A unit of measurement often used by archivists to determine how much shelf space a collection uses or requires. This method only takes into account the width of a collection, in contrast to cubic feet, which takes into account the three dimensions of a collection (i.e., length x width x height of all containers in a collection).

LOCKSS (Lots of Copies Keep Stuff Safe): A distributed digital preservation model where copies of digital information are kept at multiple sites across a network of institutions. If a failure occurs somewhere in the network, then information can be restored from these copies.

Lone arranger: An individual who is the only staff of an archives.

Lossless compression: A data compression method that does not discard any information, thus making it appropriate for archival masters.

Lossy compression: A data compression method that discards select information to optimize for file size or data transmission requirements. The effects of lossy compression become more noticeable—both for audio and visual assets—the more aggressively it is applied.

LP (long play): On video recorders, a setting that allows for tapes to record from one and a half to two times as much content as SP (standard play). For example, a two-hour VHS tape recorded at LP can record up to four hours of content. With respect to phonograph records, LP refers to a long-playing disc that can include more than twenty minutes of recorded sound.

LTO (Linear Tape-Open): A magnetic data tape format used for storing digital information; notable for its large storage capacity.

Luminance: The portion of the video signal that contains the picture information. See **chrominance**.

Mac OS Extended: A file system used on Macintosh computers; also known as HFS Plus.

Magnetic sound track: In motion picture film, a sound track held on magnetic tape and attached to the film. It is played back as the film is projected.

Magnetic tape: Magnetic particles attached to a substrate such as plastic, which can encode electromagnetic signals, often used for storing audio, video, and digital information.

MARC (Machine-Readable Cataloging): A data storage format created in the 1960s for storing and sharing library catalog records, still used often today. MARC-XML records are XML renderings of MARC records.

Master copy: The highest fidelity version of a moving image or sound asset.

MD5 (message digest 5): An algorithm widely used in digital preservation for file fixity monitoring.

MediaInfo: An open-source tool for extracting technical metadata from digital audiovisual files.

Metadata: Information about a record, which can include descriptive metadata, technical metadata, and administrative metadata.

Micro SD card: See **SD card**.

Microcassette: An analog audio recording medium, similar to the compact audiocassette, but miniaturized.

Microgroove: On phonograph records, smaller grooves (compared to those on coarse-groove discs) that were introduced in the late 1940s on 45 rpm and 33 1/3 rpm discs.

Migration: The process of moving records from one container or format to another container or format. For example, video can be migrated from a MiniDV tape to a computer file.

MII: A professional analog videotape format introduced in 1986.

MiniDisc: Digital recording technology made by Sony that uses an optical disc enclosed in a plastic container. Support for this format ended in 2013.

MiniDV: A compact digital video recording tape, used by consumers and in semiprofessional contexts to create standard-definition video.

Mirroring: A method of automatically copying content from one data store to another.

MODS (Metadata Object Description Schema): A descriptive metadata standard maintained by the Library of Congress. It is often thought of as affording more sophisticated records than Dublin Core, but without the technical complexity of MARC records.

Monetary appraisal: The process of assigning the fair-market value of a work. Contrast with **appraisal**.

Mono recording: A recording in which sound is recorded using a single channel, unlike stereo recordings, in which two channels are used. Short for *monophonic*.

MOV: The file extension for QuickTime, a video wrapper created by Apple Inc.

MP3: Abbreviation for MPEG-2 Audio Layer III, a popular lossy compressed audio codec that removes sounds that the listener should not be able to hear.

MP4: Generally the file extension for videos encoded with **MPEG4/H.264**.

MPEG (Moving Picture Experts Group): The working group that creates international audio and video standards.

MPEG4/H.264: A popular lossy video encoding format that is used on Blu-ray discs and used to distribute video over the web.

MPEG-IMX: A professional digital videotape format introduced in 2000.

MPLP (more product, less process): An archival processing strategy developed by Mark Greene and Dennis Meissner intended to reduce processing backlogs by dedicating less effort to certain labor-intensive steps, such as physical arrangement, preservation, and item-level description.

Mutoscope: An early motion picture entertainment device that included a flip-book inside a viewfinder.

MXF (Material Exchange Format): A wrapper for audio and video that can contain a wide variety of metadata.

NAS (Network Attached Storage): Usually a RAID storage system that is accessible via a network.

Negative: The reverse image produced during capture by a film camera, which is then developed to produce a positive image that can be exhibited.

Nitrate decay, also **cellulose nitrate decay:** Chemical decomposition of cellulose nitrate film base. It can be slowed or stopped by storing film in a cold and dry environment.

Nitrate film, also **cellulose nitrate film:** Highly flammable film stock that was used in the earliest motion pictures.

NTFS (New Technology File System): File system developed by Microsoft for use in Windows; used for formatting hard disks. Used in Windows NT, Windows 2000, and Windows XP, among other Windows operating systems.

NTSC (National Television System Committee): The video-encoding format and television broadcast standard used in the United States and Canada, among other countries. Includes 525 scan lines and 29.97 interlaced frames per second.

OAIS (Open Archival Information System): A model, standard, and best practice for preserving digital information.

Omeka: An open-source collection management and exhibition tool that works well for showcasing item-level records.

Open reel: A videotape or audiotape that is not enclosed in a plastic container. The reel needs to be manually loaded onto the player and the tape fed through the tape heads to the take-up reel.

Optical disc: A disc on which information is encoded visually, through impressions in plastic that can be read with a laser. Most often refers to digital discs such as CDs, DVDs, and Blu-rays.

Optical printing: The process in which film is copied to raw film, in effect duplicating the film.

Optical sound track: In motion picture film, a sound track that is printed visually as a sound wave and played back as the film is projected. Contrast with **magnetic sound track**.

PAL (Phase Alternating Line): The video-encoding format and television broadcast standard used widely in Europe, Africa, and Asia. Includes 625 scan lines and 25 interlaced frames per second.

Parity information: In the context of RAID systems, information that can be used to rebuild the contents of a disk array should a drive in the array fail.

PBCore (Public Broadcasting Metadata Dictionary): A metadata standard that is well suited for video and public broadcast content, as it includes technical fields that are unique to video.

PCM (pulse-code modulation): A format for encoding digitized audio in which the samples are stored in sequence in an uncompressed state. Used in Microsoft WAV files, Broadcast Wave files, and audio streams on CDs.

Photosite: The smallest element used in a digital camera's sensor to detect light.

Physical control: The ability to locate groups of records in their storage environment, which typically translates to boxes and box numbers (or ranges of box numbers).

Pixel: The smallest visible element used to constitute a raster image such as a photograph.

Polyester film: Durable and stable plastic film most often used today.

Positive film: Film that is used for exhibition and that shows a positive (or normal-looking) image.

Preservation: The body of knowledge and sets of practices that ensure the long-term persistence of recorded information.

Preservation assessment: A systematic process of identifying preservation issues across a set of collections or all collections held at an archives.

Preservation environment monitor (PEM): A device that monitors preservation conditions over time and can produce reports on preservation conditions.

Preservation master: See **master copy**.

Preservation metadata: Information that documents the digital preservation process, such as information about format migrations.

Preservation reformatting: See **format migration**.

Processing: The process used by archivists to arrange and describe archival material.

Progressive scanning: Display technology, such as flat-panel LCD and LED, that does not require interlacing.

PRONOM: A technical registry of file format types and variations from the National Archives of the United Kingdom.

Provenance: In archival parlance, the origin of the records, which is most often an individual, family, or organization. This contrasts with the meaning in museum parlance, which often refers to ownership history or chain of custody.

Public domain: Information that is not covered by copyright because the copyright has lapsed or because it was put in the public domain by the creator.

Quadruplex or **Quadruplex videotape:** The earliest form of videotape, introduced by the Ampex Corporation in 1956.

QuickTime: See **MOV**.

RAID (Redundant Array of Independent Disks): A hardware device that chains together one or more hard disks for the purpose of providing data redundancy, increased data access speed, or both.

Raster graphics: Method of representing images using a matrix of pixels. The number of pixels in the matrix make up the resolution of the image, and the number of bits used to represent a pixel make up its bit depth.

RCA cables: Three cables for transmitting analog video, usually comprising a yellow cable (composite video) with red and white cables for stereo audio.

RDA (Resource Description and Access): The standard for descriptive cataloging initially released in 2010 that replaced AACR2.

Reappraisal: The process in which the value of items originally deemed to have archival or permanent value is second-guessed and the preservationworthiness of the records is reevaluated.

Record: Any data or information that is in fixed form, such as information on a film reel, videotape, piece of paper, or computer file.

Relative humidity: A metric for the amount of water or moisture in the air.

Resolution: For images, the number of pixels that make up the image, both from left to right and from top to bottom. The higher the resolution, the clearer or sharper the image should be. For audio, resolution can refer to the bit depth.

Restoration: Reconstruction of a work. This topic is not addressed in this book.

Reversal film: A film type used in cameras that when processed provides a positive image that can be loaded onto a projector and exhibited.

RGB: Red, green, and blue, the colors used by most modern computers to display a full-color image.

Rip: A colloquial term used to refer to copying contents from optical discs such as CDs, DVDs, and Blu-rays. As some DVDs and Blu-rays may have built-in protections to prevent copying, which in many cases can be subverted, this practice is generally not legal by the terms of the Digital Millennium Copyright Act.

RPM (rotations per minute): The number of times a disc spins per minute. Common rpms include 78, 33 1/3, 45, and 16.

Safety film: All nonflammable film, such as acetate and polyester film.

Sampling rate: How frequently an analog signal's digital value is noted and recorded, usually measured in kHz.

Scan line: A single line, left to right, that makes up a frame of a video image.

SCSI (Small Computer System Interface): An obsolete digital interface that has been replaced by FireWire and USB; often used to connect computers to hard disks and other removable media.

SD (Secure Digital) card: A small solid-state digital storage container, often used in video cameras for capture. Also comes in smaller versions such as Micro SD and Mini SD cards.

SDI (Serial Digital Interface) ports: Ports that output uncompressed standard-definition video that can be used for migrating from SD videotapes to computer files.

SECAM (*Séquentiel couleur avec mémoire*): The video-encoding format and television broadcast standard used in France, Russia, and other countries. Includes 625 scan lines and 25 interlaced frames per second.

Series and **subseries:** Groups of similar records that originate from a common activity (e.g., Correspondence, Writings, etc.). In a hierarchy of records, a subseries is the child of a parent series.

SHA-256 (Secure Hash Algorithm 256 bits): An algorithm widely used in digital preservation for file fixity monitoring.

Shellac disc: A disc recording from the early twentieth century that is coated with a resin.

Shrinkage: Film "shrinking" because of overly dry storage conditions, occurring in acetate and nitrate film. Too much shrinkage can damage the film.

Siegfried: An open-source tool developed by Richard Lehane that uses file format signatures, such as those in the PRONOM technical registry, to determine what format a file is.

SLP (super long play): A videotape mode that allows for a tripling (or more) of total content that can be recorded to a tape (e.g., a two-hour tape can record six hours of content at SLP).

Small-gauge film: Any film with a gauge smaller than 35 mm, especially 8 mm and Super 8 mm film.

SP (standard play): The mode on a video recorder that records content corresponding to the maximum tape time (e.g., a two-hour tape can record two hours of content at SP).

Splice: To join two pieces of film using tape, cement, or other joining technology. Often used in the editing process.

Sprocket: The small holes in film used to advance it through the camera or projector.

Standard definition (SD): A video format in wide use from the 1950s to the 2000s, in which the image is made up of 480–576 scan lines.

Stereo recording: Recording of two channels of audio, often in which one channel is intended to be played back to the left ear and the other to the right ear.

Sticky shed syndrome: A condition affecting magnetic tapes in which moisture gets between the magnetic material and the plastic, sometimes causing the tape to emit a gooey substance.

Stiction: With respect to magnetic hard drives with platters, a condition in which the tape head cannot move to the desired spot and sticks to the platters, which can cause total drive failure.

Super 8 mm: Film that is 8 mm wide and that has a slightly larger image area than 8 mm film; used for personal and family use and for low-budget film productions.

S-VHS: An analog video technology that was meant to supersede VHS, as it provided 400 scan lines compared to VHS's 240 lines. It was not widely adopted.

S-VHS-C: A smaller version of S-VHS that fits in camcorders, which can be played in S-VHS players using an adapter.

S-video (separate video): An analog video connector type that separates the chrominance (color) from the luminance (picture).

SWF (Small Web Format): The file extension for files that play with the Flash player, such as vector graphics and other interactive elements. Pronounced "swiff."

Technical metadata: Information that describes attributes of the media (e.g., S-VHS tape). For computer files, technical metadata can describe things like codec, frame rate, etc.

Technicolor: A process widely used from the 1920s through the 1950s to create color motion pictures.

Telecine: Equipment that can convert film to video.

Thunderbolt: A hardware interface for connecting external devices to computers.

Time code: In professional videotapes, the code used to pinpoint parts of a tape; expressed as "hour: minute: second: frame."

Torrent file: A computer file that enables the download of files over the internet's BitTorrent file distribution system. These files often have the file extension *.torrent*.

Tracking: An option on a video player that adjusts the alignment between tape tracks and the heads of the tape player. Some players automatically adjust the tracking, whereas others can be manually adjusted, which can enhance the quality of the playback.

Transcoding: Converting from one encoding to another.

Trusted digital repository: A standard for ensuring the persistence of digital information, where the organization, resources, and technology of an institution are carefully orchestrated to preserve digital information.

Ultra HD (ultra high-definition): A new television and video format that provides for about 4,000 pixels (from left to right) of image resolution.

U-matic: A cartridge-based professional video format introduced in 1971. A higher resolution version was introduced in 1986 as U-matic SP ("Superior Performance").

USB disk: Typically any mass storage device that connects via a USB port. This includes solid-state drives and hard disks with spinning platters.

VCD (video CD): A low-resolution digital video format that is held on CDs.

VCR: Videocassette recorder, a device that records and plays back videotapes. *VCR* can also refer to "videocassette recording," an analog video format introduced in 1971 for the consumer market.

Vector graphics: Graphics created through the use of shapes with numerical characteristics (e.g., origin, width, height). Contrast with **raster graphics**.

VHS (Video Home System): A low-resolution analog video format introduced in 1976 that became the most widely used home and nonprofessional video format of the twentieth century.

VHS-C: Smaller VHS tapes that fit into VHS camcorders. Tapes can be played with a VHS player when inserted into an adapter.

Video 2000: A consumer analog video format that was introduced in 1979.

Video8: Also known as 8 mm video or Standard 8, a consumer video format that was introduced in 1984 and was used in camcorders. This format was superseded by Hi8 and Digital8.

Vinegar syndrome, **acetate vinegar syndrome,** or **acetate decay:** Decomposition of acetate film that produces a vinegar odor. Vinegar syndrome can be slowed or stopped through freezing the film. The extent of the syndrome can be measured using **A-D Strips.**

Virtual machine: A software layer that mimics hardware behavior, thus allowing old computer software to run on present-day machines (e.g., an Intel 486 PC virtual machine running Windows 3.1 on Mac OSX).

VLC Player: Open-source software for a variety of platforms that can play a wide range of media types.

WARC (Web ARChive) files: Text-based, ISO-standard file format for storing web archives with associated metadata.

WAV or **Wave (Waveform Audio File Format):** A format for saving digital sound created by Microsoft, in which the sound is encoded using pulse-code modulation (PCM).

Web archiving: Making a copy of a website or set of web pages as a means of preservation, and ensuring that that copy is faithful to the original.

Wget: A command-line tool that works on multiple platforms for downloading content from the web; a useful tool for doing web archiving.

Windows Media Player: A software product by Microsoft that can play a wide variety of media.

WMA (Windows Media Audio): A proprietary format for compressing audio created by Microsoft.

Wrapper: Also known as a file container, a wrapper contains the data (or essence) and the metadata that are read by the media player.

XML (Extensible Markup Language): A format for encoding structured information in a machine-readable format, often used to encode metadata.

YCM separation masters: Color film that is separated into its elementary colors (yellow, cyan, and magenta), with each color printed onto a strip of black-and-white film. The three strips of black-and-white film, when put together and the respective colors are shined through, can recreate the full-color image.

YCrBr: The color space used in analog video and CRT televisions, where the Y part is the luminance and the CrBr part is the chrominance (color).

YUV: A color space used in analog video, often shorthand for YCrBr.

Zoetrope: A nineteenth-century optical illusion device that shows a moving image through small openings.

Index

About the Author

ANTHONY COCCIOLO is the Dean of the School of Information at Pratt Institute in New York City, where he has taught since 2009. His research and teaching are in archives and digital preservation. He completed his doctorate from the Communication, Media and Learning Technologies Design program at Teachers College, Columbia University, and earned his B.S. in Computer Science from the University of California, Riverside. *Moving Image and Sound Collections for Archivists* received the 2018 Waldo Gifford Leland Award from the Society of American Archivists. The award recognizes writing of superior excellence and usefulness in the field of archival history, theory, or practice.

CPSIA information can be obtained
at www.ICGtesting.com
Printed in the USA
LVHW061552170422
716157LV00001B/2